Literacy for
the Twenty-First Century

LITERACY FOR THE TWENTY-FIRST CENTURY

Research, Policy, Practices, and the National Adult Literacy Survey

Edited by M CECIL SMITH

Foreword by PAUL SIMON

 PRAEGER

Westport, Connecticut
London

Library of Congress Cataloging-in-Publication Data

Literacy for the twenty-first century : research, policy, practices,
   and the National Adult Literacy Survey / edited by M Cecil Smith ;
   foreword by Paul Simon.
     p. cm.
   Includes bibliographical references and index.
   ISBN 0–275–95786–1 (alk. paper)
   1. National Adult Literacy Survey. 2. Literacy—United States.
   3. Literacy—Research—United States. I. Smith, M Cecil.
   LC151.L483   1998
   302.2'24—DC21   98–9946

British Library Cataloguing in Publication Data is available.

Library of Congress Catalog Card Number: 98–9946
ISBN: 0–275–95786–1

First published in 1998

Praeger Publishers, 88 Post Road West, Westport, CT 06881
An imprint of Greenwood Publishing Group, Inc.

Printed in the United States of America

The paper used in this book complies with the
Permanent Paper Standard issued by the National
Information Standards Organization (Z39.48–1984).

10 9 8 7 6 5 4 3 2 1

Contents

PART III. BROADER PERSPECTIVES IN ADULT LITERACY

Foreword

Paul Simon

Most of our citizens do not have any idea what a huge problem simple reading and writing is for millions of our fellow adult citizens. Most academicians do not have a much better idea what a huge problem simple reading and writing is for millions of our fellow adult citizens. This book will help to put some meat on the bare bones of our understanding. Cecil Smith and the others who have contributed to this volume deserve our thanks. Illiteracy is an easy problem to overlook, but we overlook it ultimately at our peril.

I became interested in the problem of literacy when I served in the U.S. House of Representatives. I conducted "Open Office Hours" in communities throughout my district, at which people would come in one by one to ask my help on whatever their problems might be. When citizens wanted me to look at a veteran's problem or Social Security or some difficulty that involved the federal government, the person requesting help had to sign a consent form in order for me to look at the records. I discovered that people would say, with surprising frequency, "Is it OK if my wife signs this for me?" Or "Can my husband sign it?" It stunned me to see that people who looked like other citizens in terms of dress and demeanor could not perform so basic a function as signing their name. And sometimes the person involved would very carefully, very slowly, draw his or her name. I knew it was the only thing he or she could write.

At that time I chaired a subcommittee in the House and called a hearing on illiteracy, the first such hearing in the history of Congress. I asked the Secretary of Education, "Ted" Bell, to testify, and he has since written that until he prepared for his testimony for this hearing he had no idea as to the extent of illiteracy in the nation.

After the hearing I talked with him about some type of follow-through, because he clearly shared my concern. We decided to have a series of informal breakfast meetings to discuss what could be done. One of those who joined us at these meetings was the wife of the Vice President, Barbara Bush, who has been strong on this issue.

Initially, there emerged some amendments drawn with the help of staff members Judy Wagner, William "Bud" Blakey, and Alice Johnson. We got an amendment on the Library Services and Construction Act, to encourage libraries to move into this field. We got an amendment to the Vista program, establishing the Vista Literacy Corps. We got an amendment to push literacy among homeless people. These and other amendments were all small steps that helped some people, but the numbers were small in terms of the universe of need.

Then I introduced the measure which became the National Literacy Act, which President Bush signed with Barbara Bush watching carefully. At one point the White House announced its opposition to my bill, and when I ran into the President at a social occasion I told him he might get lobbied by Barbara on this. I called her and she did! When the President started to hand the ceremonial pen to me after signing the bill, which is traditionally done for the chief sponsor, I thanked him but said that on this occasion the pen belonged to Barbara. Those who were present knew what had happened. They laughed and cheered, and she took the pen.

This book is based on a study that grew out of the National Literacy Act. It is a statistical analysis, but the statistics can hide the harsh realities that people face. Joanne Nurss's chapter on Adult Literacy and Health Care opens with quotations from two people, live people, suffering people. She has this significant line: "Particularly disturbing . . . is the finding that patients do not readily report to health care personnel that they have difficulty reading and comprehending medical forms, perhaps due to shame." After years of dealing with people who have struggled with the problem, I can assure the author that she can drop the *perhaps*. What a statistical study does not show is the overwhelming feeling of shame and embarrassment people have who cannot read and write. And over and over I have heard those who have acquired the skill late in life tell me, "It was like being imprisoned." Reading these chapters should be more than an intellectual exercise; it should be "a call to arms!"

The information and analysis in this volume provide no huge surprises. Those at the bottom of the literacy scale earn less, are less likely to vote, and are much less likely to perform functions like reading a newspaper. Forty-four percent of those in the lowest reading level are living below or near the poverty line.

One clear warning does come through: We are providing inadequate educational opportunity and demands on too many students. Sixteen percent of those with a high school diploma test at Level 1, the lowest of five literacy levels. Thirty-six percent test at Level 2. That means that the top three levels of literacy were achieved by only 48% of those with high school diplomas. More startling, 4% of those with college degrees test at Level 1 and 11% at Level 2.

If we as a nation were to really move on the problems of literacy with something more than token efforts, the result would be increased productivity for the nation, reduced crime, increased longevity (poverty and poor health are frequently Siamese twins), increased participation in the political process, and perhaps most important of all, the chance for a life with greater satisfaction for millions.

Let me make one personal footnote that I add with pride: Alice Johnson, one of the contributors, once was a valued member of my Senate staff. She may deny it, but it is true!

PART I

Issues in Adult Literacy

1

Introduction: Adult Literacy Research and the National Adult Literacy Survey

M Cecil Smith and Stephen Reder

It has been nearly half a decade since the findings from the largest assessment of American adults' literacy skills were released to the public amid a great deal of fanfare and media attention. Headlines in the *New York Times* and other large metropolitan newspapers across the country, the weekly newsmagazines, and news reports on the major networks chronicled yet another literacy crisis, as more than half of the adult population was deemed to be illiterate. Never mind that this was a gross misinterpretation of the data, perhaps designed to titillate and to sell newspapers. Two reactions to the news about adult literacy were common: the findings were met with great skepticism, as many Americans felt that this was yet another attempt to scare the public into believing that an adult education crisis was at hand; or, others, in particular many influential persons in the U.S. government, simply ignored the report, choosing to focus on other, seemingly more manageable, domestic issues.

Did the opportunity pass for the National Adult Literacy Survey (NALS) to inform research on adult literacy education, federal and state policies relevant to adult literacy education, and the practices of thousands of literacy educators? The contributors of this volume would argue that the opportunity has not passed and that much useful information can be distilled and learned from this very important survey.

A number of academics, educational policy experts, and literacy advocates have begun to utilize the NALS data and its outcomes to set educational policies, build support for the increased funding of adult literacy programs, design adult literacy education curricula, conduct further research on adult literacy skills, and disseminate information about the social and economic conditions that impact adults' literacy development.

During the course of writing this chapter, a question was posed to subscribers to the National Literacy Advocacy (NLA) listserv discussion group on the Internet. Many of the subscribers to this service are directly involved in adult literacy education service delivery (i.e., Adult Basic Education [ABE], English as a Second Language [ESL], and General Education Development [GED] programs) or are program administrators, directors of state adult education agencies, or literacy researchers. They were asked how they have made use of the NALS findings in their work. Although the sample was a decidedly limited and select one, the responses nonetheless provide some insights into the utility of the NALS data by professionals who work "on the front lines" in adult literacy education.

According to the responses, an essential use of the NALS data by program administrators has been to justify funding requests to meet increasing program needs, improve service delivery, and offer more comprehensive services. At the other end, those who distribute the funds to support adult literacy education programs must make difficult decisions, and the NALS data can be useful in this regard. For example, African-American and Hispanic adults were disproportionately represented in the lowest two levels of the NALS. Programs serving these populations might, therefore, be targeted to receive a larger portion of the available funding. State-level data also may serve as a baseline for individual states to determine how well they are doing in improving the literacy skills of their citizens.

The NALS defined literacy in the following manner: "[u]sing printed and written information to function in society, to achieve one's goals, and to develop one's knowledge and potential" (Kirsch, Jungeblut, Jenkins, & Kolstad, 1993, p. 2). This multidimensional conception of literacy stands in stark contrast to the grade-level definitions used in most previous U.S. censuses and offers a different perspective, not limited to comprehension or decoding. Several individuals on the NLA listserv reported that the NALS definition provides a basis for discussion among groups of persons in the larger community, including educational leaders, businesspersons, and advisory board members who are concerned with identifying the literacy needs of the community. Others reported that the NALS was used to augment teacher and tutor training by providing some sense of the adult literacy "problem" in the United States and within their local area. Most respondents agreed, however, that the NALS has had little impact on the day-to-day practices of their instructors, tutors, and students and the kinds of services provided, the mission of their organization, and the policies and procedures that guide the provision of adult literacy education programs and services.

It would be unrealistic, however, to expect a survey such as the NALS to have that kind of impact. What does the NALS provide to the literacy education community? It offers an accounting, from a very specific perspective, of the literacy skills and practices and the sociocultural and demographic factors that are associated with the skills and practices in the late twentieth century. It is a highly detailed snapshot of adult literacy rather than a dynamic panorama of action. Many questions that policymakers and others would like NALS to have answered are simply not addressable using only a single snapshot. For example, many would like NALS to provide clear evidence of the impact that adult education has on adult learners' literacy abilities and on the attendant social and economic outcomes (e.g., employment, civic participation). The single NALS snapshot does not contain the information needed to address such questions. Nevertheless, much can be usefully learned from analyses of the NALS that will benefit future research, policy, and practice in adult education.

The primary focus of this book concerns the results from a number of secondary analyses of the NALS and the implications of these analyses for policy, practice, and further research on adult literacy. We will see there is much to be gained from these analyses. They provide us, for example, with a more informative and certainly more complex accounting of the nature of adult literacy in the United States and the associations among various factors that are thought to impact or be impacted by literacy.

BACKGROUND ON THE NALS

The NALS developers, who previously had applied their assessment and survey methodology in similar surveys of young adults (Kirsch & Jungeblut, 1986) and Job Training Partnership Act (JTPA)/Unemployment Insurance (UI) program clientele (Kirsch & Jungeblut, 1992), assumed that adults need a range of skills to accomplish the great variety of literacy tasks that they encounter in their daily lives. The NALS therefore intended to assess literacy proficiency on three scales: prose, document, and quantitative (PDQ) literacy. Each scale reflected adults' uses of knowledge and skills in performing simulated, everyday functional literacy tasks, such as filling out a form, understanding a newspaper article, or extracting quantitative information from a graph. NALS estimated both literacy task difficulties and individuals' literacy proficiencies with scores between 0 and 500 on these literacy scales. For reporting purposes, NALS chose to categorize these scores into discrete proficiency levels. Five levels of literacy proficiency were identified representing the ability to understand and to successfully accomplish literacy tasks along a continuum from simple activities, such as signing one's name on a Social Security card, to more sophisticated tasks involving lengthy and complex written materials, such as reading an advertisement for a home equity loan and then, using the information provided, explaining how to calculate the total amount of interest charges for a loan. Among the most significant outcomes of the NALS were these findings:

- About one-half of American adults performed at the two lowest levels of literacy proficiency.
- Educational attainment was associated with literacy proficiency: those adults with few years of education were more likely to perform in the lowest literacy levels.
- Racial and ethnic group differences were also apparent: African Americans, Native Americans, Hispanics, and Asians were more likely than whites to perform in the two lowest literacy levels (Kirsch et al., 1993).

ORGANIZATION OF THE BOOK

This book is divided into three sections. This first section contains not only this introduction but three additional chapters that provide a substantive summary of the NALS and its purposes. Irwin Kirsch's chapter briefly overviews the NALS and its outcomes. Among the issues that Kirsch discusses are the connections between literacy skills and a number of social, educational, and economic variables and the distribution of literacy skills among adults in the United States.

Alice Johnson and Andrew Hartman of the National Institute for Literacy in Washington, D.C., discuss current adult education and literacy policy, how funding is determined for literacy education programs at the federal level, and the ways in which public policy regarding literacy is shaped. Their chapter describes the larger federal framework in which the NALS is situated. Finally, they call for the nationwide coordination of the many and diverse literacy education efforts across the country in order to provide more comprehensive and cost-efficient services that will significantly increase literacy learning. They describe several current initiatives that are designed to accomplish this coordination of services.

Next, Steve Reder's chapter considers the extent to which the NALS did, in fact, assess literacy proficiencies on three distinct prose, document, and quantitative scales. Drawing on evidence from both scale-level and item-level analyses of responses to the NALS tasks, Reder concludes that the NALS appears to measure a single dimension of literacy ability. For many purposes, NALS data can thus be effectively combined into a single measure of literacy proficiency. Collapsing the scales into a single proficiency measure may also facilitate the analysis and reporting of NALS data. For future NALS surveys, Reder suggests that the assessment techniques be sharpened so as to more effectively differentiate prose, document, and quantitative literacy.

The second section of the book consists of seven chapters describing several secondary analyses of the NALS database. These analyses were designed to address different questions, including, How does work influence the development of literacy? What are the relationships of different kinds of reading practices to literacy proficiencies? Do these relationships vary across racial and ethnic groups? What gender differences are found in the NALS results, and what social factors underlie these differences? Does literacy have any association with voting behavior? How does a select group of well-educated adults—community college students—fare in regard to their literacy skills? What literacy skills do learning disabled adults demonstrate? Answers to these questions provide a very broad, yet comprehensive and complex, accounting of the sociocultural and demographic factors that serve to influence adults' literacy skills and practices.

Jeremy Finn and Susan Gerber examine the significance of two contexts for developing adults' literacy skills: work and school. In particular, they want to know how work-relevant experiences might serve to either complement or compensate for schooling in the development of literacy skills and practices. Increasingly, schools have been criticized for not adequately preparing young adults for the demands of the workplace, in terms of literacy, critical thinking and problem-solving abilities, communication skills, and ability to work with others. Many entry-level workers must, therefore, acquire these skills—particularly the three Rs—on the job. Although Finn and Gerber point out that there are many discontinuities between school and work, it is likely that these two settings interact to affect the literacy behaviors of adults.

Working from the perspective of practice-engagement theory, which suggests that literacy is shaped by the social organization in which literacy is practiced, Finn and Gerber examine the extent to which the workplace promotes literacy skills. Evidence from their analyses shows that the workplace is, in fact, a context in which literacy skills are learned, practiced, and more fully developed. Thus, school does not, and probably cannot, provide all of the literacy skills necessary to function competently in the world of work.

Cecil Smith and Janet Sheehan also examine the role that different social contexts may play in the development of literacy from a practice-engagement perspective. Two studies are reported in their chapter. The first study examines the association between various literacy practices (e.g., reading different kinds of print materials such as books and periodicals) that are used to fulfill both work and personal purposes and proficiencies on the three literacy scales. These analyses show that adults who read more print contents score higher on the literacy scales than do those who read fewer contents. Although it is likely that good readers are more likely to practice reading than are poor readers, the study suggests that practice may further contribute to the development of literacy proficiencies.

The second study examined racial and ethnic group differences in literacy practices. Not unexpectedly, white American adults read significantly more newspapers and documents (for personal uses) than do other racial groups. No group differences were found in regard to reading documents for work-related purposes, suggesting that the diversity of literacy practices required in the workplace may cut across racial and ethnic lines.

Small gender differences in literacy skills were reported in the first summary of the NALS (Kirsch et al., 1993). Lynn Friedman and Ernest Davenport further examine these gender differences and describe a number of social factors that likely contribute to these observed differences in PDQ literacy across age, racial and ethnic, and educational attainment groups. Their analyses suggest that the perceived literacy gap between males and females is diminishing. Females at all age levels either outperform, or are equivalent to, males on the prose scale. Younger females (i.e., age 39 or younger) score, on average, higher than their male agemates on the document scale but lag somewhat behind males on the quantitative scale, although the gap is negligible among the youngest group (16–19 years of age). These results vary somewhat by racial/ethnic group, with the most interesting differences occurring on the quantitative literacy dimension. Generally, ethnic males and males of color tend to outperform their female counterparts, with the exception of African Americans, where females at every age score higher than males.

Exercising one's right to vote is an important civic event in a democratic society. Yet, voting has been on the decline for the past several decades. Dick Venezky and David Kaplan describe a predictive model of voting behavior based on NALS data, and they look at the relationship between literacy habits and political participation. Their model examined the predictive power of certain demographic characteristics, prose literacy proficiency, and various literacy practices on voting behavior. Their analyses show that the best predictors of voting behavior are age, education, race, and income, with prose ability and literacy practices contributing little to the model. Thus, Venezky and Kaplan speculate that education is the key variable when considering how to increase voter turnout.

The skills and abilities of community college students are often overlooked in higher education studies. The NALS results show that community college graduates typically score in the middle range of the literacy distribution, reflecting perhaps their midlevel educational attainment. As Jay Howard and Wayne Obetz suggest in their chapter, community college students' literacy abilities have advanced beyond the level of high school graduates but have not yet reached the level of college graduates. Generally, community college graduates demonstrate positive attitudes and practices in regard to literacy, suggesting that their literacy abilities will continue to improve across adulthood. Community college educators should, therefore, find some satisfaction in Howard and Obetz's analyses.

The close relationship between literacy and educational attainment is examined in more detail in a chapter by Stephen Reder. Reder distinguishes two processes underlying the relationship between educational attainment and literacy proficiency. *Literacy selection* is the process through which literacy abilities influence individuals' progress through the educational system and determines, in part, how much schooling they complete. *Literacy development* is the process through which participation in education leads to increases in basic skills and knowledge. Both literacy development and literacy selection underlie the strong association between educational attainment and literacy proficiency observed in NALS. Reder demonstrates through a structural equation model (SEM) how these reciprocal effects of literacy selection and literacy development can be empirically distinguished. He then illustrates the application of the reciprocal effects of SEM for better understanding of the distinctive social and economic impacts of literacy and education.

A small percentage of adults—about 3%—in the NALS indicated that they had a learning disability (LD). Susan Vogel and Steve Reder examine the literacy skills of these self-identified LD adults in closer detail. They note that self-reported LD among adults is not equivalent to, nor necessarily identifies, the same individuals as the more familiar form of school-identified LD. They examine the impact of such self-reported LD on NALS literacy performance. More than half of the adults who reported having a learning disability scored at the lowest level on the NALS assessment. On the other hand, nearly one-quarter of adults with LD scored at Level 3 or above, indicating that such disabilities occur over the continuum of literacy skills. Understanding how some adults are able to overcome their learning disabilities and accomplish the complexity of literacy tasks that they encounter will be informative for instructing those adults with the most severe disabilities.

The third and final section of the book consists of two chapters that are not based on analyses of the NALS data. The chapter topics are family literacy and the association between adult literacy and health care. Both of these topics are viewed as being very important in any discussions of adult literacy and so are included here to provide a larger context for understanding the NALS and its outcomes. These topics are sufficiently important that they may warrant more coverage in future NALS-like assessments. Family literacy is defined as "the ways parents, children, and extended family members use literacy at home and in their community . . . during the routines of daily living and helps adults and children 'get things done' " (Morrow, Paratore, & Tracey, 1994, no page number). There are a variety of models of family literacy and a large number of programs around the country designed to help adults and children to improve their everyday literacy skills and practices. Flora Rodriguez-Brown and Maureen Meehan describe a specific program in inner-city Chicago, Project FLAME, that was developed to assist Hispanic parents in their literacy development.

Because Hispanics are the most undereducated ethnic group in the United States, they may often not be involved in their children's schooling. Parent involvement is widely believed to be a crucial factor in children's academic success. In order to increase Hispanic parents' involvement in schools, the goals of Project FLAME are to assist parents in valuing literacy and, in turn, to promote the literacy skills of both the parents and their children. The program is designed to help parents model literacy skills and practices for their children, engage in literacy interactions with them, create a home environment that provides opportunities for literacy, and, finally, increase parent–school contacts.

The NALS results suggest that a large number of adults are likely to have difficulty with everyday literacy activities. Among these activities are reading and understanding health care-related texts, such as labels on medicines, informed consent documents, and insurance forms. Joanne Nurss describes the assessment of functional health literacy in two samples of adults recruited from large urban hospitals in two major U.S. cities. Most participants were either minority group members or indigent patients at these medical facilities. More than 40% of these individuals were found to be unable to read and understand directions for taking prescribed medicines, appointment slips, instructions for various medical procedures, and a passage describing patients' Medicaid rights. Nurss claims that this lack of functional health literacy may be a barrier to individuals' receiving high-quality health care, including accurate diagnoses. Evidence suggests that low functional health literacy is associated with hospitalization. Thus, there is a link between low literacy and rising health care costs. Adult literacy education may thus be a promising and relatively unexplored programmatic strategy for reducing the costs and increasing the quality of health care for many patients.

The National Adult Literacy Survey has provided literacy researchers and practitioners with a wealth of knowledge about American adults' literacy proficiencies. However, this information has not yet been fully disseminated in a manner that can inform public policy, suggest new ideas for literacy research, and assist in adult literacy education program development. This book was developed to fill this information gap. Historically, our society has given only nominal attention to the plight of adults whose literacy skills place them on the margins educationally, socially, and economically. If our nation is to continue to be a world leader well into the next century, we must find ways to ensure that all of our citizens possess the literacy skills that are needed to function effectively in a complex, highly technological, and information-driven culture. It is our hope that policymakers, social leaders, and educators will seriously consider the findings from the various studies of the NALS data presented in these chapters and will take the necessary action to enable all citizens to "function effectively and achieve the greatest possible opportunity in their work and in their lives" (National Literacy Act of 1991).

NOTE

The idea for this book was germinated when the first contributor was a postdoctoral fellow in adult literacy at the Educational Testing Service. Grateful acknowledgment is expressed to Irwin Kirsch for his support. Opinions expressed here are those of the contributors and do not necessarily reflect those of ETS.

REFERENCES

Kirsch, I. S., & Jungeblut, A. (1986). *Literacy: Profiles of America's young adults* (NAEP Report No. 16-PL-01). Princeton, NJ: Educational Testing Service.
———. (1992). *Profiling the literacy proficiencies of JTPA and ES/UI populations: Final report to the Department of Labor*. Princeton, NJ: Educational Testing Service.
Kirsch, I. S., Jungeblut, A., Jenkins, L., & Kolstad, A. (1993). *Adult literacy in America: A first look at the results of the National Adult Literacy Survey*. Washington, DC: National Center for Education Statistics.
Morrow, L. M., Paratore, J. R., & Tracey, D. H. (1994). *Family literacy: New perspectives, new opportunities*. Statement prepared by the International Reading Association Family Literacy Commission. Newark, DE: International Reading Association.

2

Literacy in America: A Brief Overview of the NALS

Irwin S. Kirsch

> Numbers are useful in politics, because they are more neutral than
> adjectival speech and because they express magnitude—that is,
> they can tell us not only that we confront a danger but also what
> the depth and direction of the danger are.
> —Adam Walinsky, "The Crisis of Public Order,"
> *The Atlantic Monthly*, July 1995

Some argue that numbers don't tell the story—they leave out the faces, the emotions, the personal aspects of literacy that make it such an important topic in our society. Numbers, for example, can't express the frustration that workers feel when they lose their job or are unable to find a new one because they lack the necessary education or skills; or the joy parents feel holding a child in their lap and reading a story to the child. But as Walinsky correctly points out, numbers do help us to understand the size and nature of a problem. They allow us to make comparisons and to observe changes over time. They also provide us with a means for informing policy decisions and for evaluating the effectiveness of those that have been in place for some time.

This chapter provides an overview of a number of issues associated with literacy in America—issues that initially were raised in the 1992 National Adult Literacy Survey (Kirsch, Jungeblut, Jenkins, & Kolstad, 1993) and shown to have an impact on the distribution of literacy skills. In reviewing and discussing the NALS, this chapter helps to set a context for the rest of the chapters in this volume, which provide an in-depth look at various topics of interest addressed in the literacy survey.

To gather information on adults' literacy skills, trained staff interviewed nearly 13,600 individuals aged 16 and older during the first eight months of 1992. These participants had been randomly selected to represent the adult population in the country as a whole. In addition, about 1,000 adults were surveyed in each of 12 states that chose to participate in a special study designed to yield state-level results that were comparable to the national data. Finally, some 1,100 inmates from federal and state prisons were interviewed to gather information on the literacy proficiencies of the prison population. Together, over 26,000 individuals were surveyed, representing more than 191 million adults.

Each survey participant was asked to spend approximately one hour responding to a series of literacy tasks as well as questions about his or her demographic characteristics, educational background, reading practices, labor market experiences, and other areas thought to be associated with literacy. Based on their responses to the survey tasks, adults received proficiency scores along three scales—prose, document, and quantitative—ranging from 0 to 500, which reflect varying degrees of knowledge and skill in these three literacy domains.

The three literacy scales provide a useful way to organize a broad array of tasks (some 165) and to report the assessment results. They make it possible, for example, to profile and explore the variation in skills among important subgroups in our population and to explore their relationships with various background factors. In so doing, they help us to understand the broad and diverse nature of literacy in our society.

CONNECTIONS BETWEEN LITERACY SKILLS AND SOCIAL, EDUCATIONAL, AND ECONOMIC VARIABLES

One of the first questions to ask ourselves involves the extent to which literacy is connected to individual opportunities and economic vitality. The NALS database allows us to examine the association between demonstrated skills on the three literacy scales and labor-market variables that include employment status, weeks worked, occupation, and income, as well as social outcomes and participation in educational programs of various types. Collectively, what these data suggest is that literacy has become a currency in our society. Just as adults with little money have difficulty meeting their basic needs, those with limited literacy skills are likely to find it more challenging to pursue their goals—whether these involve seeking or advancing in a job, consumer decision making, pursuing educational opportunities, or other aspects of their lives.

The data in Figure 2.1 indicate that where one is in the literacy distribution is strongly associated with the likelihood of living in or near pov-

Figure 2.1
Percentage of Adults in or near Poverty, by Literacy Level on the Quantitative Scale: 1992

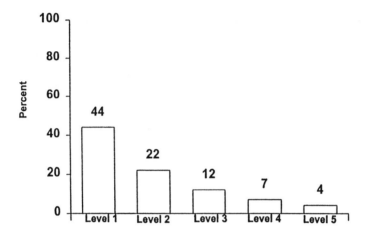

Source: National Adult Literacy Survey, 1992.

erty. On the quantitative scale, for example, 44% of adults in Level 1 reported living in or near poverty as defined by 1991 government criteria. The percentage dropped in half, to 22%, for those adults in Level 2 on the scale. As this shows, the percentages continued to decrease significantly for each successive level on the quantitative scale. Another way to look at the results is that someone in Level 1 is 11 times more likely than someone in Level 5 to be living in or near poverty and about 6 times more likely as someone demonstrating skills associated with Level 4.

The data also indicate that there is a relationship between literacy proficiency and employment status. Table 2.1 shows that individuals with more limited literacy skills are less likely to be employed than those who demonstrate more complex skills. On the prose scale, for example, some 35% of the people who are out of the workforce—that is, not employed and not looking for work—demonstrate skills in Level 1 compared to only 13% for those who are employed full-time. Among those who are unemployed some 24% perform in the lowest level. Looking at the other end of the scale, we see that only 10 to 12% of adults who are out of the workforce or unemployed demonstrate skills in the two highest levels, while about 25% of employed adults achieve these levels.

Not only were literacy skills associated with whether or not someone is in the workforce, but they also were related to the number of weeks that adults reported being employed. In Figure 2.2, adults performing in

Table 2.1
Distribution of Adults across the Literacy Levels on the Prose Scale, by Labor Force Status: 1992

Labor force status	Percent in Prose Level				
	1	2	3	4	5
Employed full time	13.0	23.8	35.8	22.6	4.8
Employed part time	14.3	25.7	36.5	20.0	3.5
Employed, not at work	14.5	24.2	37.1	20.7	3.5
Unemployed	24.0	35.4	28.7	10.5	1.3
Out of labor force	34.6	30.3	24.9	9.1	1.1

Source: National Adult Literacy Survey, 1992.

Figure 2.2
Average Number of Weeks Worked per Year by Literacy Level on the Prose Scale: 1992

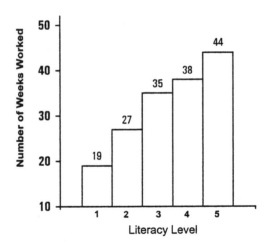

Source: National Adult Literacy Survey, 1992.

the lowest level on the document scale reported working, on average, about 19 weeks each year. The average number of weeks worked increased significantly with each successive level of literacy. That is, performance in Level 2 was associated with an average of 29 weeks, Level 3 with 35 weeks, Level 4 with 40 weeks, and Level 5 with 43 weeks.

Not surprisingly, literacy is also associated with the type of job we are

Table 2.2
Percentages of Adults in Each Literacy Level on the Prose Scale Who Were
in Selected Occupations: 1992

	Percent in Prose Level				
	1	2	3	4	5
Professionals, managers & technicians	5	12	23	46	70
Sales, clerical	15	28	34	30	20
Craft, service	43	36	27	17	8
Laborer, assembler, fishing & farming	37	24	16	7	2

Source: National Adult Literacy Survey, 1992.

likely to have access to in our society. Table 2.2 shows the percentage of adults in each literacy level on the prose scale who reported being in selected occupations. We see, for example, that among adults who perform in Level 1, some 5% reported working in professional, managerial, and technical jobs. An additional 15% were in sales and clerical positions, while 43% were in craft or service jobs, and 37% were in laborer, assembler, or fishing/farming positions. In contrast, among adults performing in Level 5 on the prose scale, some 70% were in professional, managerial, or technical positions compared to only 8% in sales and craft or 2% in laborer or assembler. Thus, while literacy does not guarantee the type of occupation one will obtain within our society, it is clearly a factor in helping employers and others sort individuals within the workforce.

Some have argued that literacy has a dual effect on individuals. It plays a role not only in the type of job we will have but also in the kinds of education and training to which we are likely to gain access. The NALS asked adults whether or not they had received any basic education training. Table 2.3 shows the results for adults 25 to 64 years of age by level of literacy. These data show that about 10% of this population reported that they had received some kind of training in reading, writing, or arithmetic outside regular formal schooling. Moreover, those demonstrating lower literacy skills were more likely to have participated in this training than those in the higher levels.

NALS also asked who provided this training. Table 2.4 reveals that about 43% of this 10% of adults said they had received this training from an employer or labor union. But here a different pattern emerges in the data. Adults in the highest literacy levels were more likely to have received this training than those with more restricted literacy skills. Thus, these data suggest that literacy plays a role not only in helping to sort our population in terms of who enters the workforce and the kind of

Table 2.3
Percentage of Labor Force Participants Who Had Ever Participated in Basic
Skills Training Programs, by Literacy Level: 1992

Literacy scale	1	2	3	4	5	All
Prose	13	12	10	7	5	10
Document	14	11	10	7	7	10
Quantitative	13	13	9	8	7	10

Note: Age group = 25 to 64.

Source: National Adult Literacy Survey, 1992.

work they will obtain but also in terms of whether they are likely to gain access to additional training and education on the job.

Table 2.5 shows the percentages of 25-to 64-year-old adults who reported being enrolled in some type of schooling by race/ethnicity and by their document literacy skills. Again, we see a clear and strong relationship between literacy skills and the likelihood of being enrolled in some type of educational program. Someone in Level 5 was three times more likely to be enrolled in school than someone in Level 1 or 2 on the document scale. This relationship also appears to hold among minority populations.

The same pattern is seen with second-chance programs. In a recent survey, the General Educational Development (GED) Testing Service and Educational Testing Service jointly conducted a national study to explore the relationships among the five GED tests and the three literacy scales. Figure 2.3 presents data indicating the strong relationship between where an individual is on the prose scale, for example, and the likelihood that this person will pass the GED test. Those who attain Level 3 or higher on the prose scale have a better than 90% chance of earning their high school equivalency certificate compared with those in Level 2, who have a slightly better than 50/50 chance, and those in Level 1, whose chance is less than 1 in 5 or 17%.

It should not be surprising, therefore, to see the relationship between literacy and earnings shown in Figure 2.4. Here we see the mean weekly earnings of adults who are employed full-time by their age and quantitative literacy level. Two points are worth noting in these data. First, among young adults (ages 16 to 24), there is no relationship between literacy and mean weekly earnings. That is, in our society, employers appear not to reward young adults for what they know and can do. These rewards come later in life when careers are pursued, and peak earning years are obtained. We see in this figure that literacy has the

Table 2.4

Percentage of Basic Skills Training Participants in the Labor Force Who Had Received This Training from Employers or Labor Unions, by Literacy Level: 1992

Literacy scale	1	2	3	4	5	All
Prose	25	40	48	56	61	43
Document	32	35	51	56	61	43
Quantitative	29	37	49	57	75	43

Note: Age group = 25 to 64.

Source: National Adult Literacy Survey, 1992.

largest effect on those who are 45 to 54 years of age. At this point in life, on average, where one is in the literacy distribution is closely associated with the amount of wages one can expect to earn. The earnings function is steepest for those who demonstrate the highest levels of literacy and flattest for those in the two lowest literacy levels.

THE DISTRIBUTION OF LITERACY SKILLS AMONG AMERICA'S ADULTS

As these data suggest, lower literacy skills may mean a lower quality of life and more limited opportunities for individuals within our society. As Carnevale and Gainer (1989) argue in their book, *The Learning Enterprise*, "the association between skills and opportunity for individual Americans is powerful and growing.... Individuals with poor skills do not have much to bargain with; they are condemned to low earnings and limited choices." The question now concerns the percentages of our adult population that demonstrate restricted skills—skills that may limit their opportunities or hinder the ability of the United States to compete in an increasingly global economy.

Figure 2.5 shows the distribution of literacy skills for the adult population 16 years of age and older. Twenty-one to 23%—or some 40 million of the 191 million adults in this country—demonstrated skills in the lowest level of prose, document, and quantitative proficiencies (Level 1). Though all adults in this level displayed limited skills, their characteristics were diverse. Many of the adults in this level performed simple, routine tasks involving brief and uncomplicated texts and documents. Others were unable to perform these tasks, and some had such limited skills in English that they were unable to respond to much of the survey.

Table 2.5
Percentages of Labor Force Participants Enrolled in School or College at the Time of the Survey, Total and Subpopulations: 1992

Levels	Total	Black	Hispanic
1	5	6	5
2	5	8	6
3	8	12	14
4	12	23	17
5	15	--	--

Note: Age group = 25 to 64.

Source: National Adult Literacy Survey, 1992.

Many factors help us to understand why so many adults in this country demonstrated such limited English literacy skills. Twenty-five percent of the respondents who performed in Level 1 were immigrants who may have been just learning to read and write English. Nearly two-thirds of those in Level 1 had terminated their education before completing high school, and a third were over the age of 65. Nineteen percent reported having some type of visual difficulty that would affect their ability to read printed or written information, and some 12% reported some type of health condition that kept them from participating fully in daily activities.

In addition to those in Level 1, some 25 to 28% of the respondents, representing about 50 million adults, demonstrated proficiencies in the next higher level of proficiency (Level 2) on the three literacy scales. While their skills were more varied than those of adults performing in Level 1, their repertoire was still considered to be limited. According to Figure 2.5, nearly one-third, or about 61 million adults nationwide, demonstrated performance defined by Level 3 on the literacy scales, and 18 to 21%, or 34 to 40 million, performed in the two highest levels of prose, document, and quantitative literacy.

Figure 2.6 shows the results by highest level of education attained. The good news in these data is that literacy and education are strongly correlated. That is, on average, the more years of schooling one attains, the higher the average score on the three literacy scales. For example, on the quantitative scale, the average score ranges from 169 (Level 1) for those reporting 0 to 8 years of schooling to 334 (Level 4) for those who pursued graduate studies or obtained a graduate degree. Other good news included the fact that there were no differences in the performance of high school graduates and those who attained the GED.

The not-so-good news is that the high school diploma has lost much

Figure 2.3
Percentages of GED Test Takers Passing the GED by Literacy Level on the Prose Scale: 1992

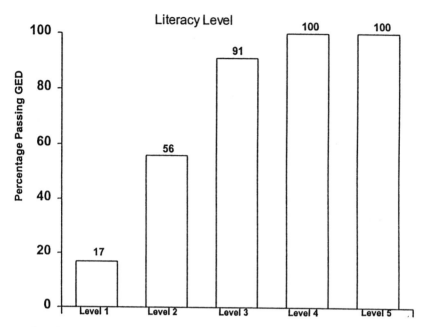

Note: Sample size of Level 5 participants is too small to provide a reliable estimate.

Source: Baldwin, Kirsch, Rock, & Yamamoto, 1995.

of its value in representing a core set of knowledge and skills. These data reveal that about 16% of those who terminated their education with a high school diploma performed in Level 1, and an additional 36% performed in Level 2. Perhaps surprisingly, some 4% of those with a four-year college degree performed in Level 1, and 11% performed in Level 2. This finding is explained somewhat by the fact that the majority of these students were either foreign-born or over the age of 65.

It is important to note that these data do not imply that individuals demonstrating low proficiencies can never succeed on more challenging tasks, that is, on literacy tasks that are more difficult or that fall at higher levels than their demonstrated proficiency. They may do so some of the time. Rather, it means that their probability of success is not as high. In other words, the more difficult the task relative to their proficiency, the lower the likelihood of responding correctly.

What implications are there for a society where so many individuals display limited skills? This is a difficult question to answer and one that is filled with emotion and personal values. Still, it seems apparent from

Figure 2.4
Median Weekly Wage of Adults Employed Full-Time by Age and Literacy
Level on the Quantitative Scale: 1992

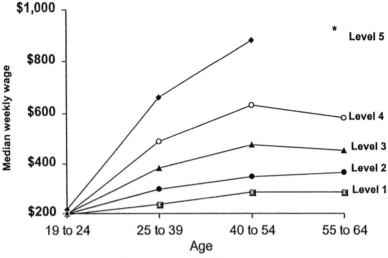

Note: Sample size is too small to provide a reliable estimate.

Source: National Adult Literacy Survey, 1992.

these data that a nation in which large numbers of adults display such limited skills has fewer resources with which to meet its goals and objectives, whether these are social, political, civic, or economic.

We live in a society in which both the volume and variety of printed and written information are growing and where increasing numbers of citizens are expected to be able to read, understand, and use these materials. Table 2.6 shows the projected mean differences in literacy by the year 2005. Using projections from the Bureau of Labor Statistics, Andy Sum, a labor economist at Northeastern University, calculated the figures in this table using the NALS data.

The first row of the table shows the average performance of the workforce on the three scales. If we assume that these represent literacy requirements, then we can calculate what might be expected to happen to scores under different assumptions. As shown here, these include looking at what happens to literacy in the high-growth occupations, low-growth occupations, all jobs, and those that are projected to decline. While overall, there appears to be equilibrium in the system, the fastest growing occupations are those that will require, on average, higher literacy skills, while occupations that are leaving the workforce are among those requiring the least amount of literacy and education. These findings are not limited to occupational projections here in the United States.

Figure 2.5
Distribution of Literacy Skills for the Adult Population 16 Years of Age and Older: 1992

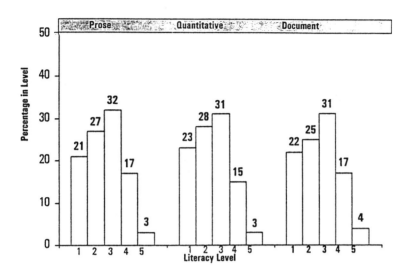

Source: National Adult Literacy Survey, 1992.

A recent study reporting results from the first-ever International Adult Literacy Survey (OECD, 1995) showed similar findings from selected countries around the world.

Perhaps the most important point to be made is the fact that many adults in our society lack literacy skills not in an absolute sense but rather in a relative sense. That is, the continuing process of social, demographic, and economic change within this country could lead to a more divided society along both racial and socioeconomic lines.

Already there is evidence of such a widening division. According to the report *America's Choice: High Skill or Low Wages!* (National Center on Education and the Economy, 1990), over the past 15 years or so the gap in earnings between professional and clerical workers has grown from 47 to 86%, while the gap between white-collar workers and skilled tradespeople has risen from 2 to 37%. At the same time, earnings for college-educated males 24 to 34 years of age have increased by 10%, while earnings for those with high school diplomas have declined by 9%. Moreover, the poverty rate for black families is nearly three times that for white families.

When we look at educational attainment, the picture is not any brighter. Figure 2.7 shows the highest level of schooling attained by selected racial/ethnic groups for both native and non-native populations.

Figure 2.6
Literacy Level and Average Literacy Proficiencies on the Quantitative Scale by Highest Level of
Education Completed: 1992

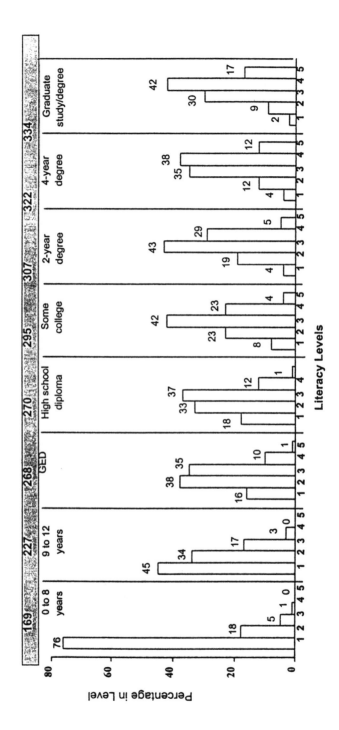

Note: Level 1 (0 to 225), Level 2 (226 to 275), Level 3 (276 to 325), Level 4 (326 to 375), Level 5 (376 to 500).

Source: National Adult Literacy Survey, 1992.

Table 2.6

Projected Differences in Mean Literacy Proficiency Requirements for Various
Subgroups of U.S. Workers: 1990 to 2005

	Prose	Document	Quantitative
Weighted mean proficiency requirement for all occupations in 1990	284	279	284
Weighted mean proficiency requirement for new jobs in high growth occupations in 2005	301	294	297
Difference in mean proficiency between new jobs in high growth occupations in 2005 and all occupations in 1990	+17	+15	+13
Weighted mean proficiency requirement for jobs in growth occupations in 2005	293	288	291
Difference in mean proficiency between new jobs in growth occupations in 2005 and all occupations in 1990	+9	+8	+7
Weighted mean proficiency requirement for lost jobs in declining occupations in 2005	252	249	258
Difference in mean proficiency between new jobs in growth occupations and lost jobs in declining occupations in 2005	+40	+39	+33
Weighted mean proficiency requirement for jobs in all occupations in 2005	286	281	285
Difference in mean proficiency between jobs in 2005 and 1990	+2	+2	+2

Source: A. Sum, *Literacy in the labor force: A report on the results of the National Adult Literacy Survey* (in press).

Among native-born populations, there is a great deal of similarity in the educational attainment of the various groups except for postsecondary experience. Here we see that larger percentages of native-born Asian Americans go on to postsecondary and college education than white Americans or African-American or Latino adults.

Among non-native populations the picture is somewhat different. Figure 2.8 shows that almost 40% of Latinos report 0 to 8 years of schooling compared with only about 10% for the other racial/ethnic groups. Among those with college education, we see that Asian adults again have the highest percentage and Latino adults the lowest percentage. These numbers are very significant when we consider the fact that more than

Figure 2.7
Percentage of the Native-Born Adult Population Reporting Levels of
Education by Race/Ethnicity

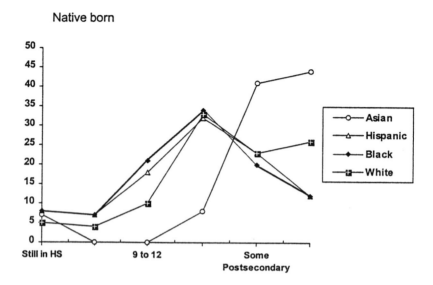

Source: National Adult Literacy Survey, 1992.

40% of the Latino population in this country is foreign-born, as is 80% of the Asian population. In addition, both of these groups are projected to grow significantly over the next decade or so.

CONCLUSION

We all have a role to play in ensuring that adults who need or wish to improve their literacy skills have the opportunity to do so. It is also important that the individuals themselves come to realize the value of literacy in their lives and to recognize the long-term benefits associated with improving their skills. Policymakers must understand that quick fixes or short-term solutions will not work. All of us must recognize that many poor, many minorities, and many of those with limited education endure distractions and disincentives to learning that prevent them from achieving higher literacy levels. Yet finding solutions aimed at improving current literacy levels for all adults is a necessary step to improving individual opportunity and to improving the quality of life in this country.

Figure 2.8
Percentage of the Non-Native-Born Adult Population Reporting Levels of
Education by Race/Ethnicity

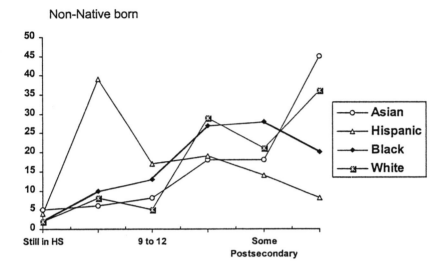

Source: National Adult Literacy Survey, 1992.

REFERENCES

Baldwin, J., Kirsch, I., Rock, D., & Yamamoto, K. (1995). *The literacy proficiencies of GED examinees: Results from the GED-NALS comparison study.* Washington, DC: American Council on Education.

Carnevale, A., & Gainer, L. (1989). *The learning enterprise.* Washington, DC: U.S. Department of Labor, Employment and Training Administration.

Kirsch, I., Jungeblut, A., Jenkins, L., & Kolstad, A. (1993). *Adult literacy in America: A first look at the results of the National Adult Literacy Survey.* Washington, DC: U.S. Department of Education, National Center for Education Statistics.

National Center on Education and the Economy. (1990, June). *America's choice: High skills or low wages! The report of the Commission on the Skills of the American Workforce.*

Organization for Economic Cooperation and Development (OECD). (1995). *Literacy, economy and society: Results of the first International Adult Literacy Survey.* Paris, France: OECD.

Sum, A. (in press). *Literacy in the labor force: A report on the results of the National Adult Literacy Survey.* Washington, DC: U.S. Department of Education, National Center for Education Statistics.

3

Adult Education and Literacy Public Policy: What It Is and How It Is Shaped

Alice Johnson and Andrew Hartman

This chapter provides an overview of federal adult education and literacy policy, including the substance of current law and funding trends; discusses how adult education and literacy policy is developed; and explains preliminary steps to address the need for more national coordination of literacy efforts. The chapter provides a context for understanding the role of the NALS in influencing current and future policy regarding adult literacy education.

CURRENT ADULT EDUCATION AND LITERACY POLICY: BACKGROUND AND OVERVIEW

The Adult Education Act

The federal government began its involvement in adult education as part of President Lyndon Johnson's Great Society efforts. The first piece of legislation to include adult education was the Economic Opportunity Act of 1964. It was followed by the Adult Education Act of 1966, which was designed to improve educational opportunities for adults, with a particular emphasis on helping them develop the skills needed for productive employment or to finish secondary school. It also provided incentives for states to spend their own funds on education, to designate a state director of adult education, and to develop state plans for allocating adult education funds locally.

In order to achieve these goals, the Adult Education Act, which is administered by the U.S. Department of Education, established a formula-based grant program that allocates funds to states to provide adult education services for three types of instruction:

1. *Adult Basic Education* (ABE): for students whose skills are below the eighth grade level;
2. *Adult Secondary Education* (ASE): for students preparing to obtain a high school equivalency diploma;
3. *English as a Second Language* (ESL): for students with limited English proficiency.

The law defines adults as persons age 16 and older who are out of school. While total enrollment in Adult Education Act programs hovers at around 4 million students per year, the number of people who would significantly benefit from literacy services is estimated at roughly 40 million.

The Adult Education Act also provides competitive grants to state and local correctional agencies for the operation of literacy and basic skills programs. This funding totaled $4.723 million in fiscal year (FY) 1997. Grant recipients are required to serve every incarcerated individual who is not "functionally literate" unless that individual is terminally ill, is serving a life sentence without parole, or has been sentenced to death.

Congress revises the Adult Education Act about every six years. It was most recently revised—and significantly expanded—in 1988. At that time, Congress created two new programs: National Workplace Literacy Partnerships and the National Programs division at the Department of Education. The Workplace Partnerships were demonstration projects that teach literacy skills necessary for the workplace through partnerships between (1) business, industry, labor organizations, or private industry councils and (2) schools, education agencies, and institutions. National Programs funds evaluation, technical assistance, and research on adult education and literacy.

The original adult education legislation grew out of the War on Poverty and the activist government philosophy that was prevalent in the 1960s. Since then, most public policy has been driven by the timing of tradition. Congress traditionally writes education laws that expire six years from the date of enactment, to be revised and updated six years later. As a result, a cycle has developed for sessions of Congress, each of which lasts two years: in any given six years, Congress will spend two years revising higher education legislation, the next two years revising elementary and secondary legislation, and the final two years revising adult and vocational education legislation.

Adult Education and Literacy Funding

Federal funding provides only about a quarter of overall literacy funding, and most programs rely heavily on funds from the state, private foundations, and individual donations. Specifically, the total federal investment in adult education and literacy (including basic state grants, Even Start Family Literacy, the National Institute for Literacy, the Department of Education's National Evaluation and Technical Assistance, and prison literacy) was $456.2 million in fiscal year 1997, while state and local funding totaled $830 million.

The Adult Education Act was initially funded at $19.9 million. In recent years, funding has increased substantially. The largest increases came between FY 1988 and FY 1994, when Congress increased funding by 121%, to $255 million, and in FY 1997, when it was boosted by $95 million to $340 million.

The factors leading to the FY 1997 increase included timely, targeted, and effective lobbying by grassroots literacy advocates nationwide. In 1994, control of Congress had shifted from Democrats to Republicans. In the winter of 1996, the Democratic administration and Republican Congress had a showdown over funding that led to an unprecedented shutdown of the federal government and an unexpected backlash from the American public. As a result, both sides were eager for an agreement. When unexpected "surplus" funding became available, both sides quickly agreed to dedicate it to education. The question was how to divide it among various education programs, most of which, unlike literacy, have lobbyists representing them on Capitol Hill.

The literacy field had been monitoring the situation, largely through the Policy Committee of the National Coalition for Literacy, an umbrella group of organizations that support literacy. Word of the possibility of a funding increase spread quickly, thanks largely to literacy listservs on the Internet, and the field responded by bombarding Congress with phone calls and faxes asking that some of the funds be earmarked for literacy.

In the meantime, Senator Jim Jeffords, one of a handful of GOP leaders crafting the Republican list of priorities, successfully argued that passage of the 1996 welfare reform bill would be driving more welfare clients to literacy programs across the country as they prepared for self-sufficiency. At the same time, Senator Paul Simon initiated a letter to the White House asking for some of this funding to be dedicated to literacy. He quickly persuaded Senator Edward Kennedy, who by this time had received hundreds of phone calls from Massachusetts, Senator Patty Murray, who had heard from constituents in Washington, and Representative Tom Sawyer of Ohio to sign on. Simon and Murray's offices then both faxed the letter to the administration's chief negotiator, chief of staff Leon Panetta, and Simon had a copy hand-delivered to the White House.

The message was not lost on the president. In his FY 1998 budget request, he proposed another significant increase for adult education state grants, to $382 million, but Congress does not seem likely to accommodate such a large increase two years in a row. The administration's request also adds $260 million in new funding for a new literacy initiative, the America Reads Challenge, which was recently enacted by Congress. Congress agreed to fund a children and family literacy initiative at that level in FY 1999, as authorizing legislation was enacted by April 1, 1998.

Potential Changes to the Adult Education Act

The 105th Congress is now considering legislation that would significantly revise the Adult Education Act. Changes under consideration include:

- Reducing state discretionary funds in adult education programs in order to increase funding for service delivery;
- Improving the overall quality of programs by setting out specific benchmarks for program outcomes and requiring states to establish acceptable levels of performance for local programs;
- Improving coordination between job training programs and adult education.

The House passed a new version of the law in May 1997, but Senate passage had not occurred by the spring of 1998, so final passage of the bill is unlikely until late in 1998. This means the changes, if they are enacted, are not likely to take effect until the year 2000.

HOW PUBLIC POLICY AROUND LITERACY IS SHAPED

Adult literacy has generally not had high priority or visibility on the public policy agenda at the national, state, or local level. The reasons for this include the following:

- There are a greater interest and empathy on the part of the public and policymakers directed toward young children. This may be, in part, because children are seen as more vulnerable, interventions at a young age are perceived to be preventive and thus more cost-effective, and there is a stronger, better-organized advocacy network for children.
- Adult education and literacy are not as well understood or appreciated as the K–12 or postsecondary parts of the American education system. Nearly all Americans have had firsthand experience with K–12 education. Adult educa-

tion and literacy programs, on the other hand, do not directly touch all lives; many people—including some policymakers—have little or no idea that such a system of education even exists.

- Adult education services are often placed in state and local agencies that are primarily focused on elementary and secondary education. As a result, adult education programs typically do not receive the support and exposure they deserve and need.

- As a field, we have not clearly defined our goals and how well we are doing in accomplishing them. We have not done a good enough job of clearly and simply describing the nature of the literacy problem in America, why the public and policymakers should be concerned about it, and what should be done to deal with it.

The *National Adult Literacy Survey* (NALS), released by the U.S. Department of Education in 1993, was the most detailed description ever produced on the condition of literacy in America. Many in the literacy field had hoped that it would address several of these concerns and contribute to making the nation's adult literacy problem a serious policy issue that demanded a greater response at the local, state, and national level. This did not happen.

Looking back at what transpired in 1993, we can now make some statements as to why. First, the report was not strongly promoted by leaders in the administration. There were other domestic policy and education issues on its agenda, and adult literacy did not fit onto the list. Second, the numbers reported in the NALS were seen as unbelievable and "hype" by many in policy positions and the media. This was largely due to the fact that initial press reports on the NALS stated that 90 million Americans were illiterate—a highly inaccurate reading of the data (Gray, 1993; Jordan, 1993). Finally, the literacy field itself was neither prepared nor equipped to take on the role of turning the NALS into a lever for policy attention.

A great deal has changed since 1993. The literacy field is much more conscious of the need to define itself in clear, easily understood terms and to demonstrate the contribution it makes to individual and societal goals. The field's infrastructure for dealing with public policy has improved significantly, and those who lead the major state and national organizations have contributed resources to make that possible. As a result, momentum for the literacy issue has increased and shows no signs of declining.

A number of other factors have helped build the momentum: the president's inclusion of literacy as a reelection campaign issue through the America Reads Challenge, which focuses on the literacy of children and families; the creation of the National Literacy Advocacy (NLA) listserv on the Internet, which provides hundreds of advocates nationwide with almost instantaneous reports of policy activity—and advocacy opportunities—around adult education and literacy; a national public awareness campaign on literacy, designed by the National Institute for Literacy and carried out by local literacy task forces in all states; the choice of the 1997 Miss America, Tara Holland, of literacy as her platform issue and her speaking about it continuously throughout the year, usually to groups that included the press; the birth of a new national organization committed to advocacy, the National Alliance of Urban Literacy Coalitions; and the increased commitment of the business community to literacy, as exemplified by Starbucks Coffee Company's creation of a new foundation that has pledged to give at least $500,000 to literacy in 1998 alone.

NEED FOR NATIONWIDE COORDINATION OF LITERACY EFFORTS

The national adult literacy delivery system is less structured than other areas of education, such as elementary and secondary education. Literacy services are provided by a variety of different agencies and organizations, including local education agencies (60%); community colleges (15%); community-based organizations (14%); public and private nonprofits, including volunteer programs (7%); and correctional facilities (about 4%). In addition to professional full-and part-time teachers, over 140,000 certified volunteers teach 250,000 adult literacy students annually through programs based primarily in libraries, churches, and community centers.

Recognizing its need for a more organized, structured system, the literacy field in the late 1980s began lobbying Congress for help in improving coordination. Congress, under the leadership of Senator Paul Simon and Representative Tom Sawyer, responded with the National Literacy Act of 1991, which defined literacy as "an individual's ability to read, write, and speak in English, and compute and solve problems at levels of proficiency necessary to function on the job and in society, to achieve one's goals, and develop one's knowledge and potential." The act authorized new and increased funding for adult education and literacy in the amount of $197.5 million per year through FY 1995. In addition to strengthening the federal commitment to literacy and ensuring that federal assistance goes to the best-quality providers serving individuals most in need, the National Literacy Act explicitly focused on improving the coordination of literacy programs. It created a new federal structure for the literacy field, consisting of the National Institute for Literacy and State Literacy Resource Centers.

The National Institute for Literacy was charged with helping to coordinate federal literacy programs, analyzing policy, evaluating program activities, operating a toll-free hot line for literacy information, promoting innovation, developing a database of literacy information, and providing fellowships to individuals in literacy-related fields. It was authorized at $15 million annually but has not been fully funded. Since 1991, it has received roughly $5 million annually to carry out its duties.

Since its creation, the institute has undertaken a number of activities designed to assist the field in its efforts to become better coordinated. One of the most successful has been the establishment of a state-of-the-art, Internet-based information retrieval and communication system, the Literacy Information and Communications System (LINCS), which can be accessed on the World Wide Web at www.nifl.gov. LINCS provides literacy stakeholders in every state—teachers, administrators, learners, volunteers, and others—with current information on instructional and research resources, technical assistance, and training. It connects the field at the local, state, and national levels and provides a timely and effective way for literacy experts to share resources and expertise with practitioners across the country and around the world. LINCS includes eight listservs that provide thousands of subscribers with a vehicle for joining on-line discussions about major literacy issues and sharing timely information, ideas, and expertise. Listservs are moderated by national literacy organizations that focus on key literacy topics, such as family literacy, ESL, learning disabilities, and staff development for literacy practitioners.

Another key initiative that is helping to coordinate the literacy field is the standards development and system reform initiative, "Equipped for the Future" (EFF). This five-year initiative aims to improve the adult literacy and lifelong learning system so that every adult has the opportunity to build the knowledge, skills, and abilities needed to fulfill real-world responsibilities as parents, citizens, and workers. EFF has helped to bring together the literacy field around a common vision through a multiyear, grassroots, consensus-building process. Literacy leaders in several states participated in an intensive, consensus-building process to create a customer-driven approach to adult literacy that will lead to the development of a set of voluntary national standards for the knowledge and skills adults need. EFF will result in curriculum, assessment, and instruction innovations for adult literacy and basic skills programs that will be nationwide.

State Literacy Resource Centers (SLRCs) provide training, technical assistance, and coordination for federal, state, and local literacy programs. Soon after they were created, however, Congress eliminated their funding. This has left it up to individual states to keep SLRC doors open and has led to a reduction in funding of some SLRCs. Most, however, have survived and are coordinating and supporting state literacy efforts in broad, interagency ways.

CONCLUSION

Despite these important steps forward, the literacy field has a long way to go before it will be able to ensure that all adults with literacy needs have access to learning the skills necessary for success in the workplace, family, and community. Traditionally, with few exceptions, literacy has not been a priority among policymakers. Slowly, this is starting to change. The late 1990s has been a time of unprecedented growth, and, as the field continues to work to make an effective case to policymakers, we are optimistic about looking forward to the most exciting times for literacy—and for making much more of a difference in the lives of adults who need to improve their skills.

REFERENCES

Gray, P. (1993, September). Adding up the under-skilled. *Time, 42*(12), 75.
Jordan, M. (1993, September). Literacy of 90 million is deficient. *Washington Post*, A1.

4

Dimensionality and Construct Validity of the NALS Assessment

Stephen Reder

INTRODUCTION

As attention increasingly focuses in the United States on the literacy skills and knowledge adults need to be productive workers and active citizens, information is being sought about adult literacy (National Education Goals Panel, 1991). The chapters in this volume examine issues and applications of adult literacy in the context of one particular national assessment of adult literacy, the National Adult Literacy Survey (NALS). The NALS assessment methodology is the most recent in a systematic series of adult literacy assessments in the United States that have been conducted by the Educational Testing Service (ETS) over the last decade. These literacy assessments have profiled various adult populations in the United States, reporting literacy proficiencies on three 0–500-point scales: prose, document, and quantitative literacy (Kirsch & Jungeblut, 1986, 1992).

The National Education Goals Panel (1991) has selected these three literacy proficiency scales as indicators of the progress of state and national efforts to meet national adult literacy goals. Understanding the construct of literacy assessed in these surveys is thus becoming increasingly important for developing effective educational, social, and economic policies.

The assessment procedures typically involve constructed responses on simulated, everyday literacy tasks such as locating and interpreting information from narrative materials (*prose* literacy tasks); identifying and filling in information on familiar forms (*document* literacy tasks); and extracting and computing with numerical information from graphs, tables, and other written materials (*quantitative* literacy tasks). Using item-response theory to calibrate and link performance across assessment instruments and populations, Kirsch and colleagues have conducted a series of parallel, large-scale assessment surveys. These surveys have profiled the prose, document, and quantitative proficiencies of various adult populations, including young adults (Kirsch & Jungeblut, 1986), clientele of federal unemployment and job training programs (Kirsch & Jungeblut, 1992), various statewide adult populations (e.g., Cosby, Howell, Carr, & Miller, 1991; Oregon Progress Board, 1991), incarcerated adults in state and federal prisons (Haigler, Harlow, O'Connor, & Campbell, 1994), and the general adult population of the United States (Kirsch, Jungeblut, Jenkins, & Kolstad, 1993).

Results of these surveys are generally reported separately for the prose, document, and quantitative scales. Adults' proficiencies on each literacy scale are profiled in relation to their demographic characteristics and their responses to survey questions about their social, educational, and economic status; perceptions and uses of literacy materials; and so forth (Kirsch et al., 1993). Both cross-tabulations and multivariate regression analyses indicate that the literacy proficiencies assessed in these studies are strongly associated with a variety of important social and economic outcomes (e.g., employment, income, poverty, voting), even after the effects of educational attainment are controlled (Ishikawa, 1994; Kirsch & Jungeblut, 1992; Reder, 1994a; Sum, in preparation).

Detailed descriptions of, and rationales for, the constructs of prose, document, and quantitative literacy underlying these assessments are available elsewhere (e.g., Kirsch & Jungeblut, 1986, 1992; Kirsch et al., 1993; Kirsch, Jungeblut, & Mosenthal, 1994; Mosenthal & Kirsch, 1994). Casual inspection of the various types of literacy materials and tasks (prose, document, quantitative) involved in the assessments lends a certain measure of face validity to the distinctions among the three types of literacy. There certainly appears to be a wide variety of everyday tasks involving written materials that can be categorized as prose, document, or quantitative literacy tasks. Furthermore, scientific advances have been made in identifying some of the features of these prose, document, and quantitative literacy materials and tasks that generate varying levels of task difficulty (Kirsch et al., 1994; Mosenthal & Kirsch, 1994).

Several rationales thus exist for accepting the distinctiveness of these three scales: their apparent face validity; the utility of the benchmarks and comparative data established through their prior use in adult literacy surveys; and the progress that has been made in identifying distinctive features of prose, document, and quantitative literacy materials and tasks. Despite these rationales, there is good reason to look more closely at the validity of the three constructs. For one thing, examination of the various literacy surveys (in the reports previously cited) reveals that the major survey results are nearly identical for each of the three scales. Although a few very small, but statistically significant, differences have been found among the scales in terms of their distributions in various subgroups of the population (Rock & Yamamoto, 1994), almost all major relationships between literacy and other important variables and outcomes (e.g., education, employment status, voting behavior, poverty status, earnings) are parallel across the three literacy scales. Survey results thus often seem redundant, with findings appearing to be reported essentially in triplicate, as it were. This pervasive pattern raises the question of whether there are really three literacy scales being assessed or perhaps just one.

This issue of the *dimensionality* of the literacy construct has important theoretical and practical ramifications. On the theoretical side, of course, it is crucial to understand the nature of the literacy construct being assessed by these surveys and instruments. The implementation of policy and programmatic goals in adult education and training ultimately are linked to such constructs. The dimensionality of the literacy construct being assessed also has important practical consequences. In terms of designing, conducting, and interpreting adult literacy surveys, for example, it makes a great deal of difference addressing three (as opposed to one or even two) separate scales. There is extra cost for developing, administering, and scoring test items from multiple scales, whether in literacy surveys or in student assessment. If fewer literacy scales need be assessed, overall measurement error can be reduced, and emerging assessment techniques such as computer-adaptive testing become more usable. There is also an economy of attention in policy discussions regarding the social and economic correlates of literacy; if the multiple scales involved are effectively redundant, then attempts to present results for each may be counterproductive when literacy concerns must contend with other problems for limited attention and resources.

There may also be additional test burden on learners, teachers, and other staff in adult education programs who wish to assess students' skills and knowledge in relation to emerging state and national standards or benchmarks. There are, for example, a commercially published versions of these assessment instruments, called the *ETS Tests of Applied Literacy Skills* (TALS), designed for use in adult education and literacy programs (Educational Testing Service, 1990). Separate assessment instruments are published and sold for the three scales. Program costs are therefore proportional to the number of scales assessed in terms of cost of testing materials, staff time for test administration and scoring, and student testing burden.

This chapter therefore explores the question of dimensionality of the

Table 4.1
Adult Literacy Surveys Conducted by ETS

Survey	Year	Population	Sample Size	Main Report
Young Adult Literacy Survey (YALS)	1985	U.S. adults in households, age 21-25	3,474	Kirsch & Jungeblut, 1986
U.S. Department of Labor - Employment Services / Unemployment Insurance (ES/UI)	1990	ES/UI program clients	3,277	Kirsch & Jungeblut, 1992
U.S. Department of Labor - Job Training Partnership Act (JTPA)	1990	JTPA program clients	2,501	Kirsch & Jungeblut, 1992
Oregon Literacy Survey	1990	Oregon adults, age 16-64	1,993	Oregon Progress Board, 1991
Mississippi Literacy Survey	1990	Mississippi adults, age 16-75	1,804	Cosby, Howell, Carr & Miller, 1991
National Adult Literacy Survey (NALS) (non-incarcerated)	1992	U.S. adults in households, age 16 and above	24,944	Kirsch, Jungeblut, Jenkins & Kolstad, 1993

prose, document, and quantitative scales underlying these assessments and surveys. The question being posed here is not whether or not in some absolute sense there *are* such multiple literacies but whether or not the assessment instruments, procedures, and surveys involved actually *measure* them separately in a distinctive and useful manner.

METHOD

Table 4.1 describes the particular surveys that will be considered in this chapter. With the exception of the Young Adult Literacy Survey (YALS), results presented here are based on secondary analyses of the public-use data sets prepared by ETS for each survey. The YALS results presented here are those published by Kirsch and Jungeblut (1986) and National Assessment of Educational Progress (1986).

Details of the individual surveys—their samples, assessment instruments and procedures, and scoring techniques—are described in the corresponding reports listed in the table. For present purposes, it is important to note several features shared by these various studies:

• Use of a literacy survey methodology that combines sophisticated population survey and cognitive assessment techniques (e.g., Campbell, Kirsch, & Kolstad, 1992).

- Reliance primarily on test items that require constructed responses to simulated functional literacy tasks rather than multiple-choice questions.

- Utilization of simulation tasks and written materials reflecting three assumed types of literacy: *prose literacy* (the knowledge and skills needed to understand and use information from narrative-like texts); *document literacy* (the skills and knowledge required to locate and use information in forms, schedules, maps, tables, and graphs); and *quantitative literacy* (the knowledge and skills needed to apply arithmetic operations to numbers embedded in written materials).

- Use of *item response theory* for developing and calibrating test items in ways that permit linking results across studies involving different populations and different sets of assessment items. Individual assessment items are assigned difficulties on one of the prose, document, or quantitative literacy scales. Individuals' proficiency scores are estimated for each of the three scales based on responses to a battery of assessment items and background characteristics (Mislevy, 1991; Mislevy, Johnson, & Muraki, 1992).

- Use of *BIB-spiraling* to present different subsets of test items to survey participants (Beaton, Johnson, & Ferris, 1987). Because of cost and test burden concerns, it is not practical to administer the large number of test items to each respondent that is needed for reliable estimation of a population's proficiencies. Individual survey respondents thus received only a carefully designed fraction of the set of test items employed in a given survey. A balanced incomplete block design ("BIB spiral") grouped the pool of items into a series of nonoverlapping blocks. These item blocks were then grouped into a number of test booklets, each of which contained a subset of blocks. Each block appeared equally often in combination with all other blocks across the set of test booklets randomly assigned to respondents. This design enables efficient estimation of proficiency distributions for a population based on responses to all items presented across the test booklets randomly assigned to that population.

- An individual's proficiency on a scale is not directly observed but is a latent variable to be inferred from test performance and background characteristics. The uncertainty or measurement error associated with this inference is expressed in terms of Rubin's (1987) *multiple imputation* methodology, in which a set of *plausible values* is inferred for each individual proficiency (Mislevy, 1991). In these studies five such plausible values were estimated for each of the three literacy scales for each respondent. The more uncertainty (measurement error) associated with estimating a particular individual's proficiency score, the greater the corresponding spread expected among the five plausible values provided for that score.

The dimensionality of these prose, document, and quantitative literacy proficiencies will be investigated through the analysis of the fine structure of the assessment data provided by the adult literacy surveys. Secondary analyses of these data sets will be conducted to produce evidence of dimensionality at two levels. *Scale-level evidence* will be drawn from the pattern of intercorrelations among the plausible values generated for the three scales. *Item-level evidence* will examine and model the patterns of relationships among survey participants' responses to the individual prose, document, and quantitative literacy task items. Additional details about the methods used to gather and analyze these various types of evidence about dimensionality will be presented.

RESULTS

Two types of evidence were originally adduced for the tridimensionality of the literacy scales in the technical report from the first of these adult literacy surveys, the Young Adult Literacy Survey (YALS). The first type of evidence from YALS concerned the magnitude of the intercorrelations among the three scale scores, while the second involved a factor analysis of the interitem correlations (National Assessment of Educational Progress, 1986). The interscale correlations are scale-level evidence, whereas the pattern of interitem correlations offers item-level evidence. Each level of evidence is considered in turn.

Scale-level Evidence

The simple intercorrelations among the three literacy scales originally reported for the YALS were moderate in strength, ranging from 0.49 to 0.56 (prose-document = 0.55, prose-quantitative = 0.49, quantitative-document = 0.56).[1] According to the technical report for the YALS, the moderate size of these intercorrelations provides "further support for the notion that literacy skills can and should be separated along at least three distinct dimensions—prose, document, and quantitative skills. These important distinctions would be lost if the diverse tasks from the current assessment had been aggregated and reported on a single scale" (National Assessment of Educational Progress, 1986: III-34).

As Salganik and Tal (1989) observed, the absolute magnitude of such intercorrelations among measures is difficult to interpret unless the reliability of the measures is known. Measurement error, of course, reduces the reliability of the measures and their expected intercorrelations. An unreliable measure generally will not correlate highly with *any* other measure. Any measurement error present in the YALS would thus attenuate the observed correlation between scales. Estimates of the *disattenuated* correlations among the scale scores would provide more direct evidence about dimensionality. As will be seen later, when disattenuated interscale correlations are estimated, the resulting coefficients are much higher (in fact, close to unity), suggesting unidimensionality in the assessment.

Table 4.2 displays the intercorrelations among the three literacy scales for a series of the adult literacy surveys. The first row shows the intercorrelations for the YALS study that were described earlier. The next four rows display results from four surveys that used identical assess-

Table 4.2
Correlation Coefficients among Literacy Proficiencies in Various ETS Adult
Literacy Surveys (Correlations Calculated between First Plausible Values of
Each Scale)

Literacy Survey	Sample Size	Prose-Document Correlation	Prose-Quantitative Correlation	Document-Quantitative Correlation
Young Adult[a]	3,474	.55	.49	.56
JTPA	2,501	.63	.59	.64
ES/UI	3,277	.65	.61	.66
Oregon	1,993	.54	.48	.54
Mississippi	1,804	.71	.66	.72
National Adult	24,944	.92	.89	.91

[a]As reported by National Assessment of Educational Progress (1986, p. III–34).

ment instruments (which shared some, but not all, items with the instruments used in the YALS). The bottom row of the table displays the intercorrelations for the NALS household survey, whose assessment instruments shared some items with the YALS but not with the instruments utilized in the Job Training Partnership Act (JTPA), Employment Service/Unemployment Insurance (ES/UI), Oregon, and Mississippi studies. These coefficients were calculated directly from the first plausible values for each scale in the data sets.[2]

With the exception of the NALS data, the intercorrelations among the three literacy scales are moderate in size and roughly comparable across the series of assessment surveys. The intercorrelations in the NALS, however, are significantly higher than those from the other surveys. The NALS coefficients are on the order of 0.9 (ranging from .89 to .92), which is, indeed, a very high degree of intercorrelation among measures that still contain some degree of measurement error. The degree of intercorrelation among the three scales in NALS, on the order of 0.9, is about two to three times as strong as that in the earlier surveys.

In exploring why the intercorrelations were so much larger in NALS than in previous surveys, it was determined that there was a significant error in the computer program ETS used in the earlier surveys to impute the plausible values for individuals' prose, document, and quantitative literacy proficiencies. This error did not materially affect the estimated means or standard deviations of the individual scale scores but did result in substantially underestimated intercorrelations among the three literacy scales. A different imputation program—which corrected the earlier error—was utilized in processing the NALS data.[3]

Since the NALS-based estimates of intercorrelations among the literacy

Table 4.3
Interscale Correlations among Plausible Values*

	Prose	Document	Quantitative
Prose	-	.92	.89
Document	.92	-	.91
Quantitative	.89	.91	-

*Data are from the NALS household survey (N = 24,944). The correlation shown between a pair of scales is the average of five pairwise correlations between counterpart plausible values for the two given scales.

scales are the best ones presently available, let's examine them more closely. The coefficients in Table 4.2 are sample correlations calculated between the first plausible values produced for each scale (recall that five plausible values were imputed for each score). Parallel correlations can be calculated between the other plausible values for the scale scores: one between the second plausible values, one between the third plausible values, and so forth. Table 4.3 displays the results of averaging the five sample correlations thus calculated for each given pair of scales. The correlation coefficients in Table 4.3 are similar to their corresponding coefficients in the NALS row of Table 4.2, but they are not identical (beyond two decimal places).[4]

The high degree of intercorrelation among the prose, document and quantitative literacy scales is illustrated graphically in the scatterplots shown in Figures 4.1, 4.2, and 4.3. Each graph displays the relationship between individuals' scores on a pair of literacy scales: quantitative-by-prose (Figure 4.1), document-by-quantitative (Figure 4.2), and document-by-prose (Figure 4.3). Each plotted point represents the scores of one survey participant. Darker points reflect the coincidence of multiple individuals. For clarity, only a random 10% sample of the 24,944 household survey participants is plotted in each figure. Notice that the strong positive correlation is evident in each figure. Furthermore, these large positive correlations appear to hold throughout the range of assessed scores.

When considering the large magnitude of the intercorrelations among the three literacy scales, it is important to remember that these are still *attenuated* estimates of the underlying correlations between the scales. The underlying proficiencies are being measured with error, the impact of which is to reduce the observed sample correlations between scales. True scores (i.e., those ideally measured without error) should be even more highly intercorrelated. Although we estimate these disattenuated correlations later, using item-level modeling, a heuristic approximation can be made using the present scale-level data from NALS.

Figure 4.1
Scatterplot of Prose by Quantitative Literacy Proficiency Scores

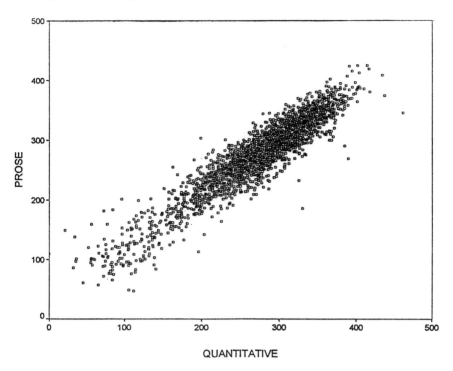

Note: Each point is a participant in the household component of the National Adult Literacy
  Survey. Darker points reflect the coincidence of multiple individuals. For clarity, a
  random 10% sample of the 24,944 household participants is plotted here.

If the five plausible values imputed for each scale score are arithmet-
ically averaged into a mean plausible value for each scale score, sample
correlations can be calculated between the mean plausible values of the
scales. By design, the mean of the five plausible values for a scale score
will have less error associated with it than will any one of the five plausible values. These mean plausible values should thus be even more
highly intercorrelated across scales than are the constituent plausible values (whose intercorrelations were presented in Tables 4.2 and 4.3). Table
4.4 shows this to be the case; the intercorrelations among mean plausible
values range between .93 and .95. This procedure, in which at least some
measurement error associated with individual plausible values is removed, provides an estimate of the (disattenuated) correlations between
true scores on the prose, document, and quantitative literacy scales.[5]
Other techniques are used later, based on modeling interitem correla-

Figure 4.2
Scatterplot of Document by Quantitative Literacy Proficiency Scores

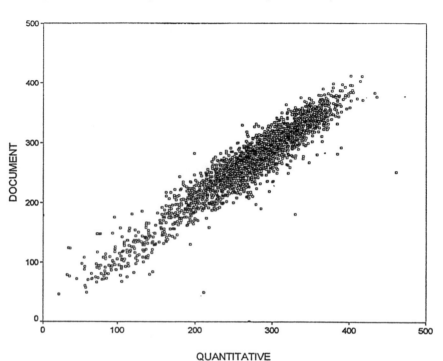

QUANTITATIVE

Note: Each point is a participant in the household component of the National Adult Literacy
   Survey. Darker points reflect the coincidence of multiple individuals. For clarity, a
   random 10% sample of the 24,944 household participants is plotted here.

tions, to estimate these disattenuated correlation coefficients. These techniques yield similarly high estimates of the disattenuated interscale
correlations, in the .95 range.

   The scale-level evidence thus offers little support for the tridimensionality of the literacy assessment scales as claimed by its developers. The
scale-level evidence originally offered in support of the three distinct
scales was found to be erroneous. The present findings of a very high
degree of intercorrelation among the NALS scales indicate that distinct
dimensions of literacy are *not* being assessed in these surveys. When
measurement error is taken into account, the disattenuated correlations
between the scales are in the .93–.95 range, a strong indication that the
same essential skills and knowledge are being assessed by the three
scales.[6]

Figure 4.3
Scatterplot of Document by Prose Proficiency Scores

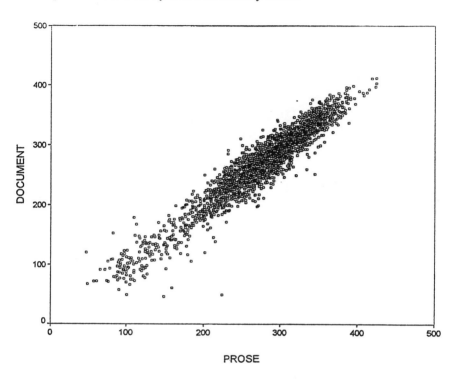

Note: Each point is a participant in the household component of the National Adult Literacy Survey. Darker points reflect the coincidence of multiple individuals. For clarity, a random 10% sample of the 24,944 household participants is plotted here.

Item-level Evidence

The second type of evidence originally offered in support of the distinctiveness of the three scales of measurement was based on classical factor analysis of the interitem correlations among individuals' responses to the cognitive items. Such factor-analytic techniques attempt to represent the pattern of individuals' responses across many items in terms of a smaller number of underlying factors (e.g., prose, document, and quantitative proficiencies). These exploratory factor analytic techniques are frequently used to assess the dimensionality of responses to a battery of cognitive items.

To consider the dimensionality of the YALS data, the matrix of interitem correlations was factor analyzed by the method of principal axes

Table 4.4
Interscale Correlations among Mean Plausible Values*

	Prose	Document	Quantitative
Prose	-	.95	.93
Document	.95	-	.94
Quantitative	.93	.94	-

*Data are from the NALS household survey (N =24,944).

(National Assessment of Educational Progress, 1986). In presenting the results of the factor analysis, the technical report examined the latent roots (or eigenvalues) for evidence of dimensionality: "An examination of the latent roots revealed three sizable factors followed by several smaller factors (roots = 18.11, 2.89, 2.30, 2.00, 1.94, 1.87, 1.79, 1.68, 1.67, 1.58, . . .). Following the logic of Cattell's (1966) scree test, the breaks in the pattern of latent roots indicated at least three salient factors with the possibility of as many as five additional factors" (National Assessment of Educational Progress, 1986: III-5).

As Salganik and Tal (1989) pointed out, the correct interpretation of this pattern of latent roots under Cattel's (1966) scree test is that there are *one* primary factor and numerous small factors. The natural break in the descending sequence of latent roots is clearly after the *first* one. The largest latent root explains more than six times the variance accounted for by the second largest one. Unfortunately, the technical report compared the target model having three factors only with models of higher dimensionality. For some reason, the technical report did not even consider models of lower dimensionality, the appropriateness of which is so clearly indicated by the analysis presented.[7] The second line of evidence originally provided for the distinctiveness of the three literacy scales within the YALS data must accordingly be discounted.

To explore these issues within the more recent surveys, parallel factor analyses of the JTPA, ES/UI, Oregon, and Mississippi data sets were carried out. These exploratory factor analyses used the method of principal components to extract factors from matrices of tetrachoric interitem correlations. Scree plots of the largest 20 eigenvalues from each analysis are shown in the four panels of Figure 4.4.

As can be seen in the scree plots, each survey exhibits the same type of scree plot, quite similar to that of the YALS study described earlier: there are a single primary factor and many smaller ones. There is absolutely no indication in these analyses that there are three factors (as opposed to one or two or four or five factors). These analyses indicate there

Figure 4.4
Scree Plots from Item Analyses of Four Adult Literacy Surveys

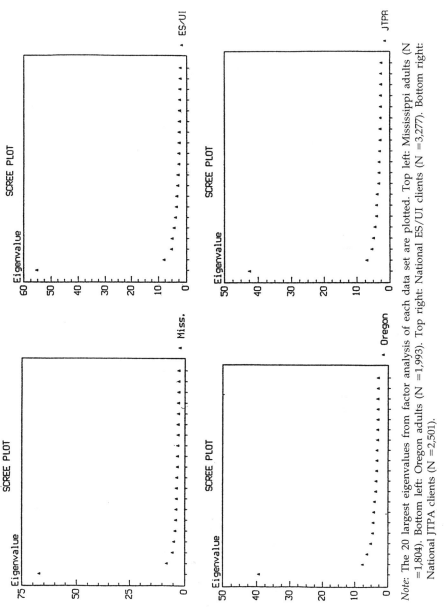

Note: The 20 largest eigenvalues from factor analysis of each data set are plotted. Top left: Mississippi adults (N =1,804). Bottom left: Oregon adults (N =1,993). Top right: National ES/UI clients (N =3,277). Bottom right: National JTPA clients (N =2,501).

Table 4.5
LISREL Confirmatory Factor Analyses (unweighted least squares)

Model	Goodness-of-Fit Index (GFI)	Degrees of Freedom	Adjusted Goodness-of-Fit Index (AGFI)	Root Mean Square Residual (RMSR)
Three factor	.974	9726	.973	.069
One factor	.973	9729	.972	.070

are but one primary factor and numerous secondary (and relatively insubstantial) ones.[8]

To test further the emerging notion of unidimensionality in these surveys, confirmatory factor analyses were carried out on the recent NALS household survey data set. The fits of two different models to the detailed pattern of observed responses data were compared. The *one-factor* model assumes that only a single factor underlies a given respondent's performance on test items. The *three-factor* model assumes three underlying factors (whose intercorrelations are to be estimated), only one of which predicts performance on any given item, depending on whether the item is designated as a prose, document, or quantitative task. In either model, a subject's performance on any given test item is assumed to depend additively on the factor involved and an error variable; errors are assumed to be uncorrelated with one another as well as with the factors. Best-fitting parameters of these models were estimated with LISREL 7 using unweighted least squares.[9]

Results of fitting the two models to the observed tetrachoric correlation matrices are summarized in Table 4.5. The fits of both models appear to be generally satisfactory. Evidently, the three-factor model does not fit these data significantly better than the single-factor model. The best-fitting three-factor model estimates intercorrelations among the latent prose, document, and quantitative factors to be very close to unity, as shown in Table 4.6. Notice how closely these interfactor correlations correspond to the estimated disattenuated interscale correlations presented in Table 4.4. There is again strong evidence here of unidimensionality in the literacy assessments.

The results of the item-level analyses thus correspond closely with those of the scale-level analyses. Both levels of evidence clearly indicate that a more parsimonious one-dimensional construct of literacy fits the assessment survey data as well as the three-dimensional construct of literacy with separate scales for prose, document, and quantitative proficiencies. A variety of methods for estimating disattenuated correlations among the three literacy scales converge on values in the .90–.95 range,

Table 4.6
LISREL Estimates of Correlations among Prose, Document, and Quantitative Factors

	Prose	Document	Quantitative
Prose		.951	.915
Document	.951		.960
Quantitative	.915	.960	

thus leaving little variance in performance to explain after a general literacy factor is taken into account.

DISCUSSION

In a recent investigation of the discriminant validity of the NALS scales, Rock and Yamamoto (1994) examined the fit of additional confirmatory factor models to selected subsets of the NALS data. Building on earlier studies of the discriminant validity of the math and verbal scales in the Scholastic Aptitude Test (Rock & Werts, 1979) and of multiple mathematics subscales in the National Assessment of Educational Progress (Muthen, Khoo, & Goff, 1994; Rock, 1991), Rock and Yamamoto were interested in the extent to which the three literacy scales can distinguish details of performance differences among critical subgroups (e.g., standard reporting groups of gender, race, and age). They examined the fit of a hierarchical confirmatory factor model to item-level data within specific subgroups of the sample. Their hierarchical factor model posited one *general literacy factor* and three *scale-specific factors* (i.e., prose, document, and quantitative) underlying performance.

Using LISREL estimation techniques, Rock and Yamamoto (1994) partitioned the variance in NALS performance into components associated with the general literacy factor, with the scale-specific factors, and with measurement error. They found that by far the largest component of variance (63–72%, depending on the subgroup modeled) is associated with the general literacy factor; a smaller, but still substantial, component with measurement error (21–28%); and the smallest components with the scale-specific literacy factors (3–13%).

In comparing the hierarchical model with the single-factor model (which involves only the general literacy factor and measurement error), Rock and Yamamoto observed, "It should be noted that the single factor model fits the data quite well for virtually all the goodness-of-fit criteria shown" (1994, p. 6). They went on to demonstrate that the less parsimonious hierarchical model nevertheless enhanced the model's ability to describe very small, but statistically significant, subgroup differences in variance components associated with the three literacy scales. After correcting for measurement error and differences in the general literacy factor, Rock and Yamamoto estimate the interfactor correlations between the scale-specific literacies to be in the range of .88–.91, in close agreement with the foregoing estimates.[10]

Rock and Yamamoto's analysis of the NALS data is generally consistent with our scale-level and item-level findings about dimensionality. They found that the more parsimonious single-factor model fits the NALS data quite well. Their hierarchical model, in which three scale-specific literacy abilities supplement a general literacy factor, adds value to the model by accounting for some very small, but statistically significant, differences among subgroups *after differences in general literacy are controlled*. Although adding the three scale-specific abilities to the model does appear to improve slightly the prediction of certain observed subgroup differences, the very small amounts of unique reliable variance associated with the scale-specific literacies are negligible for purposes of assessing an *individual's* (as opposed to a subgroup's) literacy abilities. For most practical assessment purposes, the effects of variations in the general literacy factor will dominate any observable variations attributable to the scale-specific literacies.

Although Rock and Yamamoto demonstrated that including the three scale-specific literacies in a hierarchical factor model (dominated by a general literacy factor) can account for small, but statistically significant, increments of reliable variance, their results, when weighed against the other evidence presented here, do not establish the validity or utility of the prose-document-quantitative literacy framework for most assessment purposes. The balance of the evidence indicates that the dominant feature of the *assessed* construct of literacy is a single general literacy capability. The conclusion here is *not* that only a single dimension of literacy skills and knowledge exists (as opposed to distinct prose, document, and quantitative dimensions) but rather that these adult literacy surveys are *not assessing* them in a distinctive manner.[11]

There are good reasons that the assessment instruments and procedures involved in these surveys may be failing to separate prose, document, and quantitative tasks in the manner that the assessment framework intends. Each item developed is categorized as being either a prose, document, or quantitative task. These categorizations were made on an a priori, rather than a data-driven, basis. The procedures and materials involved in many of the tasks appear to draw on elements of two or even three of the defined types of literacy tasks. For example, there is a NALS item (displayed in Campbell et al., 1992, p. 41) that requires completing a checking account deposit slip by listing two checks on the deposit slip along with the total amount deposited. Instructions for the task and the description of the two checks to be entered on the deposit slip are presented in a *prose* paragraph. To perform the task correctly, it is essential to understand the structure of the checking deposit slip, a *document*. To enter the correct total, one must correctly identify, set up, and perform the appropriate operation. This task (and many others) obviously draws on the defining features of all three types of literacy. Yet this item, like all others in these assessments, is necessarily categorized as being related to only one of the three literacies. In this case, the item happens to be classified as a quantitative literacy task.

Since many of the assessment tasks cut across the literacy categories in this manner, it should come as no surprise that the estimated proficiencies do not reflect the idealized three-dimensional structure used by the developers. As long as the assessment methodology requires complex literacy activities that cut across task categories to be assigned arbitrarily to only one of the categories, the dimensionality of performance will be correspondingly masked.

It is important to note that the conclusions drawn here do *not* imply that the results of these adult literacy surveys are necessarily any less valuable or useful. The principal implication here is that, in most circumstances, the extant data from NALS (and related surveys) could effectively be reported and interpreted with respect to a single dimension of literacy, presenting subscale results for prose, document, and quantitative literacy as appropriate. Although further development is required to extract the single underlying measure of literacy proficiency in an optimal way, one ready approximation is the arithmetical average of the corresponding prose, document, and quantitative literacy scores.

In many respects, these findings should be welcome news. A single measure of literacy proficiency can shorten and facilitate the processes of reporting survey results, of analyzing the important relationships between literacy and other educational, social, and economic outcomes, and of policy development. Furthermore, as suggested earlier, future assessment activities can be carried out in a more cost-effective manner by reducing the number of scales to be assessed.

While working with the extant adult literacy survey data in this manner should be reasonably satisfactory for many purposes, it is nevertheless important to develop improved ways of assessing the multiple sets of skills and knowledge underlying complex literacy behaviors. It is highly desirable, of course, that any changes in future assessment methodology be designed so that future survey results can be linked back to, and compared with, existing data. The adult literacy assessment methodology used in the recent surveys is thus an excellent departure point for such development. One direction for improving the assessment framework is suggested by the present findings: develop techniques for scaling given items in relation to multiple task categories and proficiency scales. Another promising direction is suggested by the recent work of Mosenthal and Kirsch (1994), who have developed techniques for specifying the information-processing features (and associated difficulties) of various types of literacy tasks. Perhaps by developing techniques for assessing individuals' information-processing capabilities directly in terms of such constituent features, the problems associated with forced-choice categorization of complex functional tasks can be minimized.

NOTES

   This paper is based on presentations at the International Reading Association North American Conference on Adolescent and Adult Literacy (February 1994 in Washington, D.C.) and at the annual meeting of American Educational Research Association (April 1994 in New Orleans). The author is pleased to acknowledge the helpful comments and assistance of Janet Baldwin, Irwin Kirsch, Andrew Kolstad, Norma Norris, Don Rock, Neal Thomas, and Richard Venezky. Any errors and the opinions expressed are my own.

   1. These correlations are between the first plausible values imputed for each scale.

   2. Data processing and statistical analysis were carried out with SPSS-X for the IBM-VM and SPSS for Windows, version 6.1.

   3. Thanks to Neal Thomas of ETS for providing this historical information (personal communication).

   4. Rubin's (1987) multiple imputation methodology implies that the interscale correlations should be estimated in this way.

   5. This is not necessarily an unbiased estimate of the disattenuated correlation coefficient (Mislevy, 1993). Unbiased, model-based estimates of the disattenuated correlation coefficients arc presented later.

   6. High interscale correlations are also present in assessment data generated with the commercial TALS instruments developed by Educational Testing Service (1990) for assessing adult literacy on the prose, document, and quantitative scales. For example, the TALS document and quantitative instruments (which are administered with separate test booklets) were used as posttest measures in a large evaluation study of literacy development among clients of California's GAIN Program, a statewide welfare-to-work program (Martinson & Friedlander, 1994). The correlation reported between quantitative and document scores in this large-scale study was 0.77. This coefficient, of course, is attenuated by measurement error present in the assessment. The reliabilities of these instruments was reported by Educational Testing Service (1990) to be in the .88–.92 range. Normalizing the observed sample correlation between the two scales by their reliabilities estimates a disattenuated correlation of 0.86.

   7. Bernstein and Teng (1989) have subsequently demonstrated that item categorization tends to spuriously influence the apparent multidimensionality, highlighting conceptual differences between factoring items and factoring scales. They conclude that criteria for dimensionality applicable to scale-level data are inappropriate for discrete item-level data.

   8. It should be noted that the correlation matrices in these analyses were not

positive-definite due to the BIB-spiraling design of the assessments. If all subjects respond to every cognitive item, then the sample interitem correlation matrix is always positive-definite. With BIB-spiraling, the sample interitem correlations are estimated from different subsets of respondents, frequently resulting in nonpositive definite correlation matrices. Research on the effects of such BIB-spiraling on apparent dimensionality suggests that analysis of data generated by BIB-spiraling tends to *overestimate* the dimensionality of the resulting sample correlation matrices (Kaplan, 1993; Zwick, 1987). Although this might seem to be of little concern here, where we have such strong evidence of unidimensionality (which should not, of course, entail an *overestimate* of the number of dimensions), a cautionary note is still appropriate. There were numerous small, negative eigenvalues in each principal components analysis. Some recently developed factor analytic techniques for binary data are not as sensitive to such limitations (Mislevy, 1986). These techniques, however, usually require much larger sample sizes than those available from most of these literacy surveys, given the large number of items involved.

9. It was necessary to exclude a few of the 166 NALS items from this analysis because of no variability or lack of covariability with other items. A few pairs of items that were either very easy or very difficult had no covariance in the sample. Recall that despite the apparently large sample size (24,944), a given pair of items taken from different BIB-spiral blocks was administered to only a subsample of respondents (approximately 1/26 of the total sample or approximately 1,000 respondents received any given assessment booklet). One data coding adjustment was made for the purposes of this analysis. Some assessment tasks involved the use of written materials (e.g., an accompanying newspaper) that were not part of the assessment booklet. There were occasions on which such supplementary prompts were not available during the assessment. Such occurrences were recorded with a special code value. These occurrences were treated as missing data (i.e., not reached) for the purposes of this item-level analysis. Also note that the effective sample size was 23,624, since no test booklet was returned for scoring from 1,320 of the 24,944 household survey participants (plausible values for scale scores were nevertheless imputed for these 1,320 individuals based on their background characteristics).

10. Rock and Yamamoto's (1994) methodology required contrasting the performance of subsamples that received disjoint subsets of items. This requirement was apparently implemented by analyzing data from subsamples whose assigned test booklets contained disjoint item blocks. Unfortunately, because every NALS test booklet contained a common block of "core" items in addition to the three variable BIB-spiraled item blocks, it appears that overlapping items were administered to the analytical contrast groups. The impact of this partial overlap on the results of Rock and Yamamoto's analysis is not known.

11. A recent study (Baldwin, Kirsch, Rock, & Yamamoto, 1995) administered both the NALS and GED Tests to a national sample of 1,573 GED examinees. GED examinees, of course, are a much more homogeneous population with respect to literacy proficiencies than the general adult population in the NALS survey. As expected, Baldwin et al. report lower disattenuated correlations (in the .77–.82 range) between NALS scales among this more homogeneous population. These disattenuated correlations, though they are somewhat smaller than those found among the general adult populations (for which the NALS instru-

ments were designed), are still sufficiently large to indicate the presence of a single dominant literacy factor, even among this restricted population. Baldwin et al. argue that the relatively minor variations in the pattern of scale scores across subpopulations indicate that the NALS scales are measuring different things. This argument is difficult to evaluate because it is not clear why the particular subpopulations used to illustrate it are the critical ones for their point, when many other subpopulations (not presented) do not show corresponding patterns of difference across scales. At best, this argument indicates that in some situations it is useful to present scale (really subscale) information as well, a point not in dispute here.

REFERENCES

Baldwin, J., Kirsch, I. S., Rock, D., & Yamamoto, K. (1995). *The literacy proficiencies of GED examinees: Results from the GED-NALS Comparison Study*. Washington, DC, and Princeton, NJ: American Council on Education and Educational Testing Service.

Beaton, A. E., Johnson, E. G., & Ferris, J. J. (1987). The assignment of exercises to students. In A. E. Beaton (Ed.), *Implementing the new design: The NAEP 1983–1984 technical report* (pp. 97–118). Princeton, NJ: Educational Testing Service.

Bernstein, I. H., & Teng, G. (1989). Factoring items and factoring scales are different: Spurious evidence for multidimensionality due to item categorization. *Psychological Bulletin, 105*(3), 467–477.

Campbell, A., Kirsch, I. S., & Kolstad, A. (1992). *Assessing literacy: The framework for the National Adult Literacy Survey*. Washington, DC: National Center for Education Statistics, U.S. Department of Education.

Cattel, R. B. (1966). The scree test for the number of factors. *Multivariate Behavioral Research, 1*, 140–161.

Cosby, A. G., Howell, F. M., Carr, J. C., & Miller, L. (1991). *The Mississippi Literacy Assessment*. Starkville: Mississippi State University.

Educational Testing Service (1990). *ETS Tests of Applied Literacy Skills*. New York: Simon & Schuster Workplace Resources.

Haigler, K. O., Harlow, C., O'Connor, P., & Campbell, A. (1994). *Literacy behind prison walls: Profiles of the prison population from the National Adult Literacy Survey*. Washington, DC: National Center for Education Statistics, U.S. Department of Education.

Ishikawa, M. (1994). *Workplace literacy and the nation's unemployed workers* (draft). Washington, DC: U.S. Department of Labor.

Kaplan, D. (1993). *The impact of BIB-spiraling induced missing data patterns on goodness-of-fit tests in factor analysis*. Philadelphia: National Center on Adult Literacy, University of Pennsylvania.

Kirsch, I. S., & Jungeblut, A. (1986). *Literacy: Profiles of America's young adults* (NAEP Report No. 16-PL-01). Princeton, NJ: Educational Testing Service.

————. (1992). *Profiling the literacy proficiencies of JTPA and ES/UI populations: Final report to the Department of Labor*. Princeton, NJ: Educational Testing Service.

Kirsch, I. S., Jungeblut, A., & Campbell, A. (1991). *The ETS Tests of Applied Literacy*. Princeton, NJ: Educational Testing Service.

Kirsch, I. S., Jungeblut, A., Jenkins, L., & Kolstad, A. (1993). *Adult literacy in America: A first look at the results of the National Adult Literacy Survey.* Washington, DC: National Center for Education Statistics, U.S. Department of Education.

Kirsch, I. S., Jungeblut, A., & Mosenthal, P. B. (1994, March). "Moving towards the measurement of adult literacy." Paper presented at the National Center for Education Statistics (NCES) meeting, Washington, DC.

Martinson, K., & Friedlander, D. (1994). *GAIN: Basic education in a welfare-to-work program.* New York: Manpower Demonstration Research Corporation.

Mislevy, R. J. (1986). Recent developments in the factor analysis of categorical variables. *Journal of Educational Statistics, 11,* 3–31.

———. (1991). Randomization-based inference about latent variables from complex samples. *Psychometrika, 56*(2), 177–196.

———. (1993). Should "multiple imputations" be treated as "multiple indicators"? *Psychometrika, 58*(1), 79–85.

Mislevy, R. J., Johnson, E. G., & Muraki, E. (1992). Scaling procedures in NAEP. *Journal of Educational Statistics, 17*(2), 131–154.

Mosenthal, P. B., & Kirsch, I. S. (1994). "Defining the proficiency standards of adult literacy in the U.S.: A profile approach." Paper presented at the National Reading Conference, San Diego, December.

Muthen, B. O., Khoo, S., & Goff, G. N. (1994). *Multidimensional description of subgroup differences in mathematics achievement data from the 1992 National Assessment of Educational Progress.* Los Angeles: Graduate School of Education, University of California.

National Assessment of Educational Progress (1986). *Young Adult Literacy Assessment: Technical report.* Princeton, NJ: Educational Testing Service.

National Education Goals Panel (1991). *National Education Goals report.* Washington, DC: Author.

Oregon Progress Board (1991). *The Oregon literacy survey: Measuring adults' functional skills.* Salem, OR: Author.

Reder, S. (1994a, February). NALS raises vital equity issues. *Connections,* n.p.

———. (1994b). *The nature and impact of GED training in Oregon.* Salem, OR: Office of Community College Services.

Rock, D. A. (1991). Subscale dimensionality. In *The NAEP 1990 technical report.* Princeton, NJ: Educational Testing Service.

Rock, D. A., & Werts, C. E. (1979). *Construct validity of the SAT across populations— An empirical confirmatory study.* Princeton, NJ: Educational Testing Service.

Rock, D. A., & Yamamoto, K. (1994). *Construct validity of the adult literacy subscales.* Princeton, NJ: Educational Testing Service.

Rubin, D. B. (1987). *Multiple imputations for nonresponse surveys.* New York: John Wiley & Sons.

Salganik, L. H., & Tal, J. (1989). *A review and reanalysis of the ETS/NAEP Young Adult Literacy Survey.* Washington, DC: Pelavin Associates.

Sum, A. (in preparation). *The National Adult Literacy Survey: Labor Report.* Washington, DC: National Center for Education Statistics, U.S. Department of Education.

Zwick, R. (1987). Assessing the dimensionality of NAEP reading data. *Journal of Educational Measurement, 24,* 293–308.

PART II

The Contexts of Adult Literacy

5

Work, School, and Literacy

Jeremy D. Finn and Susan B. Gerber

The purpose of this study was to examine the roles of work and schooling as they relate to literacy proficiency and literacy-related activities among American adults. The specific question addressed was, How do work experiences complement and/or compensate for schooling in the development of literacy proficiency and literacy habits?

Recent years have seen an outcry from employers about the poor academic preparation, not to mention lack of basic literacy skills, among members of the workforce. In survey after survey employers lament the inability of their incoming employees to perform day-to-day literacy-related tasks. To cite a few examples, New York Telephone reported in 1987 that fewer than 16% of 22,800 applicants for jobs passed a test of basic skills, including vocabulary. In a poll conducted by *Business Month* ("A poor report card," 1990), 27% of employers indicated that they reject more than half of all entry-level candidates because of lack of basic skills, defined as the three Rs. Poor writing skills were cited by almost two-thirds of the respondents as being among the most troublesome. Poor mathematics skills were listed by 27% of the respondents, poor reading skills by 26%, and poor overall communication skills by 33%.

Employers' complaints are often seen as an indictment of an educational system that is graduating youngsters ill-prepared to join today's workforce. Indeed, there is enormous variability in the literacy skills of our high school graduates.

However, we must also weigh the extent to which preparation for postschooling employment should be a primary goal of our public

schools. Besides the diverse requirements of different jobs, two significant school–work discontinuities need to be considered. First, literacy
skills are often utilized differently in the workplace from how they are
taught and practiced in schools. It has been noted that job-related reading
is done in a more information-rich context (U.S. Departments of Education and Labor, 1988) and involves a wider variety of materials (Mikulecky, 1982). Others have noted the greater number of documents that
are characteristic of the workplace and the need to understand and interpret diagrams, flowcharts, graphs, symbols, and so on (Carnevale,
Gainer, & Meltzer, 1990; Guthrie, Seifert, & Kirsch, 1986; Heath, 1983).
More than 42% of writing in the workplace involves filling out forms,
while another 22% is memorandum or letter writing, and 25% involves
recording or summarizing completed work (Carnevale, Gainer, &
Meltzer, 1990). There have been few if any comparisons of how mathematics is used in school and at work.

Second, the literacy demands of many jobs are changing dramatically
and will continue to change over the coming years. The move toward a
service economy is instrumental in these shifts. A 1987 Hudson Institute
report estimated that between 1985 and 2000, the nation would see an
8.8% decrease related to goods construction and a 32.9% increase in
service-related jobs. Because service firms are generally smaller than
manufacturing firms, most new jobs are in small businesses. At the same
time, the downsizing of large companies that began in 1995 will continue. These factors, coupled with our increased reliance on computers
and technology, mean that employees will be asked to perform a greater
variety of tasks—many of them relatively complex in nature. As part of
the Hudson Institute analysis, jobs were given "skill ratings" on a 1–6
scale. For example, machine setters had a rating of 1.8, farmers a rating
of 2.3, teachers a rating of 4.2, and scientists a rating of 5.7. Estimates
indicated that jobs in the skill range from 1.5 to 2.4 would decline from
31% to 23% of the workforce, while those with skill ratings of 3.5 and
higher would increase throughout the 1990s.

While school–work discontinuities are recognized widely, little research has examined how the two settings interact or how they jointly
affect behavior. Among the studies that examined both contexts, Kohn
and Schooler (1983) posited an elaborate interactive model with two central components, the "ideational flexibility" of the employee and the
"substantive complexity" of the job. Results of their analyses, conducted
primarily with males, indicated a reciprocal relationship. The effect of
complexity on ideational flexibility was immediate; current job complexity was found to affect one's current thinking processes. The effect of
ideational flexibility on complexity, however, was delayed; ideational
flexibility was found to predict the complexity of an individual's future
(but not present) jobs. While the study was one of the first to document

the effects of employment on workers' cognitive functioning, the findings are limited by a definition of ideational flexibility that was largely general intelligence, by a single index of schooling in a long list of independent variables, and by the extraordinary intricacy of the models tested.

Some research has been performed on reading practices based on the premise that literacy activities—not just literacy skills—vary as a function of both education and workplace demands (e.g., Heath, 1983; Kirsch & Guthrie, 1984; Guthrie, Seifert, & Kirsch, 1986). Recent theoretical developments portray how literacy practices and literacy skills develop through a process of socialization within a particular context, for example, school or the workplace (see Reder, 1994, for an overview). According to "practice-engagement theory" literacy is shaped by the "structure and organization of the social situations in which literacy is encountered and practiced" (Reder, 1994, p. 48). Specific literacy practices may take on meaning for an individual both because they are taught or required and because they involve interpersonal interactions, for example, observing others, demonstrating competence, collaborating with others. This meaningfulness of literacy activities promotes engagement and, as a result, skill acquisition. The present study examined the role that workplace practices may play in promoting literacy skills.

OCCUPATIONAL CLASSIFICATIONS AND LITERACY

Our study did not ask whether schooling can prepare students for postschool employment or whether this is an appropriate goal. Instead it examined the extent to which the workplace is, for many, an alternative setting in which literacy skills are practiced and learned. This effect is best understood by examining specific occupational classifications since occupations vary dramatically in their literacy demands. These differences are seen both in the skills needed to be selected for certain positions and in on-the-job training that is provided in some settings to enhance employees' abilities to perform specific kinds of tasks. Our study used two kinds of evidence to examine these relationships: respondents' own reports of where they learned certain literacy skills and data showing statistical relationships among occupation, job-related literacy activities, and literacy proficiency.

Some prior research has examined the relationship of occupation with literacy. For example, Guthrie, Schafer, and Hutchinson (1991) performed an intricate path analysis of the associations among literacy achievement, literacy activity (prose reading time; variety of documents read) with the occupational statuses of adults aged 21–25 years. Analyses were performed separately for prose and document literacy. According to the authors, this study provided the first quantitative evidence of literacy's being associated with occupation after controlling for background characteristics such as parents' occupation, parents' education, and years of schooling. Results indicated that occupational status is directly associated with both types of literacy activity and, through the mediating effects of activity, indirectly associated with literacy proficiency. The study viewed occupational status as the dependent variable and did not consider the possible influence of occupational status on literacy activity or of activity on proficiency.

A detailed analysis of the literacy demands of 50 occupations was produced by the U.S. Department of Labor (1992). For each occupation, employees, supervisors, and job trainers rated a series of skills on a scale from "not critical" to "extremely critical" for performing the job. Average ratings for reading, writing, and arithmetic were obtained that ranged from 1 (not critical) to 5 (highly critical). The ratings display some noteworthy features. First, it is not the case that professional, managerial, or even technical/supervisory jobs are always the most demanding in every skill. An "order filler," for example, is judged to need a reading level of 4.80, while opticians were judged to need a reading level of 3.75. Second, some jobs that are particularly demanding in terms of reading and/or writing tend to be less demanding with regard to arithmetic, and vice versa. Secretaries, for example, received a writing rating of 5.00 and an arithmetic rating of 2.75, while carpenters received an arithmetic rating of 4.00 and a writing rating of 2.67. Other occupations are intensive across all three skills, for example, food service managers, accountants, and equipment technicians. The converse of this is not true, however; no job received proficiency levels below 3.00 for even two of the basic skills.

The relationships examined in the present investigation are illustrated in Figure 5.1. Research to date portrays literacy as an outcome of youngsters' home backgrounds and their educational experiences and also as a set of skills that facilitate employment and income (the dark arrows in Figure 5.1). There is little need to reexamine these connections; a considerable legacy of evidence documents the association of educational attainment with literacy (e.g., Guthrie, Schafer, & Hutchinson, 1991; Kaestle et al., in press) and of literacy with income and employment (e.g., Finn, in press). The present study considered other dimensions, namely, the perspective that the workplace may also serve as a learning environment to encourage and/or support literacy proficiency (the broken line in Figure 5.1) and the central role that literacy practices may have in mediating these relationships. Practices undertaken in an individual's personal (nonwork) life were viewed as inextricably connected with literacy skills. Literacy practices performed at work were viewed as a mechanism through which the workplace may promote literacy proficiency.

Figure 5.1
Relationships Examined in Study of Work, School, and Literacy

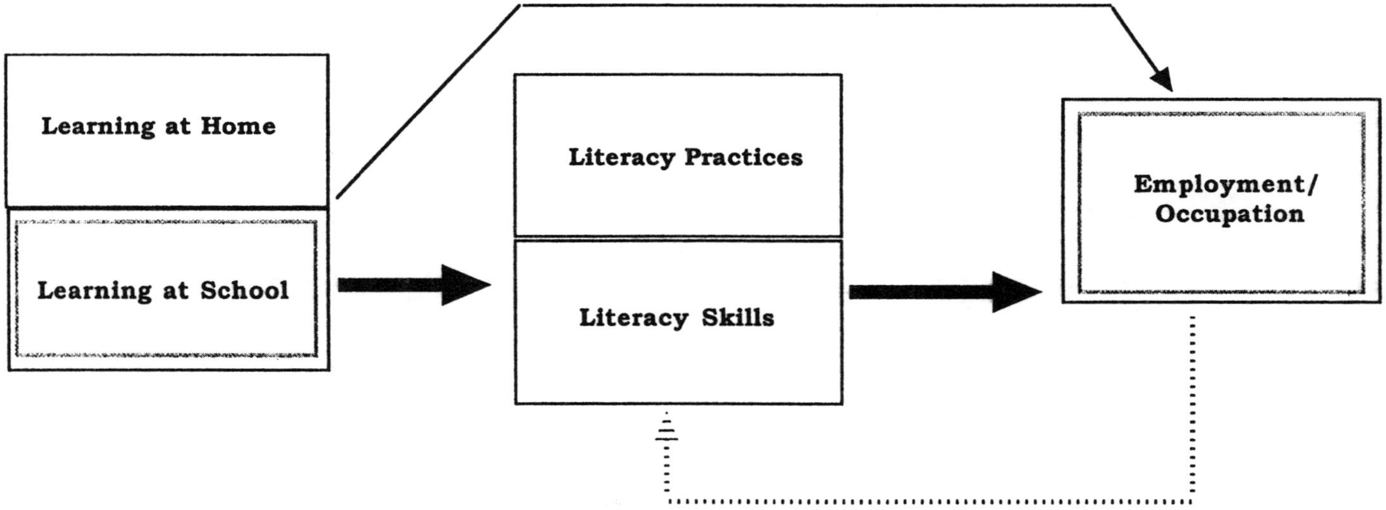

METHOD

Participants

Participants for the study were respondents to the U.S. Department of Education's National Adult Literacy Survey (NALS) conducted in 1992. A nationally representative sample of adults, ages 16 and older, was contacted in their homes and asked to provide demographic information and to complete a booklet of literacy tasks taking approximately 45 minutes (see Campbell, Kirsch, & Kolstad, 1992, for further details). Respondents were paid $20 for their cooperation.

The total NALS sample consisted of just over 26,000 individuals. For our study, we selected nonprison respondents who had attended school in the United States; individuals born outside the United States were included only if they attended American schools from age 10 up. Respondents were eliminated who did not learn to speak English before attending school or who did not report that they "usually speak English" at the time of the survey. Additionally, individuals enrolled in school at the time of the survey were eliminated from the analyses. The remaining sample consisted of 21,522 adults, of whom 73.7% were white, 18.9% were African-American, and 6.1% were of Hispanic origin. By age classification, 14.1% were between 16 and 24 years, 64.4% between 25 and 54 years, and 21.4% were 55 years or older. The loss of respondents from the total survey was fairly evenly spread across demographic subgroups except for individuals of Hispanic origin; about one-half of the original sample of Hispanic adults was eliminated by the requirements of attending an American school and speaking English currently. For the portion of the study that examined differences among occupational classifications, individuals who were unemployed at the time of the survey were also eliminated, reducing the sample size to 17,457.

Measures

The NALS Background Questionnaire elicited information from each respondent including race/ethnicity, sex, age, and educational attainment (high school noncompleter, high school graduate, any postsecondary experience), employment status, and occupation. Occupations were classified originally into 43 categories according to Bureau of Census codes and were recoded into nine broader categories for this study, following Mikulecky (in press).

One question required respondents to reflect back on their school experiences and state where they had learned each of three types of skills: reading newspapers, magazines, or books; reading graphs, diagrams, or maps; writing letters, notes, memos, or reports. The response categories for each were "mostly in school," "mostly at home or in the community," "mostly at work," or "did not learn."

Literacy Practices

The Background Questionnaire asked respondents about current literacy-related activities. Parallel sets of questions were asked about literacy practices for personal use and about practices at work. The first question in each set asked about the frequency of reading a wide range of materials, including letters, magazines, reports, and instructions. The second question asked about the frequency with which the individual writes letters or memos, forms, or reports or articles. A third question asked about the frequency of use of mathematical operations. Responses to each question were coded from 1 ("never") to 5 ("every day"). Responses to all three questions were averaged to obtain a Personal Literacy Practices index and a Job Literacy Practices index for each respondent.

Literacy Proficiency

Each respondent was administered a test of literacy proficiency that assessed three domains. Prose literacy was defined as "the knowledge and skills needed to understand and use information from text that include[s] editorials, news stories, poems, and fiction" (Kirsch, Jungeblut, Jenkins, & Kolstad, 1993, p. 3). Stimulus materials included a range of written material including newspaper articles, instructions, an editorial, and a poem. Document literacy was "the knowledge and skills required to locate and use information contained in materials that include job applications, payroll forms, transportation schedules, maps, tables, and graphs" (p. 3). Quantitative literacy was defined as "the knowledge and skills required to apply arithmetic operations, either alone or sequentially, using numbers embedded in printed materials; for example, balancing a checkbook, figuring out a tip, completing an order form, or determining the amount of interest from a loan advertisement" (pp. 3–4). The scales are described in greater detail in Chapter 2.

Procedures

The research consisted of a secondary analysis of the NALS data using cross-tabulation and multiple regression procedures. Cross-tabulations were performed with the larger sample (21,522) to examine the percentages of respondents who attributed their literacy skills to school, to home or the community, or to work and average literacy proficiencies for each group. Two sets of regressions were performed. In the first analysis, literacy practices at work was the dependent variable, and occupation the primary independent variable; educational attainment, race/ethnicity, gender, and age were included as control variables. Next, literacy proficiencies and personal literacy practices were the dependent variables, and job literacy practices and occupation were the primary independent variables. Because of the many relationships examined in these analyses, results were considered to be statistically significant only when the achieved significance level was .01 or smaller, or when an entire set of results displayed a common pattern (even if some achieved significance only at the .05 level).

Three features of the NALS data required special attention. First, certain subpopulations were oversampled in conducting NALS, for example, African-American and Hispanic households. Thus, sampling weights were derived for each respondent so that the "weighted" sample would reflect the American adult population accurately. All of our analyses were conducted with weighted data. Second, in NALS sampling, several housing units were chosen within each housing tract, and, for large families, more than one respondent may have been chosen within a household. This may produce "clustering," that is, less variability in the sample than would be obtained from a simple nationwide random sample. Thus, the procedure for estimating appropriate standard errors in this investigation was the "jackknife" approach (see Johnson, 1989). Third, because of time constraints only a portion of the literacy test was administered to each respondent. Through item response theory (IRT), the "scores" for each respondent consisted of five "plausible values," that is, five estimates of the score on the full test given the respondent's pattern of right and wrong answers and demographic characteristics (see Mislevy, Beaton, Kaplan, & Sheehan, 1992). Analyses must consider variability among the plausible values together with sampling variability. Fortunately, Educational Testing Service has recently produced statistical software that accommodates all three complexities (Jirele, 1995).

RESULTS

The first analysis examined the extent to which adults identify the workplace as a setting where literacy skills were developed. The percentages of the sample who stated that they learned three sets of skills in school, at home, or at work are given in Table 5.1 together with the average proficiency scores for each subgroup. Two patterns pervade these results. First, school was identified as the predominant source of learning for all three skills for the total sample and for each education subgroup. Second, proficiency scores increase significantly with increased educational attainment regardless of where the respondent reported learning the skill.

Other differences were skill-specific. For example, a substantial percentage of individuals stated that they primarily learned to read prose

Table 5.1
Percent of Adults Who Attribute Their Skills to Schooling, to Home or Community, or to Work, and Mean Literacy Proficiency

| | Where did you primarily learn to... | | | | | | | | |
| | read newspapers, magazines, or books? | | | read graphs, diagrams, or maps? | | | write letters, notes, memos? | | |
	School	Home	Work	School	Home	Work	School	Home	Work
PERCENTAGES[a]									
Overall	61.2 (0.5)	37.6 (0.5)	1.1 (0.1)	83.0 (0.3)	10.1 (0.3)	6.9 (0.2)	74.0 (0.5)	15.0 (0.3)	11.1 (0.3)
Educational Attainment									
Dropout	58.9 (1.0)	39.3 (1.0)	1.8 (0.3)	71.2 (1.0)	18.5 (1.0)	10.3 (0.7)	66.9 (1.1)	26.1 (0.9)	7.0 (0.8)
HS	64.2 (0.7)	34.8 (0.7)	1.1 (0.2)	82.5 (0.6)	9.5 (0.5)	8.0 (0.4)	77.9 (0.6)	12.3 (0.5)	9.8 (0.4)
Post-HS	59.6 (0.8)	39.6 (0.8)	0.9 (0.1)	88.8 (0.4)	6.9 (0.3)	4.3 (0.3)	73.7 (0.6)	11.9 (0.5)	14.4 (0.5)
MEANS[b]									
Overall	282.9 (0.8)	280.5 (1.2)	255.0 (6.5)	287.5 (0.7)	260.5 (2.5)	273 (2.3)	277.8 (0.8)	253.8 (2.0)	291.8 (2.1)
Educational Attainment									
Dropout	228.3 (1.6)	217.8 (2.1)	211.5 (12.6)	228.3 (2.3)	212.0 (3.4)	227.3 (4.8)	225.2 (1.9)	199.3 (2.6)	229.5 (4.3)
HS	276.5 (1.2)	275.0 (1.2)	253.7 (7.8)	277.4 (0.9)	268.7 (3.0)	280.0 (2.8)	269.9 (1.0)	262.3 (2.4)	278.6 (2.3)
Post-HS	317.8 (1.0)	317.4 (1.2)	303.7 (4.3)	318.0 (0.9)	307.6 (3.5)	311.3 (2.8)	310.0 (0.9)	304.7 (2.3)	316.0 (1.9)

Note: Standard errors in parentheses.
[a]Row percentages sum to 100.
[b]Prose proficiency for reading newspapers, magazines, or books; quantitative proficiency for reading graphs, diagrams, or maps; document proficiency for writing letters, notes, memos, or reports.

at home or in the community (37.6%); the percentages are similar for dropouts, high school graduates, and those with postsecondary education. Few respondents indicated that the workplace was a significant source of learning to read prose, and their mean proficiency scores were substantially below those of the other groups.

Both home and work were identified as significant sources of learning to read technical materials. Interestingly, over 10% of high school dropouts reported that they had learned these skills at work, followed by 8% of high school graduates and 4.3% of adults with postsecondary experience. Furthermore, among dropouts and high school graduates, average proficiency scores were *at least as high* as for those who reported learning these skills at school. These results suggest that for adults who have not continued their education, the workplace may be a place to acquire additional learning.

Overall, the workplace was identified by more respondents as the primary source of learning to write (11.1%). This, too, varies with educational attainment, from 7% of high school dropouts to 9.8% of high school graduates to over 14% of those with postsecondary experience. Here the results are even more provocative, however, since for dropouts, high school graduates, and those with postsecondary schooling alike, document proficiency is at least as high or higher than among individuals who learned to write at school. The "advantage" of learning to write at work (291.8–277.8) corresponds to approximately .21σ.

Occupation, Practices, and Proficiency

The nine occupational classifications used in this study are indicated in Table 5.2. These are accompanied by a brief description of the literacy tasks associated with each set of occupations, summarized from U.S. Departments of Education and Labor (1988) and U.S. Department of Labor (1991, 1992). Mean scores for each classification on the Job Practices index—the frequency with which literacy activities are required at work—as well as the Personal Practices index and the proficiency scales are given in Table 5.3.

As with the Department of Labor's (1992) ratings, significant variability is revealed among classifications. In general, occupations in which high percentages of workers have attended college are associated with high proficiencies and practices. At the other extreme, workers in some occupations rarely or never engage in literacy activities at work, for example, farmers, semiskilled laborers, and service workers. Differences among the classifications in personal literacy practices were generally smaller than those for job practices.

The first regression analysis examined the relationship of occupation with job-related literacy practices controlling for gender, age, race/eth-

Table 5.2
Description of Nine Occupational Classifications

Occupational Classification	Percent of Sample	Specific Occupations	Typical Literacy Tasks
Professional	15.1%	Architect/Surveyor; Engineer; Mathematician/Computer Scientist; Natural Scientist; RN; Health Diagnostics; Other Health (Pharmacists, Therapists); Accountant/Auditor; Teacher; Other Professional (Counselors, Lawyers).	Read to understand, communicate ideas to various audiences, identify relevant details from written material, "read-to-understand," integrate new and old material.
Managerial	7.9%	Public Executives & Managers (Administrator); Private (Financial Manager); Other Manager (Funeral Directors, Analysts).	Read to understand, communicate ideas to various audiences, identify relevant details from written material, "read-to-understand," integrate new and old material.
Technical	6.9%	Engineering Technical; Health Technician; Science Technical; Other; Adjustors & Investigators; Computer Equipment Operators; Supervisors.	Read technical manuals, "read-to-do," complete detailed forms.
Sales	11.5%	Sales Representatives; Sales Supervisors; Other Sales (Cashiers, Vendors).	Complete forms, read labels, write bills-of-sale.
Clerical	15.6%	Information Clerks (Hotel, Receptionists); Secretaries, Typists; Administrative Support (Clerks).	Proofread written documents, organize information, complete simple forms.
Skilled service workers	6.9%	Personal Service Occupations (Barbers); Public Safety; Health Services (Aides).	Complete forms, write simple reports, understand written instructions.
Farming	2.2%	Farm Managers/Operators; Farming/Fishing/Hunting.	
Skilled workers and trade laborers	9.4%	Construction Crafts (Plumbers); Craft Production (Mechanics, Repairers).	Complete simple forms, understand diagrams and charts.
Semi-skilled workers and service workers	24.6%	Transportation Operatives (Truck Drivers); Fabric Assemblers; Inspectors; Other Assemblers; Operators; Clean Equipment/Handle Laborers (Garbage Collectors); Other Service (Crossing Guard, Janitor).	

Table 5.3
Mean Outcomes for Nine Occupational Classifications

Occupational Category	Percent with Postsecondary Education		Job Practices		Literacy Proficiencies						Personal Practices	
					Prose		Document		Quantitative			
Professional	91.2	(.6)	2.69	(.01)	332.8	(1.3)	324.1	(1.3)	329.5	(1.2)	2.56	(.02)
Managerial	74.8	(1.3)	2.88	(.01)	319.5	(1.9)	310.3	(1.7)	321.3	(1.7)	2.48	(.02)
Technical	63.3	(2.0)	2.74	(.02)	309.5	(1.9)	306.3	(2.0)	308.7	(1.9)	2.40	(.02)
Sales	47.1	(1.6)	2.52	(.02)	296.0	(2.0)	289.2	(1.7)	296.4	(1.9)	2.40	(.01)
Clerical	44.8	(1.1)	2.57	(.02)	297.4	(1.3)	290.4	(1.5)	293.4	(1.4)	2.39	(.02)
Skilled service workers	32.3	(1.8)	2.24	(.03)	275.5	(1.3)	269.9	(2.8)	271.7	(2.6)	2.34	(.03)
Farming	28.2	(3.2)	2.03	(.05)	259.8	(4.1)	256.7	(4.3)	269.5	(4.8)	2.15	(.05)
Skilled workers–Trade laborers	23.7	(1.4)	2.44	(.03)	275.2	(2.1)	273.8	(2.0)	282.2	(2.3)	2.27	(.02)
Semi-skilled laborers and service workers	19.6	(.7)	1.98	(.02)	265.9	(1.2)	262.2	(1.2)	264.6	(1.2)	2.14	(.02)

Note: Standard errors in parentheses.

Table 5.4
Regression Analysis Predicting Job Literacy Practices

Predictor	Simple Correlation	Standard Regression Weight
Gender (F-M)	-.06	-.11***
Age[a]		
Young	-.17	-.12***
Old	-.07	-.08***
Race[b]		
African-American	-.11	-.06***
Hispanic	-.02	.00
Education[c]		
Dropout	-.24	-.11***
Postsecondary	.24	.05***
Occupation[d]		
Professional	.14	.00
Managerial	.18	.06***
Technical	.11	.03**
Sales	.06	-.02
Skilled service	-.07	-.10***
Farming	-.09	-.12***
Skilled trade	.01	-.09***
Semi-skilled	-.24	-.31***

Note: Significance levels*$p < .05$, **$p < .01$, ***$p < .001$.
[a]Regression weights for Young (16–24)–Middle (25–54); Old (55+).
[b]Regression weights for African-American–White; Hispanic–Nonhispanic White.
[c]Regression weights for Dropout–High School; Postsecondary–High School.
[d]Regression weights for each occupation compared with (−) clerical workers.

nicity, and educational attainment. The results are summarized in Table 5.4. Each occupational classification was compared with clerical workers, a relatively large group whose outcomes are near the center of the distribution on each measure. Six of the eight separate contrasts are statistically significant, five of them at the .001 level. The four control variables in the analysis accounted for about 12.1% of the variation in job practices. When occupational classification is added, the percentage of explained variation is increased to 20.8%; thus occupation uniquely accounts for 8.7% of variability in job literacy practices. Although the increase in explanatory power is not large, it reflects clear and pronounced differences in the literacy tasks required by occupations in the nine classifications.

Table 5.5
Regression Analyses Predicting Proficiency and Personal Practices

| | Proficiency | | | Personal |
Predictor	Prose	Document	Quantitative	Practices
Gender (F-M)	.04**	.01	-.05***	.08***
Age[a]				
Young	.03*	.06***	.01	.01
Old	-.11***	-.16***	-.08***	-.02*
Race[b]				
African-American	-.23**	-.24***	-.27***	-.02*
Hispanic	-.09***	-.09***	-.11***	-.02**
Education[c]				
Dropout	-.20***	-.19***	-.21***	-.06***
Postsecondary	.27***	.26***	.24***	.12***
Occupation[d]				
Professional	.12***	.11***	.10***	.03*
Managerial	.06***	.05***	.06***	-.01
Technical	.01	.03**	.02	-.02
Sales	.00	-.01	.01	.03
Skilled Service	-.04***	-.03**	-.03**	.05***
Farming	-.06***	-.04*	-.04**	.02
Skilled Trade	-.06***	-.04*	-.03	.02
Semi-Skilled	-.09***	-.08***	-.08***	.04**
Job Practices	.08***	.10***	.12***	.38***
Percent of explained variation:				
All variables	42.6%	41.2%	41.3%	19.5%
Occupation and job practices[e]	4.1%	3.7%	3.9%	12.1%

Note: Standardized regression weights; Significance levels*$p < .05$; **$p < .01$, ***$p < .001$.
[a]Regression weights for Young (16–24)–Middle (25–54); Old (55 +).
[b]Regression weights for African-American–White; Hispanic–Nonhispanic White.
[c]Regression weights for Dropout–High School; Postsecondary–High School.
[d]Regression weights for each occupation compared with (−) clerical workers.
[e]Independent of all other predictors.

It is likely that further variability would be revealed if a finer classification of jobs was examined.

The regression results for predicting literacy proficiency are given in Table 5.5. The findings for all three types of literacy are parallel. After controlling for gender, age, race/ethnicity, and educational attainment, occupation categories and job literacy practices account for 3.7% to 4.1%

of the three proficiencies. That the percent of explained variability is small reflects the many antecedents of literacy, including those encompassed by the model and a host of other experiences that were not part of this investigation. At the same time, most of the differences among occupational classifications are significant at the .01 or .001 level—six of eight comparisons for prose and document proficiency and five comparisons for quantitative proficiency. The relationships of work-related literacy practices with all three proficiency scales are also statistically significant, highlighting a possible mechanism through which work may influence literacy proficiency; that is, literacy may be learned from practice, whether the practice is provided at school or elsewhere.

The right-hand column of Table 5.5 gives the results for predicting personal literacy practices. While a smaller percentage of variation is explained by the complete model (19.5%), much of that is attributable to occupational differences and to job literacy practices. Although several differences among occupations are significant, for the most part there is little evidence that the workplace has a direct impact on adults' personal practices. If it does have an effect, it is mediated by work-related literacy activities; the effect of job practices on personal practices, controlled for all other variables, is highly statistically significant.

DISCUSSION

While research repeatedly documents a strong relationship between schooling and literacy, the workplace is also a distinct context in which literacy activities are undertaken. Most occupations involve a substantial literacy component. At the same time, occupations vary in the extent to which they require employees to engage in literacy-related tasks. This investigation summarized two kinds of data indicating that the workplace is a place not only where literacy skills are practiced but also where they are learned and developed.

Respondents' reports about where they acquired their literacy skills confirm that the workplace can be an important learning environment. While most adults attribute their literacy skills to formal schooling, noteworthy numbers of adults report that they learned to read technical materials and to write various documents at work. Among dropouts and high school graduates, learning to read technical documents at work was associated with quantitative proficiency that is about the same as for those who learned at school. Respondents who learned to write documents at work had document proficiencies that were as high or higher than for those who learned at school. The workplace may actually provide more opportunity to engage in these practices than does school and may, as a result, promote competence.

Regression analyses supported two primary conclusions. First, reports of actual job practices confirm that occupations vary substantially in the extent to which they require employees to engage in literacy activities. A broad range of literacy tasks, including reading various materials, writing memos, forms, or reports, and performing arithmetic operations may be required, depending on the nature of the job performed. Second, differences in work-related practices are related to literacy proficiency above and beyond schooling and demographic factors. Engagement in literacy activities at work may, indeed, provide a mechanism whereby the workplace contributes to literacy competence.

The findings of this investigation have implications for both research and policy. First, any model of literacy learning should consider the *multiple contexts* in which learning occurs and the *practice* or *engagement* that the settings provide. The simple model represented by Figure 5.1 includes both components—multiple contexts and literacy practices—but further elaboration is needed. We need to ask whether the effects of school and work are *separate* or *complementary* or *summative*. We need to ask whether some skills may be attained more efficiently in one setting or the other.

The study also has implications for calls to strengthen the links between schooling and the requirements of the workplace. On one hand, employers continue to criticize our schools for failing to prepare graduates who possess basic reading, writing, or arithmetic competencies, not to mention specialized skills useful in the workplace. On the other hand, educators confront an expanding array of obstacles in their attempts to provide instruction, for example, increasingly diverse student population, decreasing resources that limit access to materials, support staff, specialized programs, increased violence in the schools, and others. To expect the same educational system to prepare students with skills needed on the job, especially when the demands of the workplace are becoming more specialized and/or technical, may be unrealistic.

Partnerships between industry and schools may have to place greater responsibility for teaching job-relevant skills on the shoulders of business. At the same time, this study confirmed that school noncompleters (and high school graduates) have the lowest proficiency levels, whether these individuals attribute their learning to school, to home or community, or to work. It is possible that functional literacy courses—emphasizing such skills as reading and writing documents and performing arithmetic operations to solve problems encountered in daily life—would be beneficial, especially in schools serving high-risk populations. Minority students from low-income homes too often see little real value to what school offers (Mickelson, 1990; Taylor, 1991). A curriculum with components that are clearly relevant to postschooling experiences may be both appealing and useful.

Caveats

All of our findings must be qualified by the limitations of the NALS data. Establishing cause-and-effect relationships is precluded both because of the nonexperimental nature of the study and because the data collection was cross-sectional, providing no information about time sequences. The self-report nature of the data raises problems of accuracy in reporting. In the present study this may be especially problematic with regard to the "where did you learn . . ." questions. However, to the extent that the interviews required factual reporting and that memories and perceptions were not totally inaccurate, we have supported the thesis that the workplace can be viewed as an environment in which significant literacy learning takes place.

NOTE

This chapter was completed while the first author was Visiting NAEP Scholar at Educational Testing Service. The research reported here was supported by a grant from the American Educational Research Association (AERA), which receives its funds for its AERA Grants Program from the National Science Foundation and the National Center for Education Statistics (U.S. Department of Education) under NSF Grant #RED-9255347. Opinions reflect those of the authors and do not necessarily reflect those of the granting agencies.

REFERENCES

Campbell, A., Kirsch, I. S., & Kolstad, A. (1992, October). *Assessing literacy: The framework for the National Adult Literacy Survey*. Washington, DC: National Center for Education Statistics.

Carnevale, A. P., Gainer, L. J., & Meltzer, A. S. (1990). *Workplace basics: The essential skills employers want*. San Francisco: Jossey-Bass.

Finn, J. D. (in press). School noncompletion and literacy. In C. Kaestle, L. Mikulecky, J. D. Finn, S. Johnson, & A. Campbell, *Adult literacy and education in America: Results from the National Adult Literacy Survey*. Washington, DC: National Center for Education Statistics.

Guthrie, J. T., Schafer, W. D., & Hutchinson, S. R. (1991). Relations of document and prose literacy to occupational and societal characteristics of young black and white adults. *Reading Research Quarterly, 26*, 30–48.

Guthrie, J. T., Seifert, M., & Kirsch, I. S. (1986). Effects of education, occupation, and setting on reading practices. *American Educational Research Journal, 23*, 151–160.

Heath, S. B. (1983). *Ways with words: Language, life, and work in communities and classrooms*. New York: Cambridge University Press.

Hudson Institute (1987). *Workforce 2000: Work and workers for the twenty-first century*. Indianapolis, IN: Author.

Jirele, T. J. (1995). *User guide for the NAEP/SPSS analysis modules for crosstabulation and regression.* Princeton, NJ: National Assessment of Educational Progress.

Johnson, E. G. (1989). Considerations and techniques for the analysis of NAEP data. *Journal of Educational Statistics, 14,* 303–334.

Kaestle, C., Mikulecky, L., Finn, J. D., Johnson, S., & Campbell, A. (in press). *Adult literacy and education in America: Results from the National Adult Literacy Survey.* Washington, DC: National Center for Education Statistics.

Kirsch, I. S., & Guthrie, J. T. (1984). Adult reading practices for work and leisure. *Adult Education Quarterly, 34,* 213–232.

Kirsch, I. S., Jungeblut, A., Jenkins, L., & Kolstad, A. (1993). *Adult literacy in America.* Washington, DC: U.S. Government Printing Office.

Kohn, K. L., & Schooler, C. (1983). *Work and personality: An inquiry into the impact of social stratification.* Norwood, NJ: Ablex.

Mickelson, R. A. (1990). The attitude-achievement paradox among black adolescents. *Sociology of Education, 63,* 44–61.

Mikulecky, L. (1982). Job literacy: The relationship between school preparation and workplace actuality. *Reading Research Quarterly, 17,* 400–419.

———. (in press). Education for the workplace. In C. Kaestle, L. Mikulecky, J. D. Finn, S. Johnson, & A. Campbell, *Adult literacy and education in America: Results from the National Adult Literacy Survey.* Washington, DC: National Center for Education Statistics.

Mislevy, R. J., Beaton, A. E., Kaplan, B., & Sheehan, K. M. (1992). Estimating population characteristics from sparse matrix samples of item responses. *Journal of Educational Measurement, 29,* 133–162.

A poor report card. (1990, May). *Business Month, 135* (5), 8–9.

Reder, S. (1994). Practice-engagement theory: A sociocultural approach to literacy across languages and culture. In B. M. Ferdman, R. Weber, & A. G. Ramirez (Eds.), *Literacy across languages and cultures* (pp. 33–74). Albany: State University of New York Press.

Taylor, R. L. (1991). Poverty and adolescent black males: The subculture of disengagement. In P. B. Edelman & J. Ladner (Eds.), *Adolescence and poverty: Challenge for the 1990's* (pp. 139–162). Washington, DC: Center for National Policy Press.

U.S. Department of Education & U.S. Department of Labor (1988). *The bottom line: Basic skills in the workplace.* Washington, DC: Author.

U.S. Department of Labor (1991). *What work requires of schools: A SCANS report for America 2000.* Washington, DC: Author.

———. (1992). *Skills and tasks for jobs: A SCANS report for America 2000.* Washington, DC: Secretary's Commission on Achieving Necessary Skills.

6

Adults' Reading Practices and Their Associations with Literacy Proficiencies

M Cecil Smith and Janet K. Sheehan

Reading practices refer to the use of reading skills for specific purposes as they occur in particular contexts (Guthrie & Seifert, 1984; Kirsch & Guthrie, 1984). Among the significant characteristics of reading practices are that they are communicative activities that promote various forms of individual development (e.g., cognitive, social, aesthetic). Social contexts shape the purposes for reading, and, in turn, these purposes determine the subject matter and texts selected by readers (Guthrie & Greaney, 1991). Literate adults engage in many different reading practices in the workplace, at home, in leisure settings, and at school (Guthrie & Greaney, 1991; Guthrie & Seifert, 1984; Guthrie, Seifert, & Kirsch, 1986; Kirsch & Guthrie, 1984; Scribner & Cole, 1981). For example, people read documents, forms, customer orders, and technical reports at work, while the materials commonly read at school consist of textbooks, work sheets, directions, and brief papers such as book reports (Mikulecky, 1982).

A number of literacy researchers have examined the contributions of reading practices to the development of reading abilities and general knowledge among readers (Anderson, Wilson, & Fielding, 1988; Buswell, 1937; Gray & Rogers, 1956; West, Stanovich, & Mitchell, 1993). Anderson et al., for example, found that time spent reading books, but not newspapers or magazines, predicted the reading achievement of intermediate grade students. As students' reading abilities improve, they are likely to use reading as a way of learning about the world. Guthrie and Greaney (1991) contend that individuals who read for knowledge learn more than those who read for other purposes. West, Stanovich, and Mitchell (1993), in a study comparing adult readers to nonreaders, confirmed this claim. This and other research evidence (e.g., Gray & Rogers, 1956; Kirsch, Mosenthal, & Rock, 1988; Scribner & Cole, 1981; Stanovich, 1993; Taylor, Frye, & Maruyama, 1990) supports what has come to be called practice-engagement theory (Reder, 1994) and converges on the hypothesis that reading practice promotes the development of literacy skills.

The *National Adult Literacy Survey* (NALS; Kirsch, Jungeblut, Jenkins, & Kolstad, 1993) provides a comprehensive database for investigating the relationships among adults' reading practices and their literacy skills. The NALS data allow analyses of reading practices occurring within two broad social contexts—personal situations (i.e., home) and work. Adults' literacy skills, or proficiencies, were measured on the NALS prose, document, and quantitative (PDQ) literacy scales.

Two studies are reported in this chapter that examined practice-proficiency relationships within the NALS sample. The first study examined the everyday reading practices of adults with respect to newspapers, magazines, books, and brief documents and the association of these practices with proficiencies on the PDQ literacy scales. The second study examined differences in practices and proficiencies among the diverse racial and ethnic groups represented in the NALS. Because social contexts are so significant in the development of literacy abilities, and these contexts are very diverse—particularly among racial and ethnic groups in the United States—it is important to examine how reading practices may vary across race and ethnicity and the associations of these practices to literacy abilities. The analyses for both studies are based on weighted (i.e., population) data.

STUDY ONE

This study was conducted by the first author. Although the NALS sample consisted of more than 26,000 individuals aged 16 and older, only adults ages 19 and older were included in this study. The rationale for excluding 16–18 year olds is most young people in this age range do not engage in the same kinds of reading practices as do older adults (Mikulecky, 1982). Thus, the resulting sample size was just under 25,000.

Reading Practices

NALS respondents completed a questionnaire asking for background and personal information, in addition to the literacy assessment. Respondents reported the extent of their reading practices in regard to uses of five categories of print materials: newspapers, magazines, books, personal documents, and work-related documents. Respondents were queried about how often they read a newspaper (e.g., every day; a few times a week; once a week; less than once a week; never) and asked to indicate the sections of the newspaper (e.g., news, sports, editorial pages, comics, classifieds, television listings, advice columns) that they read. They then indicated the number of magazines they look at or read in English on a regular basis (e.g., 0, 1, 2, 3–5, or 6 or more). Respondents also indicated which, among eight categories of books (e.g., fiction, recreation, current affairs/history, science/social science, reference, etc.), they had read during the previous six months. Next, respondents indicated the frequency with which they read a series of different document types for personal use (i.e., at home) and for work (e.g., every day; a few times a week; once a week; less than once a week; never). Among the document types were letters and magazine articles (prose), reference books and instructions (document), and diagrams, bills, and tables (quantitative).

Two categories of readers were derived from these data: high-and low-activity readers. Individuals who indicated that they did not read any of the print categories were considered to be low-activity readers. High-activity readers were defined as those adults who reported reading (1) a newspaper at least once a week and reading at least five parts of it; or (2) three or more magazines; or (3) three or more categories of books; or (4) four or more types of personal documents every day or a few times a week; or (5) four or more types of work documents every day or a few times a week; or (6) any combination of the preceding text materials.

Research shows that adults who engage in specific reading activities, such as document reading, develop skills for performing closely associated tasks (e.g., locating information) that do not generalize across different reading contexts and text materials (Kirsch & Guthrie, 1984; Kirsch et al., 1988; Scribner, 1984; Sticht, 1982). Therefore, associations were examined between literacy proficiencies and reading practices involving the five categories of text materials. Comparisons were made between high-and low-activity readers within each text category (i.e., high-activity newspaper reading, low-activity newspaper reading) in regard to PDQ proficiencies. The cut point for distinguishing between high-and low-activity readers corresponds approximately to that point that divides the distribution in half. In this way, all available data were used in the analyses.

Results of Study One

Because respondents were classified as either high-or low-activity readers for each text category, 32 distinct reading practice patterns were generated (see Table 6.1). Next, these patterns were aggregated into six groups of practices ranging from low or no reading activities for all five text categories to high-activity reading for all texts. Then, the mean PDQ literacy proficiencies were calculated for each practice in order to determine which practices are most advantageous in terms of literacy proficiency. The mean PDQ proficiencies associated with each practice pattern are shown in Table 6.1.

Next, to illustrate the effects of a particularly important social-contextual factor on literacy abilities, the extent to which individuals having different levels of education engage in the various reading practices was examined. As can be seen in Table 6.2, adults with greater educational attainment are more likely to read multiple print contents than are those who have low educational attainment. Nearly two of three adults with less than a high school education report low or no reading activity, while slightly more than two out of five adults with a college education read among all five types of print materials.

Specific Practices

Newspaper reading is pervasive among American adults. One-half of adults read a newspaper every day, and nearly nine out of ten read a newspaper once a week or more frequently. Magazine reading is also widespread: on average, 81% of adults read or look at least one magazine on a regular basis. Because of the manner in which the book reading question was posed in the NALS, it is impossible to determine precisely the full extent of adults' book reading practices. However, 83% of adults indicate that they had read (or looked at) at least one book in the six months prior to the survey—a finding consistent with previous studies (Stedman, Tinsley, & Kaestle, 1991). Estimates were not obtained on the total number of books read, but the average number of book categories read equaled 3.0, suggesting that many adults read a diverse selection of books.

Most adults receive correspondence, junk mail, and work-related memoranda, study directions and instructions for consumer products, calculate their checking account balances, scan the newspaper for advertised bargains, or rely on directories to locate addresses and phone numbers. It seems reasonable to assume, then, that document reading is a commonplace, daily event. However, the percentage of adults who indicate high reading activity (i.e., a few times a week or more frequently) for four or more documents for either work-related or personal documents was very low. Only about a fourth (27%) of the adult population indicated reading four or more documents for personal use every day, and 16% reported reading as many documents while at work. Document reading appears to be limited to prose materials (e.g., memos and reports). High-level quantitative document reading (i.e., diagrams, invoices) is virtually nonexistent, regardless of context. These findings may account for the poor performance of adults on the document tasks, as

Table 6.1
Mean PDQ Proficiency by Reading Practice Patterns

Practice Pattern	P	D	Q	Mean *gain* in PDQ by no. of contents read P	D	Q
0 contents group						
00000	201	197	197			
1 content practice patterns						
00001	251	247	252	57**	58**	60**
00010	243	242	241			
00100	274	270	270			
01000	236	236	238			
10000	267	268	274			
2 contents practice patterns						
00011	266	258	263	23**	20**	21**
00101	284	277	279			
00110	286	279	279			
01001	264	260	263			
01010	254	247	249			
01100	286	282	282			
10001	283	283	292			
10010	279	280	288			
10100	301	300	306			
11000	258	262	271			
3 contents practice patterns						
00111	292	282	284	13**	12**	10**
01011	275	267	274			
01101	287	282	284			
01110	290	285	282			
10011	295	292	302			
10101	301	296	300			
10110	312	309	312			
11001	283	281	285			
11010	290	288	295			
11100	295	297	298			
4 contents practice patterns						
01111	297	288	289	11**	11**	13**
10111	311	303	309			
11011	290	292	299			
11101	305	301	304			
11110	313	309	311			
5 contents practice patterns						
11111	309	304	306	5	7	4

Note: The practice pattern sequence is work documents, personal documents, books, magazines, and newspapers. There are 32 reading activity patterns. 0 = low activity ("less than once a week," "never"); 1 = high activity ("every day," "a few times/once a week"); *Example:* 00100 = Very low or no reading activity on work documents, personal documents; high activity on book reading; very low or no activity on magazines and newspapers.
*significant @$p<.05$.
**significant @$p<.001$.

Table 6.2
Percent of Educational Attainment Groups at Each Reading Content Level

Number of Print Contents Read

	0	1	2	3	4	5	Total
1	58.2	34.3	24.2	18.9	11.7	5.9	27.1
2	29.2	37.8	33.3	30.3	22.8	20.9	30.7
3	8.4	16.9	22.5	23.3	28.1	30.6	20.8
4	4.3	10.9	20.0	27.6	37.4	42.6	21.5
Total =	100.0	100.0	100.0	100.0	100.0	100.0	100.0

Note: 1 = Less than high school diploma; 2 = High school or GED diploma; 3 = Some post high school education; 4 = College degree or greater.

less than one in five adults (18%) performed at the two highest levels on document literacy (Kirsch et al., 1993).

When the 32 individual reading practices are aggregated into six groupings of practice patterns, based on the number of print contents read (i.e., 0–5), nearly one-third of adults (29%) are found to regularly read any three or more text categories. For the remaining two-thirds (71%) of the adult population who read two or fewer text types, this lack of practice with diverse kinds of printed materials is likely to negatively impact their literacy abilities. Of course, a large percentage of adults fared poorly on the PDQ literacy assessment (Kirsch et al., 1993). Next, the associations between particular reading practices and adults' PDQ literacy proficiencies are described.

Association of Reading Practices with Literacy Proficiencies

Mean scores on the PDQ scales for each reading practices grouping (i.e., reading no text materials or reading any single, any two, any three, any four, or all five types of texts) were compared. Adults who are high-activity readers of any single text category—regardless of the type of text read—score an average of 57, 58, and 60 points higher on the prose, document, and quantitative literacy scales, respectively, than adults who do not read. While gains in literacy proficiencies diminish with the addition of each text type, the differences are significant up to a ceiling of four types. So, adults who read any two text types score about 22 points higher on the PDQ scales as compared to those who read only a single type of text. Reading any three text types results in a difference of about 11 points on the PDQ scales as compared to reading only two types of texts. Reading any four text categories results in a difference of nearly 12 points as compared to reading any three. These comparisons are significant (p<.001), but there are no differences in average PDQ scores between reading four or five categories of texts. These results parallel Anderson et al.'s (1988) findings that, among middle school children, time invested in reading yields large returns in reading ability initially, but achievement gains diminish as more and more time is devoted to reading.

Two print categories—work documents and books—are most clearly associated with higher PDQ literacy proficiency. Ten percent of adults restrict their reading to only work documents, however; another 5% report reading only books. Generally, most people who read these types of print materials read other types as well. Among all 32 reading practice patterns, the highest eight practices—in terms of PDQ proficiency—involve reading various combinations of work documents and books. The associations between reading specific text materials and PDQ literacy proficiencies are described next.

Books

Book reading is associated with generally high literacy proficiencies as compared to the other print materials. Adults who read only books have mean PDQ scores equal to 274, 270, and 270, respectively. Closer examination of the book categories shows that adults who read fiction have the highest prose (M=269) and document (M=263) literacy scores, followed by those who indicate the *other* category (M=261, prose; M=259, document). Data were not obtained on the typical kinds of books that constitute the *other* category, so a more detailed analysis is not possible. There is no difference in quantitative literacy proficiency between fiction readers and those who read from the *other* books category (M=264 for both categories), suggesting that this latter category captures a rich variety of textual and linguistic forms. Book reading, in combination with other print materials, is associated with high PDQ scores. Other surveys confirm that book readers also generally read other print contents, in particular, newspapers and magazines (Book Industry Study Group, 1984).

Documents

Reading documents at work is associated with high PDQ literacy scores, while reading only personal documents contributes very little to literacy proficiencies. Apparently, not all documents are created equally, in terms of providing some literacy benefits. Documents found in the workplace are likely of a more technical nature, written at a higher readability level, but likely to be more context-specific than are documents found in the home. About 10% of adults report reading only work-related documents, while less than 5% report that their reading is limited to just personal documents. The data show that most adults read other kinds of text materials in various combinations with documents for work and personal purposes.

Magazines

Magazine reading by itself contributes very little to literacy abilities. Adults who read only magazines have low mean PDQ scores. Most magazine readers read other types of text materials. Twelve percent of adults report regular reading of six or more magazines.

Newspapers

Individuals who read only newspapers on a regular basis (i.e., at least once a week) have mean PDQ literacy scores of 251, 247, and 252, respectively. Because newspaper reading is so commonplace and an important information source for many adults, regular readers may demonstrate greater literacy proficiencies than those adults who read the paper infrequently. Adults who reported frequent (i.e., at least once a week) and extensive newspaper reading (i.e., at least five newspaper sections) were compared to those who reported low or no newspaper reading on PDQ literacy scores. On each scale, high-activity readers significantly outperformed low-activity readers across three different kinds of newspaper reading activities: (1) reading the main news, editorials, and financial pages; (2) reading home/fashion/health, sports, and book/movie reviews; and, (3) reading comics, ads, television/movie listings, and advice/horoscope columns.

Adults who read multiple sections of the newspaper outperform those who read only a few sections. For example, adults who read only one newspaper section have an average prose score of 227, while those who read two sections have an average score of 246. Adults who read six or more newspaper sections average 288 on prose. The patterns are similar for document and quantitative literacy.

Reading Practices by Education Interactions

Because educational attainment has an important relationship to the development of individuals' reading practices and skills (Gray & Rogers, 1956; Kirsch, Mosenthal, & Rock, 1988), a series of two-way analyses of variance (ANOVA) were performed in order to examine the interactions between four educational attainment levels and six reading pattern groupings on PDQ literacy. Across the three ANOVAs, all main effects and interactions were significant ($p < .001$). Plotting of cell means revealed a much larger gap between low-and high-activity readers for those with less than a high school education than among the remaining three educational groups. This pattern is similar across all three literacy scales. In other words, among less well educated adults, engaging in reading practice can make an appreciable difference in promoting literacy proficiencies. This practice effect remains true at higher educational levels, but other variables likely have a mediating effect on literacy proficiencies (e.g., exposure to a wider range of reading materials) at the upper levels of education. When non-English speakers are removed from the analyses—in order to eliminate the confound that occurs because these persons are unlikely to read English-language print sources—the main effects sizes are reduced, but the interactions remain significant. These findings demonstrate the importance of educational attainment as a predictor of literacy proficiency, as well as the critical role of reading practices in shaping adults' literacy skills.

STUDY TWO

Kirsch et al. (1993) reported that white adults significantly outperformed all other racial/ethnic groups in the NALS. The average prose literacy of white adults, for example, was 26 to 80 points higher than that of any of the other nine racial/ethnic groups. Although the first study showed education to be a significant factor in PDQ performance and reading practices, educational differences among the racial and ethnic groups do not fully account for the PDQ performance differences among these groups. Given the impact of race and ethnicity on social roles in this country and the different educational opportunities available to racial and ethnic minorities, it is likely that different kinds of reading practices will be apparent for these groups. It is important to note that blacks and Hispanics were oversampled in the NALS so that they would be adequately represented in the final sample.

Procedures

These groups were compared on reading practices in a series of regression analyses for each of the five categories of print materials. The racial and ethnic groups were white, black, Hispanic-Cuban; Hispanic-Mexican; Hispanic-Puerto Rican; Hispanic-Central and South American; Asian and Pacific Islander; and Native American. Age, occupational status, educational attainment, and prose literacy proficiency were controlled in all analyses.

Reading practices were determined in the same manner as in the first study. However, for this study, quantitative scores were derived for each print category. Newspaper reading was scored as the number of newspaper sections read per week (i.e., 11 sections × 7 days; score range: 0–77). Magazine reading was scored as the number of magazines read "on

Table 6.3
Regression Coefficients and Probability Values for Differences among Ethnic Groups in Reading Practices Controlling for Age, Occupational Status, Level of Education, and Prose Proficiency Level

	Magazines		Books		Newspapers		Work Docs.		Personal Docs.	
1	0.009	p>.05	-0.002	p>.05	0.18*	p=.008	0.02	p>.05	0.09*	p=.001
2	-0.007	p>.05	0.03	p>.05-	0.262	p>.05	-0.106	p>.05	-0.16*	p=.012
3	0.066*	p=.002	0.149*	p=.000	0.73*	p=.005	0.248	p>.05	0.25*	p=.020
4	0.1065*	p=.000	.1518	p=.000	1.34*	p=.000	0.0051	p>.05	0.291*	p=.000
5	-0.044	p>.05	-0.168*	p=.002	-1.571*	p=.005	0.1169	p>.05	0.118*	p>.05
6	0.0008	p>.05	0.044	p>.05	-0.331	p>.05	-0.225	p>.05	0.056	p>.05
7	-0.100	p>.05	-0.132	p>.05	-0.202	p>.05	-0.553	p>.05	-0.484	p>.05

Note: 1 = Whites vs. others; 2 = Asians and Pacific Islanders vs. Native Americans, blacks, and Hispanics; 3 = Native Americans vs. blacks and Hispanics; 4 = Blacks vs. Hispanics; 5 = Cubans vs. Central and South Americans, Mexicans, and Puerto Ricans; 6 = Central and South Americans vs. Mexicans and Puerto Ricans; 7 = Mexicans vs. Puerto Ricans.

a regular basis" (0–6). Book reading was scored as the number of book categories read in the previous six months (0–8). Personal document reading was scored as the number of prose, document, and quantitative contents read per week (e.g., six categories × 7 days; score range = 0–42). Work document reading was scored in the same manner as personal documents.

The question of interest in this study was, Do reading practices involving newspapers, magazines, books, and documents vary among different racial and ethnic groups, when controlling for age of the respondent, prose proficiency score, employment status (i.e., working/ not working), and educational attainment?

Results

Whites were found to read significantly more newspapers and personal documents than the other racial and ethnic groups (see Table 6.3). Asians and Pacific Islanders read significantly more personal documents than Native Americans, blacks, and Hispanics. Native Americans read significantly more magazines, books, newspapers, and personal documents than blacks and Hispanics. Blacks read significantly more newspapers and personal documents than Hispanics. Hispanics of Central and South American and Puerto Rican origin read significantly more personal documents than Cuban Hispanics. No other comparisons between Hispanic groups were significant.

Perhaps the most surprising finding in our analyses is that Native Americans read more printed materials (except for work documents) than American blacks and all Hispanic groups. Given the traditionally poor educational attainment of Native Americans in this country, we find this to be remarkable. Among the Hispanic groups, caution is required in interpreting differences in reading practices. The differences found in our study pertain, of course, to printed materials written in English, and many Hispanics (both those who are native to the United States and immigrants) may prefer to read Spanish-language materials rather than English-language texts.

It is also interesting to note that no differences in the reading practices among the racial and ethnic groups were found for work documents. Although the reasons for this are unclear, it may be that the diversity of practices required in the workplace cuts across all racial and ethnic groups. However, given that equal occupational opportunities remain a goal rather than a reality for many racial and ethnic minorities, this explanation is an unsatisfying one.

SOME CONCLUSIONS WITH IMPLICATIONS

The findings from both studies support a practice-engagement perspective on literacy development. Practice-engagement theory, which has been developed by social cognitive theorists (Reder, 1994; Scribner & Cole, 1981), links practice to skill and assumes that

the development and organizational properties of an individual's literacy are shaped by the structure and organization of the social situations in which literacy is encountered and practiced. Literacy development . . . is driven by qualities of individuals' *engagement* [italics in original] in particular literacy practices. (Reder, 1994, p. 48)

Individuals acquire literacy through their participation in various literacy practices, in multiple social contexts, according to Reder (1994). American adults engage in many reading practices that include the use of a broad array of text materials. These practices take place in social contexts ranging from home to work and in other formal institutional settings. Evidence from the NALS suggests that these practices are likely to contribute to the development of adults' literacy proficiencies. Individuals who are more proficient readers may, however, simply be more inclined to read a variety of print materials (Stanovich, 1986), so determining a cause–effect relationship between reading practice and literacy proficiency is a task yet to be accomplished by literacy researchers.

Gray and Rogers (1956) claimed that maturity in reading is evidenced by an individual's valuing of reading and engaging in a broad array of reading practices. They found that educational attainment indirectly influences reading maturity by way of its impact on social roles and participation. Social roles are an important determinant of individual reading practices because they influence adults' choices of reading materials. The results of our research show that more than one-half of the adult population in the United States reads at least two types of print materials on a regular basis, indicative of reading "maturity" within a substantial segment of society. In most cases, the selected reading materials consist of different combinations of books, magazines, and newspapers. Given widespread beliefs about declining U.S. educational standards, it is noteworthy that less than one in five American adults can be described as nonreaders. However, these nonreaders perform at the lowest levels on the PDQ tasks. Certainly, educational efforts need to be directed to assisting individuals to develop literacy proficiencies that will enable them to use print to meet personal, social, and occupational needs. As Stedman et al. (1991) suggested, concern for the literacy skills of our nation's students must be rooted in concern for adults' reading habits because adults demonstrate the value of reading to children and students through their literacy behaviors.

Our studies also suggest that motivating adults to broaden the range of reading materials that they use in their everyday lives should be an important goal in adult education. This seems particularly true in programs directed toward members of racial and ethnic minorities whose reading practices are likely to have been muted by poor-quality schooling in childhood. Regardless of demographic characteristics, adults' reading practices that involve the use of multiple printed materials are the hallmark of reading maturity (Gray & Rogers, 1956).

Newspapers are the most widely read printed materials among adults, but book readers and those who read documents in the workplace perform best on the NALS literacy tasks. Document reading, however, is uncommon among adults. Individual and social-contextual (i.e., education) factors may contribute to this lack of document reading. Because adults are likely to skim documents such as reference materials, recipes, invoices, and bills, they may not be fully cognizant of the extent of their document reading and will underreport it in surveys (Guthrie & Greaney, 1991). Adults may avoid documents that include complex features such as diagrams and tables that seem incomprehensible. One study (Stamm & Jacoubovitch, 1980) found that subscribers to two metropolitan newspapers rarely looked at the tables (e.g., stock prices, box scores, weather data) published in these newspapers. Reading instruction in school rarely focuses on how to read and understand documents, but if more attention were given to document reading and interpretation, future generations of adults may be undaunted by documents. Of course, students of all ages must be encouraged to develop a broad repertoire of reading practices involving diverse texts, including prose, documents, and quantitative materials. More generally, efforts must be directed toward developing the reading skills and practices of socially and economically disadvantaged adults in ways that will result in higher literacy abilities for members of these groups.

Our findings demonstrate the positive association between practice and the skillful use of cognitive abilities related to literacy. Cognitive psychology research has demonstrated the cumulative effects of practice on experts' performances in domains such as chess (Chase & Simon, 1973; deGroot, 1966). It is widely acknowledged that massed practice in any number of activities leads to enhanced performance. Our analyses show that regular reading of even a single type of print materials (e.g., newspapers) is related to significant literacy achievement. Encouraging newspaper reading and making newspapers widely available to low-literate adults may be effective for developing their literacy skills.

Limitations of the Study

The research reported in this chapter is subject to the limitations of the NALS. The full extent of adults' reading practices was not assessed in the NALS. For example, how much time and effort do adults devote to reading? This information would be useful in further clarifying the relationships among different reading practices and literacy skills. Because there were no NALS data pertinent to the linguistic quality and complexity of the different kinds of print materials that adults read, it is impossible to determine if particular types of texts have a greater impact on literacy proficiencies than other types (e.g., prose versus technical materials). Despite these limitations, the data allow for a conservative examination of the relationship between reading practices and literacy proficiencies. In sum, the broad types of reading practices assessed by the NALS appear to contribute to adults' literacy skills with varying degrees of effectiveness. Literacy research now must move beyond correlational studies to include experimental studies that determine how reading practice impacts literacy development.

NOTE

The first study was conducted when the first contributor was a postdoctoral fellow in Adult Literacy at the Educational Testing Service. Gratitude is expressed to Irwin Kirsch, Norma Norris, and Don Rock for their invaluable assistance.

REFERENCES

Anderson, R. C., Wilson, P. T., & Fielding, L. G. (1988). Growth in reading and how children spend their time outside of school. *Reading Research Quarterly, 23,* 285–303.

Book Industry Study Group. (1984). *The 1983 consumer research study on reading and book purchasing.* New York: Book Industry Study Group.

Buswell, G. T. (1937). How adults read. *Supplementary Educational Monographs, No. 45.* Chicago: University of Chicago Press.

Chase, W. G., & Simon, H. A. (1973). Perception in chess. *Cognitive Psychology, 4,* 55–81.

deGroot, A. (1966). Perception and memory versus thought: Some old ideas and recent findings. In B. Kleinmuntz (Ed.), *Problem-solving* (pp. 19–50). New York: Wiley.

Gray, W. S., & Rogers, B. (1956). *Maturity in reading: Its nature and appraisal.* Chicago: University of Chicago Press.

Guthrie, J. T., & Greaney, V. (1991). Literacy acts. In R. Barr, M. L. Kamil, P. Mosenthal, & P. D. Pearson (Eds.), *Handbook of reading research,* vol. 2 (pp. 68–96). New York: Longman.

Guthrie, J. T., & Seifert, M. (1984). *Measuring readership: Rationale and technique.* Paris: UNESCO.

Guthrie, J. T., Seifert, M., & Kirsch, I. S. (1986). Effects of education, occupation, and setting on reading practices. *American Educational Research Journal, 23,* 151–160.

Kirsch, I. S., & Guthrie, J. T. (1984). Adult reading practices for work and leisure. *Adult Education Quarterly, 34,* 213–232.

Kirsch, I. S., Jungeblut, A., Jenkins, L., & Kolstad, A. (1993). *Adult literacy in America: A first look at the results of the National Adult Literacy Survey.* Princeton, NJ: Educational Testing Service.

Kirsch, I. S., Mosenthal, P. B., & Rock, D. A. (1988). *The influence of reading patterns on the proficiencies of young adults.* Unpublished manuscript. Princeton, NJ: Educational Testing Service.

Mikulecky, L. (1982). Job literacy: The relationship between school preparation and workplace actuality. *Reading Research Quarterly, 17,* 400–419.

Reder, S. (1994). Practice engagement theory: A sociocultural approach to literacy across languages and cultures. In B. M. Ferdman, R. M. Weber, & A. G. Ramirez (Eds.), *Literacy across languages and cultures* (pp. 23–74). Albany, NY: SUNY Press.

Scribner, S. (1984). Studying working intelligence. In B. Rogoff & J. Lave (Eds.), *Everyday cognition: Its development in social context* (pp. 9–40). Cambridge: Harvard University Press.

Scribner, S., & Cole, M. (1981). *The psychology of literacy.* Cambridge: Harvard University Press.

Stamm, K. R., & Jacoubovitch, M. D. (1980). How much do they read in the daily newspaper: A measurement study. *Journalism Quarterly, 57,* 234–242.

Stanovich, K. E. (1986). Matthew effects in reading: Some consequences of individual differences in the acquisition of literacy. *Reading Research Quarterly, 21,* 360–407.

————. (1993). Does reading make you smarter? Literacy and the development of verbal intelligence. In H. W. Reese (Ed.), *Advances in child development and behavior* (vol. 24, pp. 133–180). New York: Academic Press.

Stedman, L. C., Tinsley, K., & Kaestle, C. F. (1991). Literacy as a consumer activity. In C. F. Kaestle, H. Damon-Moore, L. C. Stedman, K. Tinsley, & W. V. Trollinger, Jr. (Eds.), *Literacy in the United States: Readers and reading since 1880* (pp. 149–179). New Haven, CT: Yale University Press.

Sticht, T. (1982, January). *Evaluation of the reading potential concept for marginally literate adults* (Final Report FR-ET50–82–2). Alexandria, VA: Human Resources Research Organization.

Taylor, B. M., Frye, B. J., & Maruyama, G. M. (1990). Time spent reading and reading growth. *American Educational Research Journal, 27*, 351–362.

West, R. F., Stanovich, K. E., & Mitchell, H. (1993). Reading in the real world and its correlates. *Reading Research Quarterly, 28*, 35–50.

7

Literacy Gender Gaps: Evidence from the National Adult Literacy Survey

Lynn Friedman and Ernest Davenport

INTRODUCTION

Cognitive gender differences are heavily debated topics today, undoubtedly because the feminist resurgence in the 1960s and 1970s challenged both the morality and the inevitability of male dominance in the economic and political worlds. Betty Friedan's *The Feminine Mystique*, published in 1963, was the inspiration for many research-oriented psychology texts (e.g., Maccoby, 1966; Wittig & Petersen, 1979). Hard evidence on cognitive gender differences has, however, come primarily from school-age samples with little ethnic diversity. Opportunities to examine data over a larger spectrum of ages and settings have been rare.

Prior to the mid-1970s, school samples often showed small gender differences in favor of females on verbal tasks and in favor of males on mathematical tasks (Maccoby & Jacklin, 1974). In the early school years, girls outperformed boys even in mathematics. Few gender differences in mathematics appeared before the students reached the middle school years. These often appeared in the more abstract subjects such as algebra and geometry, though there were some reports of greater male ability in more practical problem-solving tasks (see, e.g., Swafford, 1980). As we come to the close of the twentieth century, advances in communication have made data such as those gathered by the 1992 National Adult Literacy Survey (NALS) readily available to researchers. Such data provide opportunities to examine gender differences on a large (i.e., national) scale.

The overall NALS results do not follow school patterns. Divided simply by gender, the prose scale shows no gender difference. Men do, however, score significantly higher on the document and quantitative scales (Kirsch, Jungeblut, Jenkins, & Kolstad, 1993). These scales do not test algebra, geometry, or other higher math proficiency—in fact, they have a strong verbal component. The highest-level NALS document tasks require the reader to extract information from complex displays containing multiple distractors and to make high-level, text-based inferences; however, these tasks do not use any mathematical or scientific symbolism. Tasks at the highest quantitative level involve making appropriate series of calculations. Correct responses result from patient and detailed analysis of very tangible tasks.

The NALS is intended to measure adults' competence in dealing with economic and cultural life in mainstream society. Cognitive gender differences research has, on the other hand, generally focused on human abilities. For example, the tests used in reports of school-age quantitative gender differences are aimed at teasing out differences in students' potential for creative mathematical reasoning. Explanations of cognitive gender differences ordinarily emphasize either societally or genetically induced traits. Most theorists readily admit that both environment and biology are at play; however, they generally believe one or the other is the more important source. Those emphasizing societally induced traits might interpret the NALS results as indicating that adult women eventually lose all verbal advantages they show at school age because they are relegated to more menial tasks than men upon leaving school. The opposing explanation might be that the genetic capabilities of males are suppressed in the artificial, female-dominated school world and develop fully only in adulthood.

The goal of this chapter is to present patterns of gender performance taking account only of age groups and ethnicity. We omit much information collected by the NALS that may have some relevance to gender differences. Our choice of variables has sprung from traditional debates over explanations of cognitive gender differences. The reasons that these variables are the focus of debate are considered later in this chapter. A brief summary of the history of research on cognitive gender differences will provide the background for present debates.

OVERVIEW OF RESEARCH

Research through the 1970s

Rigorous empirical research on gender differences is not much more than a century old. As group testing became more frequent over the twentieth century, reviews of all published research on gender differences were included in psychological reference materials. In 1946, "psychological sex differences" were the topic of the 19th and last chapter in the standard reference *Manual of Child Psychology*, edited by Leonard Carmichael. The chapter was written by Lewis Terman and his associates, and they remarked then, "An adequate summary of available data on sex differences in mental abilities would require a fair-sized volume" (p. 986). As the midcentury mark passed, Eleanor Emmons Maccoby became a well-known name in psychological gender difference analyses. Maccoby produced two books devoted entirely to the review of studies on gender differences. Her second book, *The Psychology of Sex Differences* (Maccoby & Jacklin, 1974), became a necessary resource for all gender differences researchers. These narrative reviews generally agreed on the direction of differences in specific abilities. No one was willing to hazard a conclusion on general ability; Terman et al. (1946) stated that no consistent pattern of gender differences could be found over differing age groups and that the differences found were generally small. Maccoby (1966) and Maccoby and Jacklin (1974) remarked that most tests of general ability had been standardized to remove gender differences.

Reports on verbal abilities varied; Terman et al. (1946) found that though girls developed language skills at earlier ages than boys, later vocabulary growth showed no significant differences. Terman and Tyler (1954) did note differences in favor of females on some speeded reading comprehension tests. Maccoby and Jacklin (1974) stated that gender differences in favor of females on verbal ability were fairly well established in almost all areas, including fluency and comprehension.

In quantitative areas, research summaries were more consistent. According to Terman et al. (1946), sex differences in favor of males in the sciences clearly exist and increase with the ages of the students. Mathematical skills also show fairly consistent gender differences in favor of males, differences that emerge in the middle school years. Terman et al. further reported that gender differences "progressively favor boys as we go toward the more complex levels of arithmetic reasoning" (p. 992). Maccoby (1966) and Maccoby and Jacklin (1974) emphasized the age, or school grade level, at which these differences appear.

Until the mid-1980s, these assessments were common: girls excelled in verbal areas, boys in quantitative ones. The gap in quantitative areas grew with the age of the subjects. Some of these results remain true today. However, research has produced several different results in general verbal and mathematical abilities. These results are primarily due to a review technique, meta-analysis, believed to be more objective than the narrative review.

Meta-Analysis and Gender Difference Studies

In the late 1970s and 1980s, meta-analysis, a set of statistical techniques for reviewing studies, entered a period of rapid growth. Researchers collected studies on a certain topic, either all studies in the literature or a random sample of them. They coded variables common to all their pool of studies and used various statistical techniques, usually based on linear models, to calculate average effects for the topic of interest. Because of the objectivity required for conducting a meta-analysis, this tool has had tremendous impact on gender difference studies. The particular set of statistical techniques developed by Hedges and Olkin (1985) became the basis for a large number of gender difference reviews by researchers (Becker & Hedges, 1984, 1988; Friedman, 1989, 1995; Hyde, Fennema, & Lamon, 1990; Linn & Petersen, 1985).

These meta-analytic reviews noted declines in almost all verbal and mathematical gender differences in studies published in recent years. Hyde and Linn (1988) were prepared to assert that there are no gender differences in verbal ability, at least at that time, in American culture, in the standard ways that verbal ability has been measured. Friedman (1989) and Hyde et al. (1990) found studies to indicate that gender differences in mathematics had decreased over the years, even since 1974. The only cognitive ability that did not appear to be susceptible to decline was a particular kind of spatial reasoning ability, the ability to recognize rotations of whole objects in three-dimensional space (Hilton, 1985; Linn & Petersen, 1985).

Age and academic advancement of the subjects were particularly influential study variables, as was the year in which the study was done. Rosenthal and Rubin (1984) used the year in which the study was published as an independent variable. They found diminishing gender differences over time and remarked that "in these studies, females appear to be gaining in cognitive skill relative to males rather faster than the gene can travel" (p. 711). Becker and Hedges (1984) noted that the selectivity, or educational advancement, of the sample studied played an influential role. Friedman (1996) noticed that the largest gender differences in mathematical tests were now only about one-third of a standard deviation and almost always occurred on college or graduate entrance examinations.

Meta-analysis remains primarily a review technique. However, it has contributed widely to synthesizing results in as objective a way as possible. The results from recent meta-analyses indicate that gender gaps in verbal skills are so small as to be insignificant and that gender gaps in mathematical skills are decreasing. These results have been confirmed in a large meta-analysis conducted by Myers (1997). It is less well known that the ratios of males to females in extremely high score ranges in mathematical tests are declining.

Rationale for the Variables Used

The historical overview just given is of research on gender differences in human abilities. The NALS data focus on competencies in daily living as opposed to mental capabilities. However, results from the study of human abilities foreshadow those from NALS.

The heredity–environment dichotomy underlies controversies about gender differences. Most early researchers believed that heredity was by far the most important factor in abilities. The evidence given for such beliefs relied heavily on twin studies: Sir Francis Galton (1883) stated the following: "In solution of the question whether a continual improvement in education might not compensate for a stationary or even retrograde condition of natural gifts, I made inquiry into the life history of twins, which resulted in proving the vast preponderating effects of nature over nurture" (pp. 216–217). Galton's studies were anecdotal, however, and Sir Cyril Burt's more statistical ones were later discredited. More recent twin studies tend to report similarities in intelligence in monozygotic twins reared apart; however, the similarities seem to depend on the test used (Bouchard, 1983) and do not generalize to twins of different sexes.

Most research on cognitive gender differences today considers environmental factors. These variables are, after all, the ones that can be manipulated most easily. Moreover, many researchers are as convinced that nurture prevails over nature as Galton was of the contrary (e.g., Friedman, 1989). Many biological factors may have contributed to male dominance of power structures: size, muscular configuration, and so on. These may have led to economic dominance, necessitating intellectual development not required of women. Many environmental variables have been suggested as explanations for gender differences, teachers' attitudes toward their students, for example. However, few firm conclusions have come from these. With regard to teachers' attitudes, we have, on one hand, researchers proposing that "[l]iterature on the success of science and math programs for female students indicates that strategies that emphasize cooperation and team building work best for promoting performance in these fields" (Banziger, 1992, p. 280). On the other hand, some researchers have compared classrooms and found that teachers who encourage "autonomous learning behaviors" produce greater gains in their female students (Koehler, 1986).

Socioeconomic status (SES) is an often investigated environmental factor. One of its measures is income: however, Myers (1997) reports that regular attendance at school and early achievement are far more reliable predictors of achievement than poverty level.

Differential course taking is another frequently addressed environmental factor. In the past it has been found to account for some, but not all, of the gender imbalance in mathematics and science. Recently, however, females have increased the amount of mathematics taken in high school at higher levels than males (Smith, 1996). They have also increased their proficiency in mathematics exam taking, even on college entrance examinations such as the mathematics portions of the Scholastic Aptitude Test and the American College Testing Service Test (Friedman, 1996).

Reports of differential course taking and of selective samples can take place only after elementary school and will depend on age. Age is always an important factor in gender difference studies. The range of ages in school youth is approximately 15 years: the age range in the NALS data is more than 70 years. It is unlikely that gender differences remain constant over this period for three reasons. First, regardless of whether environmental or biological factors explain gender differences, it is true that an unpracticed skill is soon lost. Second, the feminist pressures of the 1960s and beyond should have shaped younger adults' preferences and skills if environmental factors have any influence. Third, the process of aging has biological consequences: until recently, these consequences were uniformly thought to be of a declining cognitive system that is inescapable and irreversible. Such declines would influence memory abilities and thus literacy skills.

The National Center for Education Statistics (NCES) used two age groupings in their early analysis of the PDQ scales of the NALS. The first corresponded to stages in educational and economic development, and the second was an approximately even division into intervals of ten years. We chose the first, as it was more consonant with developmental theories (e.g., Erikson's stages of life).

We found that we required a further split of older adults than was used in the NALS report. Gender differences in the quantitative scale become dramatic after age 65. The reason suggested for this in the early report was that women live longer than men, and proficiencies drop with age. Thus, we divided older subjects into those between 65 and 80, inclusive, and those over 80. The age groups we used were 16–18 years of age; 19–24; 25–39; 40–54; 55–64; and the two oldest age groups.

Friedman's (1989) meta-analysis had found that when minority samples are studied, the gender differences in quantitative tasks are smaller. For this reason and because of well-known differential patterns of socialization in ethnic groups, ethnicity was an important variable in our analysis. Five ethnic groups, black, Hispanic, Asian, U.S. Indian/Alaskan, and white, were considered separately. Although the NALS data had five different codings for Hispanic groups, we combined them for our analyses. We also combined the Asian and Pacific Islander categories. One more category, "other," was used in NALS but was disregarded in our analyses, as we had little idea of what this category might mean.

The NALS uses a sample of adults that is representative of the U.S.

population. The data set contains large amounts of background information on the respondents. Five plausible scores were given to each individual on each of the three scales. Within scales, these scores are very highly correlated, however. We used the first score given to the individual on each scale in our analyses. Because the sampling was stratified, individuals were assigned weights to ensure that the sample was representative of the population. For testing, we halved the weights so that the degrees of freedom would be halved, rendering conservative tests.

RESULTS

Age Patterns in Gender Differences

When broken down by age groups, the NALS results are far more consonant with results from school research. Controlling for age, only the quantitative literacy scale shows differences that are statistically significant. Female and male means and sample sizes and weights, along with adjusted t-and p-values, are shown for the three scales in Table 7.1.

No overall gender differences are statistically significant on the prose scale. Contrary to overall reports of no gender differences on the prose scale, the 25–39-year-old age group shows a trend toward a gender difference in favor of females, with a mean difference in favor of females of −5.05 and an adjusted p-value of .069. Mean differences in every age group except the 65–80-year-olds favor females.

The document scale shows even less disparity. The two youngest age groups show mean differences in favor of females. Weak trends in favor of males appear for adults 40–64 and 65–80 years of age, with adjusted p-values of .17 and .12, respectively.

The quantitative scale shows overall age group means forming a quadratic curve, with a peak between 40 and 54 years of age. However, gender differences in quantitative scores themselves show far less steady patterns. No gender differences appear for ages 16–18 nor for ages 19–24. Those in the 25–39 age group have a mean difference of about six points in favor of males (adjusted p-value of .0543). The difference is more extreme in the next age group, 40–54 years: the mean difference between males and females is 12.5, with a statistically significant difference, p=.0005, even at our adjusted levels. The gap decreases and is nonsignificant for those aged 55–64 but then increases dramatically for those between 65 and 80, with a p-value of 0. For adults over age 80 mean differences are nonsignificant.

Ethnic Patterns across Age Groups

Not all ethnic groups contribute to this pattern of gender differences. Black American families have often displayed very different cultural pat-

Table 7.1
Overall Age Group Statistics by Gender

Age Group	Male Mean	Male n	Male Wgt.	Female Mean	Fem. n	Fem. Wgt.	Diff. in means	Adj. t-value[a]	Adj. p-value
				Prose Scale					
1	269.62	593	366.8	273.88	623	313.3	-4.26	-0.63	.53
2	277.2	1329	805.7	283.78	1748	787.3	-6.58	-1.48	.14
3	281.76	4062	1979	286.81	5330	2125	-3.64	-1.82	.07
4	285.5	2731	1383	286.30	3376	1471	-0.80	-0.24	.81
5	256.8	1171	587.4	261.73	1729	687.6	-4.93	-0.99	.32
6	238.64	695	742.1	237.29	1131	896.9	1.35	0.31	.75
7	192.47	109	115.7	200.62	266	189.6	-8.15	-0.78	.44
				Document Scale					
1	272.02	593	366.8	273.65	623	313.3	-1.63	-0.24	.81
2	278.28	1329	805.7	282.45	1748	787.3	-4.17	-0.95	.34
3	281.88	4062	1979	281.82	5330	2125	0.06	0.03	.97
4	280.55	2731	1383	276.10	3376	1471	4.45	1.36	.17
5	250.36	1171	587.4	249.57	1729	687.6	0.79	0.16	.87
6	226.55	695	742.1	219.77	1131	896.9	6.78	1.57	.12
7	182.98	109	115.7	182.52	266	189.6	0.46	0.05	.96
				Quantitative Scale					
1	269.13	593	366.8	266.71	623	313.3	2.42	.9	.7002
2	277.94	1329	805.7	276.92	1748	787.3	1.02	.22	.8298
3	286.32	4062	1979	280.61	5330	2125	5.71	1.93	.0543
4	292.53	2731	1383	280.12	3376	1471	12.41	3.47	.0005
5	264.78	1171	587.4	257.4	1729	687.6	7.38	1.39	.1661
6	247.83	695	742.1	223.14	1131	896.9	24.69	5.24	0
7	194.4	109	115.7	184.12	266	189.6	10.28	.92	.3602

[a]Adjusted t-values are approximately half the size of those printed out by the program in
SAS Proc GLM.
[b]Age Groups: 1 = 16–18 years of age (generally school youth); 2 = 19–24 years of age
(entry level career age); 3 = 25–39 years of age (early career years); 4 = 40–54 years
of age (middle career years); 5 = 55–64 years of age (late career years); 6 = 65–80
years of age (early years of retirement); 7 = over 80 years of age (late years of retirement).

terns from those of white families. The parent who encourages education
is often the mother; sometimes the mother is the more educated of the
parents. The NALS data for blacks show no significant gender differences: all standardized mean differences have adjusted p-values greater
than .5. However, mean differences favor females on all three scales. For
16–18-year-olds, these data show that there may be new patterns developing since the late 1970s. The National Association for Educational
Progress (NAEP) data for that era showed that, although females did

better in mathematics than males at 13 years of age, at age 17 males were doing better than females (e.g., Jones, Burton, & Davenport, 1984). The NALS data show a ten-point mean difference in favor of females for the 16–18-year age group.

Other minority groups show no consistent or marked patterns. On the quantitative scale, Hispanics have a mean difference in favor of males in the 40–54-year age group of about 19 points, though the adjusted p-value of this difference is >.20. Other groups also show no significant differences. Sometimes mean differences are large, even as much as 60 points: this is the size of the difference favoring females among U.S. Indian/Alaskans ages 19–24 on the quantitative scale. However, adjusted p-values were always larger than .10.

Of all ethnic groups, only whites show statistically significant differences favoring male performance. On the prose scale, mean differences favor females even in this ethnic group, with the exception of the non-significant difference for those ages 65–80. All other ethnic groups have differences in favor of females on the prose scale in this age group. On the document scale, white males in this same age group show a statistically significant difference compared with white females, with an adjusted p-value of .046. No other significant differences appear.

It is the quantitative scale for which differences are most dramatic. No gender differences are significant among the youngest three age groups, 16–18, 19–24, and 25–39 years. In fact, in the youngest group, the difference slightly favors females. However, white males outperform white females at ages 40–54 and 65–80. Whites older than 80 have a difference in means of about 14 points, not significant and considerably smaller than the 30-point difference found among 65–80-year-olds, which is statistically significant. Thus, the fact that females live longer than males does not appear to explain the gender difference in older adults.

As the quantitative scale is the only one having interesting figures, we show only the results for the age/ethnicity cross-classification. Table 7.2 contains the male and female means and adjusted t-values for gender differences in means, by both age group and ethnicity. We have also included sample sizes and the sum of the (halved) normalized final weights for each group.

Educational Level

Because we found such a sudden drop in white female scores among 65–80-year-olds (i.e., females who would have begun school between 1915 and 1930), we hoped that the analysis of mean educational levels might explain this phenomenon. In fact, differences in educational level are unremarkable in any ethnic group but whites; these differences are marginally significantly in favor of males in three age groups, from 40

Table 7.2
Statistics on the Quantitative Scale for Groups by Gender, Age Group, and Ethnicity

Age Group	Male Mean	Male n	Male Wgt.	Female Mean	Fem. n	Fem. Wgt.	Diff. in means	Adj. t-value
				Black				
1	232.14	119	50.3	242.5	147	56.18	-10.36	-0.63
2	237.49	211	81.77	243.91	390	116.4	-6.42	-0.53
3	238.27	618	213.4	239.97	1120	271.4	-1.7	-0.22
4	224.39	391	121.2	228.88	619	166.7	-4.49	-0.45
5	201.28	182	57.60	203.4	264	65.54	-2.12	-0.14
6	162.56	124	63.4	166.41	223	77.19	-3.85	-0.27
7	135.31	18	5.70	137.93	44	14.05	-2.62	-0.06
				Hispanic				
1	234.63	95	47.27	224.69	106	43.48	9.94	0.56
2	229.49	231	123.4	235.97	279	107.4	-6.48	-0.58
3	214.34	548	232.3	214.04	719	248.6	0.3	0.04
4	223.94	235	97.39	205.01	301	112.9	18.93	1.62
5	204.37	91	42.3	183	149	54.21	21.37	1.23
6	150.28	55	33.65	152.87	81	47.26	-2.59	0.14
7	47.34	5	3.4	102.13	16	6.42	-54.79	0.33
				Asian				
1	289.42	13	11.21	265.63	8	4.68	23.79	0.51
2	283.11	37	25.85	283.57	37	17.90	-0.46	-0.02
3	266.47	93	47.88	261.85	101	55.08	4.62	0.28
4	257.79	58	33.28	267.05	42	23.32	-9.26	-0.41
5	284.25	14	8.64	229.73	9	5.34	54.52	1.17
6	176.79	8	17.68	186.36	9	14.91	-9.57	0.32
7	22.5	1	1.85	95.17	1	1.57	-72.67	-1.13
				US Indian/Alaskan				
1	233.37	7	5.27	232.94	7	6.058	0.43	0.01
2	229.17	11	9.82	288.51	16	11.77	-59.34	1.63
3	263.22	24	18.24	262.59	46	28.00	0.63	0.02
4	286.03	10	7.44	262.98	10	7.63	23.05	0.53
5	221.9	6	3.74	232.84	13	8.68	-10.94	0.21
6	144.23	2	2.1	159.88	6	5.12	-15.65	0.23
7	142.48	3	2.14	81.06	1	.76	61.42	0.53
				White				
1	283.08	358	250.5	283.63	350	200.8	-0.55	-0.07
2	295.12	834	560.15	291.9	1020	532.2	3.22	0.63
3	305.99	2764	1461	300.61	3328	1510	5.38	1.74
4	307.32	2030	1119	295.6	2399	1157	11.72	3.31[a]
5	287.21	874	472.7	272.1	1289	550.2	6.11	1.15
6	264.16	505	624.1	234.66	811	751.9	29.5	6.45[a]
7	206.75	82	102.6	192.6	203	166.6	14.15	1.30

[a]Highly statistically significant results: i.e., $p<.01$ for these results.

to 80 years of age. Females over age 80 have a slightly higher educational level than males in their age cohort.

DISCUSSION

Summary

Adults over age 80 have witnessed almost all the major events of this century: they saw World War I through children's eyes, witnessed the depression at its worst, were adults during World War II, and have been through confined regional wars and varying economic cycles since. This is the age group at which gender differences are most striking. These differences are dominated by the white ethnic group; this group also shows differences in favor of males in educational level.

Adults between ages 55 and 64 were children during the depression and World War II and had reached adulthood by the time of the publication of Friedan's (1963) book *The Feminine Mystique*. In this age group there is a narrowing of the gender gap in quantitative performance. This is due to a greater decrease in males' mean performance; it may be that males are finding quantitative skills less necessary to their work performance in these late career years. Whites show a considerable gender difference in educational level.

Those adults between 25 and 39 years of age show no significant gender differences, though the gender discrepancy in quantitative scores is larger than in younger groups. Differences in educational level are hardly perceptible except among Asians, with males having a higher level of education. The two youngest age groups in the NALS show almost identical performances on the quantitative and document scales; females hold a slight advantage on the prose scale. Though many in the 19–24-year-old group are still in school, this group has educational levels close to those of 25–39-year-olds. This suggests that educational attainment levels are rising. Quantitative performance is at its peak in these younger students except among Native Americans and whites.

The effects of history vary across ethnic groups. Blacks and whites have very dissimilar patterns of gender differences. Black females almost always outperform black males on all three scales. On the other hand, white males ages 40–54 and 65–80 solidly outperform females on the quantitative scale; they show a tendency to do so on the document scale as well.

Conclusions

The NALS data indicate that we are doing better at educating black and Asian minorities than ever before: the quantitative data show the highest means for ages 16–24 in these ethnic groups. Still, the means for these young age groups fall well below those of whites. Language differences may be part of the problem, but levels are lower for blacks than for the Asian minorities and whites. Gender differences are small for all ethnic groups in young adulthood.

Even adults aged 25–39 show almost no mean gender difference in educational attainment across all ethnic groups and only small gender differences in quantitative performance. Young women are coming to be as economically and politically capable as are young men. We have noted the improvements of school-age females in academic test performance over the years; young women's performances on the NALS literacy scales echo these gains.

On the other hand, the sudden drop in older white females' quantitative performance from means of approximately 272 for those aged 50–64 to 235 for those at ages 65–80 is unsettling. A similar decline occurs in the document scale, from about 263 to 229. Even on the prose scale, mean scores decline from 276 to 246. Educational level is apparently a factor here, as there is a drop of almost one level of attainment. Women aged 65–80 often become widowed and responsible for the financial affairs of their households at these times. It seems possible that offering very practical seminars on financial matters might improve the quantitative performance of females in this age group. At ages 80 and over, males drop close to equity with the females on the quantitative scale, are nearly equal on the document scale, and score below females on the prose scale. Females have higher educational attainment than males in this group.

Genetic effects are not apparent in the NALS data. Educational attainment explains most ethnic differences. Moreover, gender effects differ with ethnicity, so if there is a "math gene" operating, it is hard to explain why it functions so differently across the different ethnic groups. Not surprisingly, educational attainment is a powerful factor in many of the NALS results. Environmental effects are clear in these data. How to best use this evidence—that is, how we can promote gender and ethnic equity—remains our task. We look forward to further demographic and cultural analyses of the NALS data, similar to Myers' (1997) analysis of Minnesota state data, to inform our future efforts toward equity.

REFERENCES

Banziger, G. (1992). Women-in-the-science program at Marietta College—Focusing on math to keep women in science. *Journal of College Science Teaching, 21,* 279–283.

Becker, B. J., & Hedges, L. V. (1984). Meta-analysis of cognitive gender differences: A comment on an analysis by Rosenthal and Rubin. *Journal of Educational Psychology, 76,* 583–587.

————. (1988). The effects of selection and variability in studies of gender differences. *Behavioral and Brain Sciences, 11*, 183–184.

Bouchard, T. J., Jr. (1983). Do environmental similarities explain the similarity in intelligence of identical twins reared apart? *Intelligence, 7*, 175–184.

Carmichael, L. (Ed.). (1946). *Manual of child psychology*. New York: Wiley.

Friedan, B. (1963). *The feminine mystique*. New York: Norton.

Friedman, L. (1989). Mathematics and the gender gap: A meta-analysis of recent studies on sex differences in mathematical tasks. *Review of Educational Research, 59*, 185–213.

————. (1995). The space factor in mathematics: Gender differences. *Review of Educational Research, 65*, 22–50.

————. (1996, April). "Tests of mathematical reasoning: Do they cause trouble for women?" Paper presented at the annual meeting of the American Educational Research Association, New York.

Galton, F. (1883). *Inquiries into human faculty and its development*. London: Macmillan.

Hedges, L. V., & Olkin, I. (1985). *Statistical methods for meta-analysis*. Boston: Academic Press.

Hilton, T. L. (1985). *National changes in spatial-visual ability from 1960 to 1980* (Research Rep. No. RR-85–27). Princeton, NJ: Educational Testing Service.

Hyde, J. S., Fennema, E., Lamon, S. J. (1990). Gender differences in mathematics performance: A meta-analysis. *Psychological Bulletin, 107*, 139–155.

Hyde, J. S., & Linn, M. C. (1988). Gender differences in verbal ability: A meta-analysis. *Psychological Bulletin, 104*, 53–69.

Jones, L. V., Burton, N., & Davenport, E. (1984). Monitoring the mathematics achievement of black students. *Journal for Research in Mathematics Education, 15*, 154–164.

Kirsch, I. S., Jungeblut, A., Jenkins, L., & Kolstad, A. (1993). *Adult literacy in America: A first look at the results of the National Adult Literacy Survey*. Washington, DC: National Center for Education Statistics.

Koehler, M. C. S. (1986). Effective mathematics teaching and sex-related differences in algebra one classes (Doctoral dissertation, University of Wisconsin–Madison, 1985). *Dissertation Abstracts International, 46*, 2953A.

Linn, M., & Petersen A. (1985). Emergence and characterization of sex differences in spatial ability: A meta-analysis. *Child Development, 56*, 1479–1498.

Maccoby, E. (1966). *The development of sex differences*. Stanford, CA: Stanford University Press.

Maccoby, E., & Jacklin, C. (1974). *The psychology of sex differences*. Stanford, CA: Stanford University Press.

Myers, S., Jr. (1997). *Analysis of the 1996 Minnesota Basic Standards Test data* (Tech. Rep.). Minneapolis: University of Minnesota, Humphrey Institute of Public Affairs, Roy Wilkins Center for Human Relations and Social Justice.

Rosenthal, R., & Rubin, D. (1984). Further meta-analytic procedures for assessing cognitive gender differences. *Journal of Educational Psychology, 74*, 708–712.

Smith, T. M. (1996). *The condition of education* (NCES 96–304). Washington, DC: U.S. Government Printing Office.

Swafford, J. (1980). Sex differences in first-year algebra. *Journal for Research in Mathematics Education, 11*, 335–346.

Terman, L., and Associates. (1946). Psychological sex differences. In L. Carmichael (Ed.), *Manual of child psychology*. New York: Wiley.

Terman, L., & Tyler, L. (1954). Psychological sex differences. In L. Carmichael (Ed.), *Manual of child psychology* (2d ed.). New York: Wiley.

Wittig, M. A., & Petersen, A. C. (1979) (Eds.). *Sex-related differences in cognitive functioning: Developmental issues*. New York: Academic Press.

8

Literacy Habits and Political Participation

Richard L. Venezky and David Kaplan

Voting is a form of political participation that is characterized by high accessibility to the average citizen and low resource expenditure—time, money, motivation, and so on (Kleppner, 1982). Unlike other forms of political participation such as contributing to political parties or candidates, campaigning, or belonging to political clubs, voting can be done with a minimum of time, effort, and expenditure. Voting is also a right and a responsibility considered vital to the American style of democracy, yet beginning in 1960 a long downward trend occurred for the percentage of those eligible to vote who actually voted. This occurred even though more and more barriers to registration and voting were removed during this same period. This trend continued through the 1988 presidential election, which had the lowest voter turnout since the 1920s. The 1992 presidential election, in which 55.4% of the eligible voters actually voted, marked the end of this 28-year decline, although the percentage turnout did not exceed that of 1968 (Cook, 1993), and in the 1994 and 1996 national elections voter turnout declined sharply. Analyses of demographic and sociopolitical characteristics have provided some insights into why these declines occurred.

The goal of this chapter is to develop a predictive model of voting behavior and to estimate the parameters of the model using data from the National Adult Literacy Survey (Kirsch & Jungeblut, 1986). First we present a literature review of the salient predictors of voting behavior. This review specifically examines demographic variables, sociopolitical variables, and the relative strengths of each. A brief discussion of registration and voting is also provided. Next we present specific survey results of the literacy habits and voting behavior of the NALS respondents, followed by a logistic regression of voting behavior on demographic variables and literacy variables. The chapter concludes with a discussion of the policy implications of the results.

PREDICTORS OF VOTING BEHAVIOR

Demographic Factors

Voter turnout studies (e.g., Kleppner, 1982; Lipset, 1981; Teixeira, 1992; Verba & Nie, 1972) have focused on two sets of individual variables: demographic (education, occupation, income; age, residential mobility, marital status, race, geographic region, sex) and sociopolitical (partisanship, political efficacy, campaign newspaper reading). Among the core Socioeconomic Status (SES) demographic variables, higher education, income, and occupational status have been associated with higher tendencies to vote. Older citizens have exhibited higher turnouts than younger citizens, a difference that holds up when adjustments in voting rates are made for education, income, and sex. In the 1984 presidential election, as an example, persons 55–64 years of age had nearly twice the self-reported voting rate as persons 18–20 (72.1% vs. 36.7%). Among these core demographic variables, education generally is found to be the strongest predictor of voting behavior (e.g., Wolfinger & Rosenstone, 1980).

Age, residential mobility, and marital status constitute a rootedness factor that is characterized by stability and experience and that relates positively to voting behavior. Older persons have more voting experience than younger persons; therefore they find the mechanics of voting to be less a barrier to their presence in the ballot booth. Higher residential mobility implies a higher need for reregistration and reestablishment of political ties, costs that tend to decrease the probability of voting. Married persons living with their spouses tend to vote at higher rates than single persons or married persons living alone, due to the sharing of information about the particulars of voting and of the candidates and their positions.

Parallel to the rootedness variables are race, region of the country, and sex, which constitute a political distancing grouping. Those who feel they are on the inside, that is, who consider themselves socially, racially, and geographically close to the centers of power (white, male, non-South), tend to vote at higher rates than those who feel they are on the outside. Male turnout in the past has exceeded female turnout, but this difference has been gradually disappearing, especially as more and more women enter the labor force and become concerned about their economic viability (Farah & Klein, 1989). Similarly, white turnout rates have been higher than black rates, but most of this gap is due to differences in education and income and has been declining (Leighley & Nagler, 1992).

Sociopolitical Factors

Partisanship, political efficacy, and campaign newspaper reading, all of which index a form of engagement, are the main sociopolitical factors that have been investigated in voter turnout studies. Partisanship and political efficacy are similar but not always closely related. Partisanship indexes degree of identity with a specific party candidate or issue, while political efficacy denotes the degree to which persons feel they have any influence over governmental activities. Individuals with strong partisan identifications tend to be more likely to vote (Teixeira, 1987), while those who are highly cynical of the ability or willingness of government to assist them or others they care about tend to vote less. In general, persons who have high political efficacy take a stronger interest in campaign issues and in candidates and tend, therefore, to be more partisan. However, one could be strongly partisan but possess low political efficacy.

Related to partisanship is identity politics—the tendency of voters to develop political allegiances based on demographic features shared with specific candidates. For example, almost 80% of the Catholics who voted in the 1960 presidential election voted for the Catholic candidate, John F. Kennedy. Similarly, a large number of Protestant voters who might normally have voted for a candidate with Kennedy's political positions voted for his opponent as a reaction to his religion (Plutzer & Zipp, 1996). Gender identity appears to have played an important role in the 14 gubernatorial and Senate races in 1992 in which women were candidates. Identity politics and partisan politics can create tensions when they pull voters in opposite directions, for example, when Democratic women have the opportunity to vote for a female Republican candidate.

Exactly how partisanship and political efficacy interact over time is difficult to predict. In 1990, for example, a *Times-Mirror* poll found that 57% of those surveyed nationally agreed that "people like me don't have any say about what government does" (McWilliams, 1993, p. 196), a result that presaged a low turnout for the 1992 election. Yet by November 1992, the apparent closeness of the race and the voters' sense of economic threat from the recession led to higher partisanship and therefore to the highest turnout since the 1960s.

Campaign newspaper reading, an indicator of intellectual engagement and of understanding, is also highly related to turnout. This factor derives from general, year-round habits of media use. Chafee and Yang (1990) found differences in voting habits according to how individuals gained their political knowledge. Television-dependent citizens were found to vote less, to be less understanding of, and less involved in, political campaigns, and to be less likely to have well-formed reasons for their political choices. Analyses of campaign media coverage have concluded that newspapers present the greater range and depth of issues, have more partisan bias, and require more active and more creative reader engagement. In contrast, television coverage is more structured and less intellectually demanding, requiring less initiative by the viewer (Shaffer, 1981).

Television news coverage, furthermore, has over the past decade tended to give less direct coverage to the candidates, showing "reporters more and candidates less" (McWilliams, 1993, p. 198). The average campaign news sound bite, that is, "direct television footage of what the candidate and others actually say," fell, according to one count, from about 12 seconds in the 1984 campaign to about 9 seconds in the 1988 campaign (Lemert, Elliott, Bernstein, Rosenberg, & Nestvold, 1991, p. 1). In reaction to this trend, candidates in the 1992 campaign turned to the "new" news and the "weird media"—talk shows, infomercials, and so on—to reach large audiences with sustained messages (McWilliams, 1993). Television's propensity to block viewers from direct access to the candidates was clearly shown in the coverage of Clinton's victory speech at the end of the 1992 election. Every network except CNN and C-Span dropped the speech after four minutes, and CNN stopped after nine minutes.

Television is, nevertheless, the most common route through which children first become aware of politics. Those who become newspaper readers generally do not begin to gain political information from this medium until early adolescence (Chafee & Yang, 1990). Newspaper reading habits, however, may shift over time. The most stable readers are those who regularly access both hard news (international news; national, state, and local politics) and soft news (news about people in the community, home and garden, crime and accidents, etc.). People who abandon newspaper reading tend to read hard news less than either stable readers or those who adopt newspaper reading after adolescence (Chafee & Choe, 1987).

Not all researchers agree, however, on the role of campaign newspaper reading. Abramson, Aldrich, and Rohde (1990), for example, argue that campaign newspaper reading, like voting, is a form of political behavior rather than a personal characteristic that measures campaign involvement. Thus, whatever factors influence political behavior act simultaneously upon both voting and campaign newspaper reading. Generally opposing this view is Teixeira (1992), who also points out that campaign newspaper reading should not be confused with overall frequency of newspaper reading. The latter variable has shown no independent effect on the likelihood of voting.

Whatever the role of newspaper reading in voting behavior, some attention needs to be paid to the types of newspapers actually read. In-depth coverage of campaigns is typical of papers like the *New York Times*, the *St. Louis Globe-Dispatch*, and the *Washington Post*, in contrast to papers, like *U.S.A. Today*, that present briefer and less in-depth coverage. Further along the journalism scale are supermarket tabloids, which tend to present news more like television, although with a greater emphasis on sensationalism. These latter newspapers were chiefly responsible during the 1992 campaign for the descent into what has been called "sexual McCarthyism," the frenzied delving into the candidates' personal lives (McWilliams, 1993, p. 198). Little attention in the past was given to the role that supermarket tabloids play in voting behavior, yet they are widely circulated throughout the country, particularly among the less educated.

Impact of Issues

It is often assumed that through newspaper reading and, to a lesser degree, through television and radio, voters obtain the candidates' messages and that these messages then have an impact on the voters' behavior at the polls. This causal chain assumes, first, that the candidates' messages are, in fact, being received and understood and, second, that the voters' behavior is at least based on this information. Both of these assumptions have been challenged. The literature on whether or not issues influence voters is divided. Classic studies such as Berelson, Lazarsfeld, and McPhee (1954) showed an electorate little interested in, and lacking knowledge on, campaign issues. Similarly, Rosenstone and Hansen (1993) found little influence of campaign factors on voting. Price and Zaller (1993), in partial contrast, claim that voters are influenced by the candidates' positions when (1) they receive adequate information on the important issues and on the candidates' positions vis-à-vis these issues and (2) the voters are able to comprehend this information.

One observed barrier to voter comprehension of issues is the "information tide" that appears when local, state, and national elections occur at the same time. Voters may not be able to distinguish, for some of the issues, to which particular contest each applies. Data from the 1988 senate election provide some support for this "confusion" hypothesis. Of 1,485 respondents who claimed to have voted in the senate race, 61.3% could recall only a single issue from the race, and 42% overall named at least one issue that was not a major campaign theme in their state (Dalager, 1996). (Thirteen percent could recall two issues correctly, and under 3% could recall a third.)

When knowledge of specific issues has been probed, generally the respondents did not show highly accurate recall or understanding of the matter. For example, Holbrook and Garand (1996) surveyed residents of Milwaukee County, Wisconsin, during the 1992 presidential election concerning their perceptions of national unemployment and inflation rates—issues of importance to that election. Accuracy of estimates was low, with 34.3% of the respondents unable to estimate any unemployment rate and 57.0% unable to estimate any inflation rate. Whether recall of an accurate quantitative indicator is a fair assessment of voter knowledge on an issue, however, is open to question. Voters might hear, for example, that, due to high inflation, prices were going up faster than wages, and therefore, more people were applying for welfare support. Similarly, one might learn that unemployment was at its lowest level in a decade without knowing the actual unemployment rate. Relative information may be sufficient to choose among candidate positions.

Relative Strengths of Predictors

The relative strengths of different sets of turnout predictors have been compared in a few studies, the most common contrasts being between systemic and individual factors. Commonly explored systemic factors include campaign mobilization, registration laws, union membership, and closeness of an election. Individual factors include the demographic and sociopolitical factors discussed before. Results have not shown any stable patterns, however. For example, Patterson and Caldeira (1983) concluded from an analysis of gubernatorial elections that systemic factors were the primary determinants of voter turnout, while Leighley and Nagler (1992) concluded for the 1984 presidential election that individual factors, particularly education, were the primary determinants of turnout.

Registration and Voting

In the Young Adult Literacy Study (YALS) (Kirsch & Jungeblut, 1986), respondents were asked in separate questions if (1) they were currently registered to vote and (2) if they had voted in a national, state, or local election in the past five years. In the initial report for YALS, hard news reading was found to relate positively to voting, as was literacy level (Kirsch & Jungeblut, 1986). However, no attempt was made to control for age, education, sex, race, or other potential explanatory variables, nor was the selection bias caused by registration considered. Registration, a necessity for voting, has also been ignored in most voter turnout studies. Although the factors that lead to registering to vote and actually voting must have a large overlap, some factors may be unique to each or more important to one than the other. Erickson (1981), for example, claimed that the factors that influenced the two processes might be different.

Others, however, have argued the opposite (e.g., Squire, Wolfinger, & Glass, 1987).

Jackson (1996) points out that registration is often more complex, more difficult, and less convenient than voting. In many states, at least until recently, registration needed to be done in advance of the time when campaign interest peaks. In an analysis of registration and voting from the 1984, 1986, 1988, and 1990 elections, Jackson found that registration depended mostly on individual characteristics such as age, education, residential mobility, and partisan intensity. In contrast, voting depended more on campaign issues, that is, political mobilization.

Although registration is usually not considered in multivariate studies of voting behavior, its role in limiting voter turnout has been analyzed. Wolfinger and Rosenstone (1980), for example, examined registration laws as barriers to voting and developed one of the first multivariate models for estimating their effects. Teixeira (1992) claims that the elimination of registration deadlines will have the largest effect of any single factor on turnout. But whether the turnout rate of registrants has been declining over the past three decades or has remained stable has not been resolved. Some (e.g., Piven & Cloward, 1988) interpret available data as showing a stable turnout; others (e.g., Teixeira, 1992) conclude that the rate of turnout of registrants has declined.

In a follow-up study of the YALS database, Kaplan and Venezky (1994) used a bivariate probit regression model with sample selection to test the independent contributions of different demographic and sociopolitical variables to registration and to voting. Separate probit regressions showed that all of the selected variables were significant predictors of both registration and voting. Separate regressions, however, fail to account for sample selection, that is, for the bias that occurs because only those registered to vote can actually vote. Bivariate probit regression with sample selection is designed to handle the problem of sample selection by incorporating a term in the voting equation that captures the fact that only those who are registered to vote can vote.

In the bivariate probit regression, only years of education and number of different types of hard news read were significant predictors of voting, given registration. For registration, these same variables plus race/ethnicity, hours per day of television watching, and degree of keeping up with government affairs were significant predictors.

VOTING PATTERNS AMONG NALS RESPONDENTS

The data for the present study were collected in 1991–1992 as part of the National Adult Literacy Survey (Kirsch, Jungeblut, Jenkins, & Kolstad, 1993). From a household screening of over 40,000 respondents, interviews were done with about 30,000 adults, ages 16 and up. Each interview consisted of a background questionnaire covering demo-graphic, educational, occupational, and literacy habits variables, plus a reading assessment composed of items that required the extraction and use of information from everyday documents—airline schedules, prod-uct labels, letters, directions, insurance descriptions, and so on.

Although the NALS assessment items were divided into three scales (prose, document, and quantitative), the extremely high correlations across these scales, ranging from .859 (prose-quantitative) to .895 (prose-document), have led us to report results for only a single scale, the prose scale. All of the data reported here are based on respondents who were born in the United States or its territories and who were 25–65 years of age and out of school. The place of birth restriction eliminates a subpop-ulation whose literacy performance may have, in part, been decreased by lack of familiarity with English and with U.S culture. The age restric-tion removes a subpopulation who are still in school or are just estab-lishing themselves in jobs or were most likely retired. Although these characteristics may not affect literacy abilities, they do influence income, voting, and literacy practices. Also excluded are the incarcerated, leaving 15,274 respondents who project to a national population of about 106 million.

The NALS background questionnaire contained only a single question on voting: "Have you voted in a national or state election in the United States in the past five years?" Possible responses were "Yes," "No," and "Not eligible to vote." Because local elections were excluded from this question, comparisons to YALS responses cannot be made. In addition, since no question was asked about registration, a bivariate probit re-gression could not be done on the NALS responses. When only univari-ate relationships are tested, with no controls for other factors, voting percentages increased with increasing education, literacy, and age. The percentage of eligible voters who voted also increased with the amount of newspaper reading, as shown in Table 8.1.

Race differences, also shown in Table 8.1 for different literacy levels, indicate that whites had the highest voting percentage at the highest literacy level, but this advantage shrank with decreasing literacy level. Blacks had the second highest voting percentage across almost all cate-gories, with Hispanics and Asians exchanging positions for third and fourth highest across the different literacy levels.

A step toward understanding more complex relationships is shown in Figure 8.1, where percentage voting is plotted against five levels of prose literacy performance for five different educational attainment levels. Within each educational level, some change in voting percentage occurs across the literacy levels, but the change is nowhere as dramatic as what occurs when voting percentage is plotted against literacy level across all educational attainment levels, indicating that when education is con-

Table 8.1
Percentages of Respondents Who Voted by Major Demographic Variables
(standard errors in parentheses)

Variable	%Who Voted
Total	72.6 (0.52)
Age	
25-44	60.2 (0.93)
35-44	73.3 (0.99)
45-54	79.9 (1.02)
45-54	82.5 (0.90)
Prose Literacy	
Level 1	57.7 (1.86)
Level 2	64.6 (2.06)
Level 3	75.3 (0.92)
Level 4	86.2 (1.02)
Level 5	92.4 (1.92)
Educational Attainment	
0-8	48.9 (3.12)
9-11+	52.6 (1.76)
HSD or GED	66.5 (0.75)
Some College	79.0 (0.79)
BA/BS	88.2 (1.03)
Post-Graduate	94.7 (0.79)
Income	
< $10,000	49.6 (2.26)
10,000-19,999	59.3 (1.78)
20,000-29,999	67.3 (1.76)
30,000-39,999	72.8 (1.12)
40,000-49,999	77.4 (1.56)
50,000-74,999	85.5 (0.97)
75,000+	91.3 (0.99)
Gender	
Male	71.3 (0.83)
Female	73.7 (0.61)
Race	
White	73.3 (0.54)
African American	71.5 (1.36)
Hispanic	62.3 (2.35)
Other	56.9 (5.40)

Figure 8.1
Percentage Voting by Prose Literacy Performance at Different Educational Attainment Levels

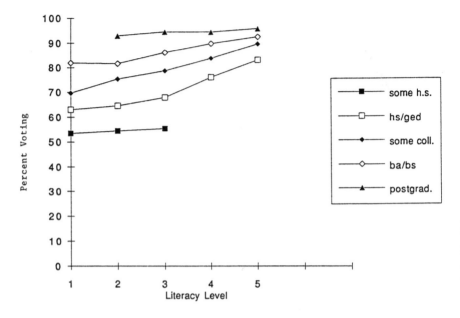

trolled, literacy performance does not have a strong effect on probability of voting. This is only a tentative conclusion, however, since age, race/ ethnicity, and other potentially influential variables other than education were not controlled in this plot.

Predicting Voting Behavior

To test the predictive power of demographic characteristics, literacy performance, and literacy activities for voting, logistic multiple regression was used. This approach allows a determination of the joint contribution of demographic variables and literacy variables in predicting the probability of responding affirmatively to the question "Have you voted in a national or state election in the United States within the past five years?" (Yes, No, Not eligible to vote). This dependent variable was coded 1=yes, 0=no. (The sample selection process removed those not eligible to vote.)

Included as predictor variables were age (in ten-year increments), sex, race/ethnicity (coded as a black–white contrast, a Hispanic–white contrast, and an other–white contrast), level of educational attainment (coded as five contrasts, each with high school graduation), household income (coded as six contrasts, each contrasted with $20,000–$29,999 income range), prose literacy (scale score), and a group of literacy practices variables. These latter variables included frequency of newspaper reading, frequency of reading on the job, number of magazines read regularly, and amount of newspaper and book reading.

The newspaper reading variables were created by constructing scales for hard news and soft news. Respondents indicated, in response to questions on the background questionnaire, which sections of the newspaper they read regularly. Hard news sections included news, editorial, and financial, giving a scale from 0 to 3. Soft news included horoscope/advice, ads, comics, and entertainment schedules, giving a scale from 0 to 4. Similarly, the book reading categories indicated by respondents were divided into hard book (current affairs, science) and light book (recreation, religion, fiction). (Descriptive statistics for all variables used in the model are shown in Table 8.1.) In what follows we refer to the criterion variable as "voting" for ease of discussion. We are cognizant that this variable is a retrospective self-report measure.

The results of the logistic regression are shown in Table 8.2. It can be seen that the predictors, taken as a whole, predict the probability of voting better than what can be explained by an intercept-only model, c^2 (35, N=15,274) = 3,745.87; p<.001. Closer inspection of the results, however, yields a picture of differential predictive ability. To aid in the interpretation, odds ratios are provided.[1] We consider an odds ratio greater than, or equal to, 1.5 as substantively significant. In addition, we are employing a one-tailed test of significance at the $a = 0.05$ level.

With respect to the main purposes of this study, literacy activities as well as basic literacy skills as measured by the prose literacy scale were not predictive of the probability of voting. However, it can be seen that, holding all else constant, the most salient predictors of voting behavior are the demographic variables of age, education, race, and income. We find that age differences of ten-year increments among the respondents increase the odds of voting 1.6 times[2] ($p < .05$). We also find that African Americans are 1.9 times more likely to vote than whites, holding all else constant ($p < .05$). (The comparison of Hispanics to whites was not significant.)

For education, using high school graduates as the comparison group, we find that those with some high school education are 1.7 times less likely to vote than those with a high school diploma ($p < .05$). Those with only two years of college do not differ from high school graduates. Those with a college diploma are 2.6 times more likely to vote than those with a high school diploma, and those with postgraduate education are 4.3 times more likely to vote than high school graduates ($p < .05$, respectively).

With regard to income, we observe that the odds of voting increase

Table 8.2
Results of Logistic Regression of Voting on Demographic Variables, Literacy
Activities, and the Prose Literacy Scale

Variable	Coefficient (std err)	z-value	odds-ratio
Age *10	0.483 (.029)	16.430**	1.62
Sex	-0.211 (.053)	-3.971**	0.81
African American	0.637 (.080)	7.977**	1.89
Hispanic	0.013 (.138)	0.092	1.01
Other	-0.314 (.193)	-1.627	0.73
Some High School	-0.504 (.111)	-4.527**	0.60
Some College	0.396 (.066)	6.033**	1.49
College	0.953 (.122)	7.835**	2.59
Post Graduate	1.461 (.193)	7.589**	4.31
Miss Inc	0.095 (.110)	0.866	1.11
Income 1	-0.437 (.127)	-3.436**	0.65
Income 2	-0.183 (.123)	-1.492	1.20
Income 4	0.221 (.092)	2.402*	1.25
Income 5	0.263 (.091)	2.882**	1.30
Income 6	0.534 (.112)	4.754**	1.71
Income 7	0.657 (.159)	4.124**	1.93
High Paper	0.376 (.078)	4.708**	1.46
Mod. Paper	0.118 (.079)	1.503	1.13
Low Paper	-0.074 (.118)	-0.627	0.81
High Job	0.153 (.076)	2.022*	1.17
Mod. Job	0.177 (.100)	1.764	1.19
Low Job	0.034 (.101)	0.334	1.03
No Job	-0.087 (.109)	-0.800	0.92
One Mag.	0.111 (.104)	1.072	1.12
Two Mags.	0.212 (.093)	2.278*	1.24
tffmag	0.219 (.083)	2.633**	1.24
six mag.	0.323 (.110)	2.941**	1.38
Hard News	0.151 (.048)	3.144**	1.16
Soft News	-0.031 (.019)	-1.583	0.97
Hard Book	0.098 (.034)	2.891**	1.10
Lt. Book	0.164 (.046)	3.586**	1.18
No Book	-0.068 (.088)	-0.775	0.93
Prose	0.161 (.052)	3.104**	1.17
Constant	-3.007 (.366)		

*= $p < .05$
***= $p < .01$
Note: Income 3 ($20,000–29,999) is the contrasted income level.

monotonically with income. For example, compared to respondents earning between $20,000 and $29,000 a year, those earning between $50,000 and $74,999 a year are 1.7 times more likely to vote (p < .05). Conversely, those below the poverty line are about two-thirds as likely to vote.

CONCLUSIONS AND POLICY IMPLICATIONS

The voting results are particularly striking for a number of reasons. First, although a lower percentage of blacks than whites reported voting in the sample used for the logistic regression analysis, once age, education, document literacy, and several other demographic and literacy practices variables were controlled, it was found that blacks had a higher probability of voting than whites. This illustrates the dangers in using univariate relationships, particularly for policy analysis.

For Asians, on the other hand, these results should be a matter of concern in that they show that for equal education, literacy, age, and so on, Asians vote at only one-half the rate that whites do. At present we have no explanation for this result. Although language barriers may still exist, even for those born in the United States, we have not investigated this with the NALS database. Second, literacy performance, as indexed by scores on the document literacy scale, does not influence voting behavior, but years of education does. This implies (but does not prove) that training people after they leave school so that their literacy performances improve will not increase the probability that these people will vote. However, each year a person remains in school does increase the probability that that person will vote.

That frequency of newspaper reading is a better predictor of voting behavior than amount of hard news read is, at first glance, puzzling, in that it is the reverse of what was found in Kaplan and Venezky (1994). In that study it was found that once registration was accounted for, only the amount of hard news read and years of education were significant predictors of voting. Persons who read all four hard news sections (national news, state and local news, editorial, and financial) were one and one-half times more likely to vote than those who read no hard news sections of the newspaper. In that study, however, separate equations were developed for registration and voting, a strategy that was not possible in the present study due to restrictions in the background questionnaire. The relative advantage in predictive power of frequency of newspaper reading over hard news reading could also be due to the limited variability in the NALS hard news variable, given that respondents were asked only if they generally read a particular section and not how much time they spent reading it. For news, in particular, large differences in reading time might exist between those who regularly skim the news on the front page and those who digest carefully all of the various news sections. Future surveys should probe not only for amount of time spent on different sections of the newspaper but also for what types of newspapers are read.

In summary, we find that if increased voter turnout is a national goal, increasing the number of years that citizens spend in school will probably do more to reach this goal than increasing either literacy levels or hard news reading. This is a speculation, however, because we do not know if a selection bias occurs in the data upon which this study was based. Both educational attainment and voting behavior might, for example, depend on a third, unspecified variable. Newspaper reading may not be important for determining voter turnout, but it may be important for ensuring informed voting. In addition, given that some earlier studies found that when registration and voting were predicted separately, campaign issues were important for the latter, the lack of ability to separate registration and voting in this study may have reduced its sensitivity to newspaper reading. We can only hope that future studies of adult literacy will attend to a wider range of variables that are important for understanding voting behavior, including whether or not respondents are registered, residential mobility, partisanship, and other forms of political participation.

NOTES

1. Odds ratios are obtained by exponentiating the logistic regression coefficient, b. For continuous variables, the odds ratio can be interpreted as an increase in the odds of the outcome's occurring for a unit increase in the predictor. For dichotomous (e.g., group dummy) variables, the odds ratio can be interpreted as how much more likely it is for the outcome to be present for the group coded 1 compared to the group coded 0 (see Hosmer & Lemeshow, 1989).

2. Within the framework of logistic regression it is possible to examine changes in the odds for different units of the predictor variable. That is, if we let c be some constant number of years (say, ten-year increments), then $exp(c*b)$, where b is the logistic regression coefficient, gives the increase in the odds for every ten-year difference in age.

REFERENCES

Abramson, P. R., Aldrich, J. H., & Rohde, D. W. (1990). *Change and continuity in the 1988 elections.* Washington, DC: Congressional Quarterly Press.

Berelson, B. R., Lazarsfeld, P. F., & McPhee, W. N. (1954). *Voting: A study of opinion formation in a presidential campaign.* Chicago: University of Chicago Press.

Chafee, S. H., & Choe, S. Y. (1987). Newspaper reading in longitudinal perspective: Beyond structural constraints. *Journalism Quarterly, 58,* 201–211.

Chafee, S. H., & Yang, S.-M. (1990). Communication and political socialization.

In I. O. Ichelov (Ed.), *Political socialization, citizenship, education, and democracy.* New York: Teachers College Press.

Cook, R. (1993, May 15). '92 voter turnout: Apathy stymied. *Congressional Quarterly Weekly Report,* pp. 1258.

Dalager, J. K. (1996). Voters, issues, and elections: Are the candidates' messages getting through? *The Journal of Politics, 58* (2), 486–515.

Erickson, R. S. (1981). Why do people vote? Because they are registered. *Politics Quarterly 9,* 259–276.

Farah, B. G., & Klein, E. (1989). Public opinion trends. In G. M. Pomper (Ed.), *The election of 1988: Reports and interpretations* (pp. 103–128). Chatham, NJ: Chatham House.

Holbrook, T., & Garand, J. C. (1996). Homo economus? Economic information and economic voting. *Political Research Quarterly, 49* (2), 351–375.

Hosmer, D. W., & Lemeshow, S. (1989). *Applied logistic regression.* New York: John Wiley and Sons.

Jackson, R. A. (1996). A reassessment of voter mobilization. *Political Research Quarterly, 49* (2), 305–330.

Kaplan, D., & Venezky, R. L. (1994). Literacy and voting behavior: A bivariate probit model with sample selection. *Social Science Research, 23,* 350–367.

Kirsch, I. S., & Jungeblut, A. (1986). *Literacy: Profiles of America's young adults* (NAEP Report No. 16-PL-02). Princeton, NJ: Educational Testing Service.

Kirsch, I. S., Jungeblut, A., Jenkins, L., & Kolstad, A. (1993). *Adult literacy in America: A first look at the results of the National Adult Literacy Survey.* Washington, D.C. National Center for Educational Statistics, U.S. Department of Education.

Kleppner, P. (1982). *Who voted? The dynamics of voter turnout, 1870–1980.* New York: Praeger.

Leighley, J. E., & Nagler, J. (1992). Individual and systemic influences on turnout: Who votes? 1984. *Journal of Politics, 54* (3), 718–740.

Lemert, J. B., Elliott, W. R., Bernstein, J. M., Rosenberg, W. L., & Nestvold, K. J. (1991). *News verdicts, the debates, and presidential campaigns.* New York: Praeger.

Lipset, S. M. (1981). *Political man.* Baltimore: Johns Hopkins University Press.

McWilliams, W. C. (1993). The meaning of the election. In G. M. Pomper et al. (Eds.), *The election of 1992: Reports and interpretations* (pp. 190–218). Chatham, NJ: Chatham House.

Patterson, S. C., & Caldeira, G. A. (1983). Getting out the vote: Participation in gubernatorial elections. *American Political Science Review, 77,* 675–689.

Paulus, D. L., & Reid, D. B. (1991). Enhancement and denial in socially desirable responding. *Journal of Personality and Social Psychology, 60,* 307–317.

Piven, F. F., & Cloward, R. A. (1988). *Why Americans don't vote.* New York: Pantheon Books.

Plutzer, E., & Zipp, J. F. (1996). Identity politics, partisanship, and voting for women candidates. *Public Opinion Quarterly, 60,* 30–57.

Price, V., & Zaller, J. (1993). Who gets the news? Alternative measures of news reception and their implications for research. *Public Opinion Quarterly, 57,* 133–164.

Rosenstone, S. J., & Hansen, J. M. (1993). *Mobilization, participation, and democracy in America*. New York: Macmillan.

Shaffer, R. (1981). A multivariate explanation of decreasing turnout in presidential elections, 1960–1976. *American Journal of Political Science, 25*, 68–95.

Squire, P., Wolfinger, R. E., & Glass, D. P. (1987). Residential mobility and voter turnout. *American Political Science Review, 81*, 45–65.

Teixeira, R. A. (1987). *Why Americans don't vote: Turnout decline in the United States 1960–1984*. New York: Greenwood.

———. (1992). *The disappearing American voter*. Washington, DC: Brookings Institute.

U.S. Bureau of the Census (1993). *Statistical abstract of the United States* (113th ed.). Washington, DC: Author.

U.S. Department of Commerce (1994). *U.S. industrial outlook 1994*. Washington, DC: Author.

Verba, S., & Nie, N. H. (1972). *Participation in America: Political democracy and social equality*. New York: Harper & Row.

Wolfinger, R. E., & Rosenstone, S. J. (1980). *Who votes?* New Haven, CT: Yale University Press.

9

Community College Literacy: Is the Middle Right?

Joseph Howard and Wayne S. Obetz

From modest beginnings at the turn of the century, community colleges have established their place in American higher education. Until 1955, there were fewer than 600 two-year colleges in the United States, but this number doubled within 20 years; in 1994 there were 1,236 public and private two-year colleges spread throughout all 50 states (Cohen & Brawer, 1996). In 1993, over 5.5 million students were enrolled in two-year colleges (National Center for Educational Statistics, 1995a), and almost half of all first-time college students—1,047,000 or 48%—were in community colleges (National Center for Educational Statistics, 1995b). The rapid growth of community colleges has led to concerns about the quality of education that they provide. While the quantitative growth of the community colleges has been impressive and is readily quantifiable, it has been more difficult to assess the quality of community college education and its impact on the literacy performance and practices of its graduates.

As part of the National Adult Literacy Survey (NALS), participants were asked to indicate their highest level of education, and over 1,000 participants said that they had earned an associate's degree. A review of the literacy outcomes and practices of the community college graduates shows that they often placed in the middle of the five-level scale devised by the NALS. The largest number of associate degree holders scored at Level 3, which is in the middle of the range. The community college graduates could also be considered in the middle of an educational range, commencing with high school and finishing with the earning of a bachelor's degree. These two middles, the midlevel of proficiency on the literacy scales and the middle position between secondary and tertiary education, will serve as the focal points when considering the prose, document, and quantitative literacy of community college graduates.

THE QUALITIES OF THE COMMUNITY COLLEGE

The placement of the community college in the spectrum of American education has shifted in the past century. Tillery and Deegan (1985) stated that in their early years, from about 1900 to 1930, community colleges were often regarded as extensions of high schools. It was not until the 1950s that colleges asserted their role in postsecondary education. Even after establishing their place in postsecondary education, community colleges were still striving to fulfill a number of goals, and these goals tended to distinguish them from four-year colleges.

One of the missions of community colleges has been to prepare students for transfer to baccalaureate colleges or universities, and this goal associates them with the baccalaureate institutions. But the community colleges usually subscribe to four other goals. In addition to transfer, they also want to (1) prepare students for careers, (2) remediate basic skills, (3) provide general education, and (4) offer community service (Lorenzo, 1994). The emphasis that community colleges place on these goals may distinguish them from four-year schools.

Besides having such varied goals, the community colleges have also been guided by the concept of open admissions, and this has resulted in a very diverse student body who, as Cohen and Brawer (1996) have pointed out, have distinctive demographic characteristics. Community college students are likely to be older than traditional college students and are likely to be female. Community colleges also enroll significant numbers of minority students. While community colleges attract many high-ability students, they also attract those who are underprepared for college study (Cohen & Brawer, 1996).

LITERACY IN THE COMMUNITY COLLEGE

It is difficult to describe literacy in the community college since the colleges have such diverse student bodies and a wide range of goals, but a few researchers have tried. Richardson, Fisk, and Okun (1983) presented a description of the literacy taught to basic skills and vocational students in community college classrooms. In these classrooms, two different types of literacy, "texting" and "bitting," were taught, but bitting was the dominant type of reading and writing that was practiced. Whereas texting required the careful reading of longer passages, bitting was the "use of reading or writing to understand or produce fragmented language when presented with specific external clues" (p. 65).

In more general terms, McGrath and Spear (1991) considered the academic culture of the community college to be in crisis since "rigorous academic practice [is] moving from the center to the periphery" (p. 37). Eaton (1994) stated that the cognitive demands of the liberal arts and transfer components of the community college were declining. Community college students "are assigned less writing, for example, and the level of demand of reading and writing assignments has decreased" (p. 35).

These critiques are mainly centered in a more qualitative assessment of the community college or open admissions classroom. What sort of quantitative assessments are available? Since community colleges have attempted to accomplish varied goals and because they enroll students with quite varied backgrounds, it has been difficult to evaluate the outcomes of a community college education. The colleges have been willing to evaluate their students' skills upon registration. According to Hutchings and Marchese (1990), "community colleges lead the way when it comes to entry-level assessment and the use of results for placement and advising of students. What has seemed harder for many of them is the assessment of outcomes" (p. 33). Part of this difficulty with assessment of outcomes stems from the view that community colleges, with their open admissions policies and diverse mission statements, need their own measures of success and cannot just mimic the success criteria used by universities (Griffith & Connor, 1994).

Cohen and Brawer (1987) reported that the General Academic Assessment (GAC), which was compiled by the Center for the Study of Community Colleges, tested over 8,000 students in urban community college systems on their knowledge of the humanities, sciences, social studies, math, and English usage. From the findings, it appeared that course completion and age were positively related to what was learned, but the nature of literacy was not explored in detail. In recent years, some of the state education systems, such as in Florida, Georgia, and Texas, have been interested in maintaining standards and have legislated that students pass competency tests before receiving an associate's degree or going on to further study within the state system (Cohen and Brawer, 1996).

While these efforts, the GAC, and the state initiatives show an interest in determining standards, they do not provide much information on literacy abilities or practices. The National Adult Literacy Survey included in its population 1,033 individuals who indicated that they had received an associate's degree, and in addition to the prose, document, and quantitative literacy tests, these individuals also completed questionnaires that provided information on their reading practices and interests. We have used the NALS data to describe the literacy of community college graduates (Howard & Obetz, 1996). One observation was that community college graduates often scored in the middle of the range, and this brings up the first consideration of the "middling" performance.

IS THE MIDDLE LEVEL SATISFACTORY?

When considering the prose, document, and quantitative literacy of community college graduates in comparison to high school and baccalaureate graduates, it appeared that the greatest number of community college graduates was in the middle level, or Level 3 (see Figure 9.1).

In this figure, the community college graduate literacy profiles resemble a bell curve, with the greatest number of respondents scoring at the middle level of literacy on the prose, document, and quantitative scales. The high school group was skewed toward the lower levels of literacy, and the four-year college group was skewed toward the higher levels.

According to Barton and Lapointe (1995), literacy Levels 1 and 2 reflect a lack of literacy. On the prose and quantitative materials, 23% of the community college graduates were at Levels 1 and 2, and on the document materials 29% were at these levels, which signals a deficiency in functional literacy and a possible cause for concern. The great majority of community college graduates, however, were in Levels 3 or 4 on the scales, with the greatest number at Level 3. A very small percentage were at the highest level of literacy, Level 5.

For the prose materials, Level 3 required that the reader make matches between the text and the question or make low-level inferences. There were no headings to assist the reader, and there could be some distracting information. On the document materials, the reader at Level 3 had "to integrate multiple pieces of information from one or more documents . . . [or] cycle through rather complex tables or graphs which contain information that is irrelevant or inappropriate" (Kirsch, Jungeblut, Jenkins, & Kolstad, 1993, p. 89). For the quantitative tasks, the respondents at Level 3 had to use the arithmetic terms proposed in the question and find two or more numbers in the text.

Level 3 was different from Level 2 in that Level 3 required more use of inferential thinking from longer text. At Level 4, which was mastered by a quarter of the community college graduates on the document materials and almost a third on the prose materials, the reader had to be able to deal with multiple sources of information and make more complex inferences. When readers reached Level 5, they were supposed to be able to do all the skills included at the preceding levels as well as disregard distracting information in dense text and use background information. On the quantitative scale at Level 3, the respondents had to use two or more numbers to perform an arithmetic function that was

Figure 9.1
Literacy Levels by Highest Level of Education

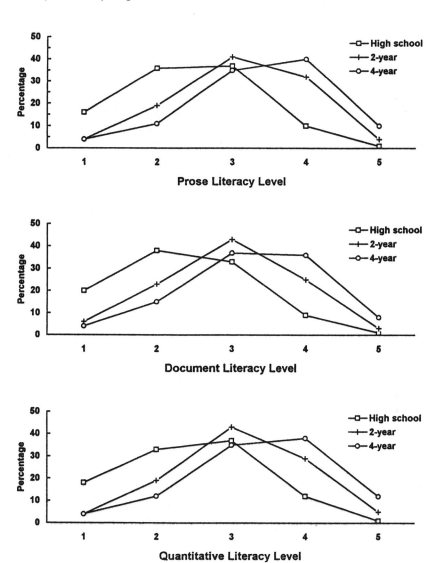

given in the problem. At the higher levels, it might be necessary to infer the arithmetic operation and to perform two or more operations.

Community college educators might have mixed reactions to the accomplishments of their graduates. On one hand, they might be encouraged, since most of the community college participants in the NALS did not place at the lower two levels on either the prose, document, or quantitative scales, which are generally considered to show lack of literacy abilities. By placing in the middle level, community colleges seem to correspond to national trends. Thirty-two percent of the population placed at Level 3 on the prose scale, and 31% each on the document and quantitative scales were at the middle level. Whereas the national population resembled the community college sample in that both peaked at Level 3, more of the national population placed in the lower levels, Level 1 and Level 2, than did the associate's degree group. On the other hand, community college educators might be dissatisfied since their graduates, despite having completed a program of study in higher education, were not in the higher end of the scales. Community colleges probably do not want just to reflect national trends; they would probably prefer to set standards and to raise the literacy levels of their graduates.

The comparison of literacy levels is only one way to investigate literacy, and it does not consider the other information that is included in the NALS. The questionnaire data on sources of information, books read, personal literacy, and literacy in the workplace provide a good deal of data that can be used to compare community college graduates with high school graduates and with graduates of baccalaureate programs. By examining these data, it might be possible to paint a richer picture of the literacy practices and uses of community college graduates and to determine whether their frequent placement at Level 3 on the literacy scales signals achievement or mediocrity.

COMMUNITY COLLEGE LITERACY IN CONTEXT

The community college graduate may be considered to be bracketed by the high school graduate and the four-year college graduate. In the NALS, there were 6,107 participants whose highest level of education was a high school diploma, 1,033 with associate's degrees, and 2,534 with bachelor's degrees. Chi-square tests were used to determine if there was an association between prose, document, and quantitative literacy achievements and the highest levels of education. For the prose scale, $x^2 = 1996$, $df = 8$, $p < .001$; for the document scale, $x^2 = 1800$, $df = 8$, $p < .001$; and for quantitative literacy $x^2 = 1795$, $df = 8$, $p < .001$. These results show a marked relationship between educational level and level of performance on the NALS scales; literacy improves with level of education. When comparing the prose, document, and quantitative levels of literacy, community colleges have distinguished themselves from high schools and also from four-year colleges. This suggests that community college students' literacy skills have advanced beyond those typical of high school graduates but have not yet reached the level of college graduates.

Table 9.1
Percentage Frequently Using Source of Information by Highest Level
of Education

	Source of Information				
Education	Television	Newspapers	Radio	Family/Friends	Magazines
High School	92.1	78.7	72.2	65.9	56.0
2-Year	90.6	83.6	73.8	66.5	65.5
4-Year	90.8	85.4	72.3	68.8	67.1

The NALS questionnaire asked the participants to indicate what materials they read for information, to tell what types of books were read, and to list the uses of reading, writing, and arithmetic on the job and at home. By examining how often some of these literacy sources were consulted or these literacy practices were used by each of the three groups, it might be possible to determine how the community college graduates resembled or differed from the two groups that bracketed them.

Sources of Information

The participants were asked about five potential sources of information: newspapers, radio, television, magazines, and family/friends. They then indicated their level of usage of these sources of information on a four-point scale, ranging from "a lot" to "none." The positive responses, "a lot" and "some," were combined for each group (e.g., high school graduates, community college graduates, and baccalaureate graduates), and the results are presented in Table 9.1.

All groups were similar in their reliance on television, radio, and family or friends for information. The community college graduates resembled the four-year college graduates in their use of print media, newspapers and magazines, for acquiring information. High school graduates were far less likely to use these text-based sources of information.

Other items on the questionnaire could be used as checks on these findings. For example, the participants in the NALS were asked how often they read a newspaper, and 79.1% of the associate degree holders said that they read the paper every day or a few times a week. Almost two-thirds of community college graduates, 63.3%, responded that they read three or more magazines a week, which was greater than for the high school graduates (42.3%) or the college graduates (59.4%).

There were reports on the amount of television watched per week.

Table 9.2
Percentage Reading Books in Past Six Months by Highest Level of Education

| | | | Type of Book | | | | |
| | | | History/ Current | | Science/ Social | | |
Education	Fiction	Recreation	Affairs	Religion	Science	Reference	Manuals
High School	44.3	28.9	25.2	35.8	12.8	48.9	56.4
2-Year	59.4	40.8	38.4	41.3	29.4	68.3	66.7
4-Year	62.1	39.0	39.1	37.3	32.4	71.8	68.2

Small percentages of the community college graduates (9.6%) and college graduates (5.2%) watched television five or more hours a week, as compared to 21.4% of the high school graduates who watched television that much. Although television was the most frequently cited source of information for all three groups, it also serves other purposes, and the questionnaire item on the amount of television watched per week may not be related to the item on sources of information. All three groups appear similar, but the two sets of college graduates view less television in general than does the high school graduate group.

College graduates, two- and four-year both, resemble the high school graduates in their reliance on radio and family or friends for information. The community college graduates are similar to the four-year graduates in their usage of print materials, newspapers and magazines, and in their viewing of television for information.

Books Read

The questionnaire asked the respondents to indicate if in the past six months they had read at least one book from seven categories. The percentages of participants who indicated that they had read a book and the types of books read are presented in Table 9.2.

The community college graduates were more likely than the other groups to have read a book on religion. In many respects, the book-reading habits of community college graduates and baccalaureate graduates seem to be similar. While the four-year college graduates read more, both groups of college graduates seem to have similar interests in reading fiction, history/current affairs, and science/social science books as well as manuals.

An item on the questionnaire asked how many times the respondents had used the library. Of the community college graduates, 18.3% used the library daily or weekly, as compared to 8% of the high school graduates and 22.4% of the four-year college graduates. While use of the library is not a direct link to books read, the community college graduates' frequency of use was similar to the college graduates' use.

It seems that the community college graduates have demonstrated positive attitudes and practices regarding literacy. They choose to read books on a range of topics, and they use the library frequently. Although the associate degree holders seem more likely than members of the other groups to prefer to read books on religion and recreation, they still have interests in other types of literature. The reading habits of the community college graduates resemble those of the four-year college graduates, and it seems that the community college group has crossed a significant threshold. Literacy seems to be a positive part of their lives, and it is not just functional. Community college graduates elect to read books, and they rely on print materials for information.

Personal Uses of Literacy

In addition to books read, the NALS asked the adults who completed the survey about the types of reading and writing they did for themselves. Six types of reading activities were listed, as were three types of writing activities. Participants could use a five-point scale, from "every day" to "never," to indicate how often they took part in these reading and writing activities for their own purposes. Table 9.3 presents the summary of the two positive responses, "every day" and "a few times a week," for both activities.

Of the three groups, community college graduates reported that they read manuals/reference books, directions/instructions, diagrams/schematics, and bills/spreadsheets more than the other two groups. On the other two categories, reading letters/memos and reports/articles, the community college group was similar to the four-year college group. Stated another way, community college students are more likely to read document and quantitative text sources than are other groups. Community college graduates' reading of prose materials is equivalent to that of individuals with a four-year degree.

The associate degree holders reported that they wrote more forms than the other two groups, and they were roughly between the high school and baccalaureate graduates in their need to write letters/memos and reports/articles.

One question asked to what extent arithmetic was used for individual needs. Of the high school graduates, 78.1% said that they used arithmetic often, 86.2% of the community college graduates did, and 88.3% of the holders of bachelor degrees did. The use of arithmetic operations played a significant role in the lives of all three groups of participants, but once

Table 9.3
Percentage Reading and Writing for Self by Highest Level of Education

| | Reading Activity | | | | | |
| | Prose | | Document | | Quantitative | |
Education	Letters/ Memos	Reports/ Articles	Manuals/ Reference	Directions/ Instructions	Diagrams/ Schematics	Bills/ Spreadsheets
High School	45.0	38.7	25.7	41.0	7.4	44.2
2-Year	54.2	50.8	36.4	45.4	13.7	52.6
4-Year	58.3	59.8	29.8	41.4	11.3	50.6

| | Writing Activity | | |
Education	Letters/ Memos	Reports/ Articles	Forms/Bills
High School	32.5	8.9	30.1
2-Year	37.2	10.9	39.2
4-Year	40.1	13.7	36.8

Note: Includes those who engaged in these activities "every day" or "a few times a week."

again the associate degree holders separated themselves from the high school graduates on this dimension and appeared more like the four-year college graduates.

The need for community college graduates to read and write technical types of materials (e.g., manuals, diagrams, forms) might be linked to personal interests and hobbies, but the NALS did not have any other questions related to this topic. Alternatively, the need for technical literacy might be linked to job requirements and professional interests, and there is more information on this in the NALS.

Literacy on the Job

The NALS questionnaire posed a number of questions that assessed the context of literacy for work-related settings. The activities and format for these questions were the same as the items on personal uses of literacy. Table 9.4 presents the summary of the two positive responses, "every day" and "a few times a week," for reading and writing activities on the job.

The community college graduates reported that they had to read di-

Table 9.4

Percentage Reading and Writing on Job by Highest Level of Education

	Reading Activity					
	Prose		Document		Quantitative	
Education	Letters/ Memos	Reports/ Articles	Manuals/ Reference	Directions/ Instructions	Diagrams/ Schematics	Bills/ Spreadsheets
High School	64.0	42.0	42.8	32.4	26.2	40.8
2-Year	81.9	60.9	60.9	40.7	37.7	46.7
4-Year	85.2	70.3	65.6	35.3	38.2	51.7

	Writing Activity		
Education	Letters/ Memos	Reports/ Articles	Forms/Bills
High School	50.2	32.5	44.5
2-Year	67.3	46.3	57.5
4-Year	73.3	48.7	58.1

Note: Includes those who engaged in these activities "every day" or "a few times a week."

rections/instructions more often than the other two groups. They were very similar to the college graduates in the need to read diagrams/schematics and more like the college graduates than like the high school graduates in the other work-related reading activities. The community college group did more writing on the job than did high school graduates and was very similar to the college group in its need to write forms and reports.

The need to use mathematics on the job was great for all three groups. Of the high school graduates, 81.4% reported frequent use of math, as compared to 88.8% of the community college graduates and 90.4% of the four-year college graduates. In the workplace, it appeared that arithmetic skills were used more often than reading and writing.

When literacy needs on the job are compared with literacy at home, it appears that the workplace demanded a considerable use of reading, writing, and math. With the exception of the reading of directions/instructions, the community college group had to use more literacy skills on the job more often than they did at home.

Literacy in the workplace could be a factor of the types of jobs that the participants held. On the NALS questionnaire, the participants were asked an open-ended question about current occupation, and the various responses were arranged in approximately 40 categories. A chi-square test was used to determine if there was an association between groupings of occupations and level of education ($x^2 = 3569$, $df = 84$, $p < .001$). Jobs were associated with educational level, and community college graduates frequently held jobs as registered nurses, secretaries, health technicians, engineering technicians, supervisors, and public safety staff.

CONCLUSION: THE CHARACTERISTICS OF COMMUNITY COLLEGE LITERACY

The predominant placement of the community college graduates at Level 3, or in the middle, of the prose, document, and quantitative literacy scales on the NALS could be reason for concern. However, viewed in the historical context of the community college's definition of its mission and purpose in American education, this medial placement might be just right. Community colleges, in the early part of this century, were viewed as extensions of high schools, but on the NALS literacy scales, the community college graduates have distinguished themselves from the high school graduates. Today community colleges do not regard themselves as part of the secondary system, and the literacy outcomes of associate degree holders are markedly different from the outcomes of the high school graduates.

Community college graduates have distanced themselves from high school graduates, but they still do not match the literacy performance of the baccalaureate college graduates. In some regards this is what is expected. Since community college degree holders have attended college for less time than the holders of four-year degrees, they have not had the opportunities to use and improve their literacy skills. On the NALS prose, document, and quantitative scales, the bachelor's degree holders usually did better than the associate's degree participants. However, when the data on reading habits and interests were examined, the community college group shared many characteristics with the four-year college group. The community college and baccalaureate college graduates relied, in similar fashion, on print sources of information. Similar percentages of both collegiate groups read fiction, history, and science books in the few months preceding the NALS interview. The reading of reports and letters done for personal use by the two college groups was similar, as was the use of arithmetic for individual needs. It appears that the college experience, either at a community college or a four-year college, allows higher education graduates to cross a literacy threshold. After earning either the associate's or bachelor's degree, the graduates share comparable literacy interests. In this regard, the community college group is strikingly similar to the four-year college group.

Of course, some of the literacy interests and needs of the community college graduates set them apart from the other two groups. Community college graduates read books on religion or recreation more than the other groups. On the job, they do more reading of directions or instructions than the high school or baccalaureate groups, and this is reflected in their reading done for personal uses.

Community colleges are educating a significant percentage of the American populace. Fortunately, the NALS results indicate that the literacy abilities that community college graduates demonstrate are sufficient to enable them to function in American society and to enjoy the personal enrichment that literacy brings.

REFERENCES

Barton, P. E., & Lapointe, A. (1995). *Learning by degrees: Indicators of performance in higher education*. Princeton, NJ: Educational Testing Service.

Campbell, A., Kirsch, I. S., & Kolstad, A. (1992). *Assessing literacy: The framework for the National Adult Literacy Survey*. Washington, DC: U.S. Department of Education.

Cohen, A. M., & Brawer, F. B. (1987). *The collegiate function of the community college*. San Francisco: Jossey-Bass.

———. (1996). *The American community college* (3d ed.). San Francisco: Jossey-Bass.

Eaton, J. (1994). *Strengthening collegiate education in community colleges*. San Francisco: Jossey-Bass.

Griffith, M., & Connor, A. (1994). *Democracy's open door: The community college in America's future*. Portsmouth, NH: Heinemann.

Howard, J., & Obetz, W. (1996). Using the NALS to characterize community college graduates. *Journal of Adolescent and Adult Literacy, 39*, 462–467.

Hutchings, P., & Marchese, T. (1990, September/October). Watching assessments—Questions, stories, prospects. *Change, 22*, 13–38.

Kirsch, I. S., Jungeblut, A., Jenkins, L., & Kolstad, A. (1993). *Adult literacy in America: A first look at the results of the National Adult Literacy Survey*. Washington, DC: U.S. Department of Education.

Lorenzo, A. L. (1994). The mission and functions of the community college: An overview. In G. A. Bakker III (Ed.), *A handbook on the community college in America: Its history, mission and management* (pp. 111–122). Westport, CT: Greenwood Press.

McGrath, D., & Spear, M. B. (1991). *The academic crisis of the community college*. Albany: State University of New York Press.

National Center for Educational Statistics. (1995a). *Digest of Educational Statistics: Post Secondary Education* [On Line]. http://www.ed.gov/NCES/pubs/D95/dtab165.html

———. (1995b). *Digest of Educational Statistics: Post Secondary Education* [On Line]. http://www.ed.gov/NCES/pubs/D95/dtab175.html

Richardson, R. C., Fisk, E., & Okun, M. (1983). *Literacy in the open access classroom*. San Francisco: Jossey-Bass.

Tillery, D., & Deegan, W. (1985). The evolution of two-year colleges through four generations. In W. L. Deegan, D. Tillery, & Associates (Eds.), *Renewing the American community college: Priorities and strategies for effective leadership* (pp. 3–33). San Francisco: Jossey-Bass.

10

Literacy Selection and Literacy Development: Structural Equation Models of the Reciprocal Effects of Education and Literacy

Stephen Reder

INTRODUCTION

Individuals and society have long believed and invested in education, in part because of the well-established economic returns to increases in schooling. The National Adult Literacy Survey (NALS) not only provides another large-scale demonstration of the connection between educational attainment and a range of social and economic outcomes but has profiled society's adult literacy proficiencies. This has enabled a detailed examination of relationships between adult literacy and the various social and economic outcomes of interest (Kirsch, Jungeblut, Jenkins, & Kolstad, 1993). Many of the strong positive associations found between adult literacy proficiency and a range of social and economic outcomes resemble those found between education and the same outcomes. Since adult literacy and educational attainment themselves are highly correlated (Kirsch et al., 1993), this raises the problem of how to disentangle the effects of adult literacy and education on these key outcomes.

The need to distinguish the effects of adult literacy and educational attainment is of more than just theoretical interest. Many adult education programs and students formulate goals of increasing literacy skills without necessarily obtaining additional educational credentials. Although many adult literacy students may seek the General Educational Development (GED) diploma and postsecondary credentials, many others participate in basic skills training without such credentials as goals, wanting to increase their skills for a variety of personal and work-related reasons

(Collins, Brick, Kwang, & Stowe, 1997; Young, Morgan, Fitzgerald, & Fleishman, 1994). The goals of many adult basic education, workplace literacy, and family literacy programs often include increased literacy skills but without concomitant attainment of additional educational credentials. Better understanding of the distinctive and overlapping ways in which basic skills and educational attainment contribute to positive social and economic outcomes is essential to formulating more effective adult education policy and programs. Such understanding would be particularly helpful, for example, in evaluating the relative costs and benefits of interventions that seek to add credentials such as postsecondary degrees versus those that seek to improve literacy abilities versus interventions that seek to accomplish both.

Joint Effects of Literacy and Education

To illustrate the joint effects of literacy and education on important social and economic outcomes, consider the NALS data presented in Figure 10.1. Median annual earnings for the year preceding the survey are displayed as a function of educational attainment and literacy proficiency.[1] Data in the figure are for individuals who reported *some* earnings during the preceding year, were *not* students at the time of the interview, and were U.S.-born, native speakers of English. Notice how earnings tend to increase regularly with both education and literacy proficiency and that relatively high levels of *both* literacy and education are required for most individuals to attain substantial incomes. Also notice that the corner cell of the table is empty because in our society very few individuals attain this highest level of literacy proficiency and lowest level of educational attainment. Elsewhere (Reder, in preparation) I have plotted similar graphs for different social and economic outcomes—for example, amount of employment, wages, poverty status, voting behavior—and the results look very similar in each case. The shape of Figure 10.1 is apparently characteristic of diverse social and economic outcomes.

Literacy Selection and Literacy Development

To disentangle the effects of literacy and education, the overall complexity of their interrelationship must be better understood as they impact individual and societal outcomes. At the simplest level, the two variables are highly correlated. Figures 10.2 and 10.3 exhibit the close linear relationship between the two. On one hand, the more education individuals complete, the better developed their literacy skills become. Figure 10.2 shows regular increases in average literacy proficiency for each additional year of schooling completed. On the other hand, the more proficient individuals' literacy abilities are, the more education

Figure 10.1
Median Earnings in Previous Year as a Function of Literacy Proficiency and Educational Attainment

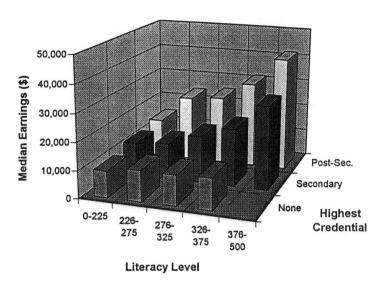

Literacy Level

Note: Adults who worked during preceding year who were not currently in school, who were born in the United States, and who spoke English before starting school.

Source: National Adult Literacy Survey, household component.

they tend to complete. With less literacy proficiency, it becomes harder to advance in the educational system. Figure 10.3 shows the converse: an increase in educational attainment for each increment in average literacy proficiency.

We term the influence of educational attainment on literacy a *literacy development* effect, and we term the reciprocal effect, the influence of literacy on educational attainment, a *literacy selection* effect. Although most researchers studying the relationship between literacy and education have emphasized the literacy development effect (e.g., Kirsch et al., 1993; Stedman & Kaestle, 1987), others have emphasized the significance of literacy for educational development, that is, the literacy selection effect (e.g., Olson, 1977). Discerning clearly the effects of important background variables such as minority status and parental education requires that we assess their effects in terms of both literacy development and literacy selection processes.

To make this discussion more concrete, consider the three diagrams in Figure 10.4. These three diagrams represent different ways in which background variables such as age, gender, parental education, and minority status are assumed to affect literacy and educational attainment.

Figure 10.2
Mean Combined Literacy Proficiency as a Function of Years of Schooling Completed

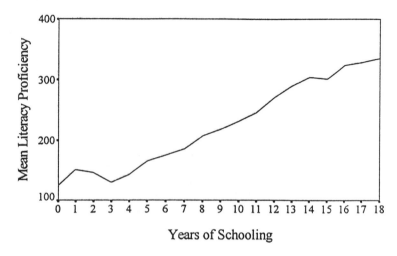

Note: Adults 16 years and older, not in school.

Source: National Adult Literacy Survey, household component.

Common to the three models is the assumption that the various background variables have direct effects on both educational attainment and literacy. These direct effects are symbolized by the paths (single-headed arrows) from the background variable box to one of the others. In the model shown in Figure 10.4(a), background variables have indirect effects on literacy that arise through the chain of direct effects leading first from background variables to education and then on from education to literacy. This class of model assumes that increasing educational attainment has direct effects on literacy but that literacy proficiency itself has no direct effects on educational attainment. This asymmetry characterizes what we term the *literacy development model* because it assumes that literacy develops through schooling.

The model shown in Figure 10.4(b), on the other hand, makes the opposite assumption about causal paths between education and literacy. This model assumes that literacy proficiency directly affects educational attainment: the higher one's literacy proficiency, the further one is likely to progress in school. But this model assumes that educational attainment itself has no *direct* effects on literacy proficiency; schooling merely "filters" or "screens" individuals according to their literacy proficiencies, such that those who go further in school tend to have higher literacy proficiency. We term this type of model a *literacy selection model* because

Figure 10.3
Years of Schooling Completed as a Function of Mean Combined
Literacy Proficiency

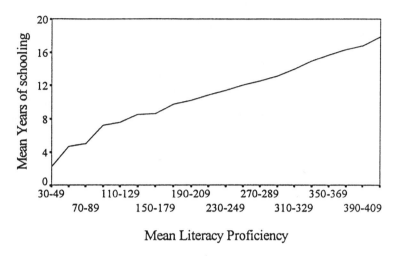

Mean Literacy Proficiency

Note: Adults 16 years and older, not in school.

Source: National Adult Literacy Survey, household component.

of the filtering or screening function of schools to effectively sort students in terms of their literacy abilities.

There is ample evidence that elements of both the literacy selection and literacy development models are useful for understanding relationships among education, literacy, and other variables of interest (Miller, 1988; Resnick & Resnick, 1977; Scribner & Cole, 1981). Figure 10.4(c) displays a model containing both selection and development effects between literacy and education. Increasing education has direct effects on literacy (development), and increasing literacy has direct effects on educational attainment (selection). We term such models, incorporating both literacy selection and literacy development effects, *reciprocal effects* models.

This chapter attempts to model and discern the relative effects of literacy selection and literacy development within the NALS data. This should be considered an initial and exploratory attempt to formalize some of these notions and to illustrate their potential usefulness in understanding and quantifying the contributions of literacy and schooling to important individual and societal outcomes. An important caveat, of course, is that we are attempting to model these inherently diachronic constructs of literacy development and literacy selection within the cross-sectional data of the NALS. We return at the end of the chapter, after

Figure 10.4
Three Models of Relationships among Background Variables, Educational Attainment, and Literacy.

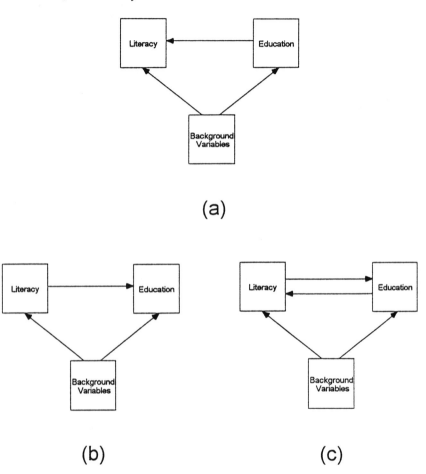

Note: All three models posit direct effects of background variables on both educational attainment and literacy. Model (a) includes direct effects of educational attainment on literacy. Model (b) includes direct effects of literacy on educational attainment. Model (c) includes reciprocal direct effects between educational attainment and literacy.

examining the fit of various models to the cross-sectional NALS data, to consider the limitations of this approach and the need to model longitudinal data.

METHOD

The population of interest in this inquiry was individuals age 16 and older who were born in the United States, spoke English before entering

Table 10.1
Variables Used in the Analyses

Variable	Coding
AGE	Years of age at time of interview (16 and above)
AGE^2	= AGE X AGE
GENDER	0 if female, 1 if male
MINORITY	0 if white & non-Hispanic, else 1
YRSED	if no secondary diploma, = highest grade completed (0-11); high school diploma/GED = 12; some college, no degree = 13; 2 yr college degree= 14; more than 2 yrs college, no degree = 15; B.S./B.A. = 16; postgraduate, no degree = 17; postgraduate degree = 18
PARENTED	Higher of mother's and father's YRSED, each computed as above
LD	1 if self-identified as having a learning disability, else 0
LITERACY	Average of 5 values imputed for prose, 5 for document and 5 for quantitative literacy (15 values averaged)
LOGEARN	log of annual earnings for year preceding interview

school, and were not students at the time of the NALS survey. Of the 24,944 NALS household survey respondents, 18,170 satisfied these criteria. The corresponding population in the 1990 U.S. census from which this target subsample of NALS is drawn numbers 141,253,694.[2]

To explore the literacy development, literacy selection, and reciprocal effects models, structural equation models were estimated and evaluated. Structural equation modeling (SEM) is based on analysis of the fit between an observed covariance matrix among a set of variables and the covariance matrix expected if the theory and measurement assumptions of the SEM are assumed to hold (Joreskog, 1973). Whereas conventional path analytic models could have been constructed for the literacy development and the literacy selection models, a structural equation model is more useful here, in part, because of the simultaneous effects of education and literacy on one another (Goldberger, 1972).[3] Structural equation modeling and estimation were conducted with LISREL 7 and AMOS Version 3.51 software.

The variables used in the following SEM analyses are described in Table 10.1. Comments on several of these variables are in order. Because of the complexity of the effects of age in life span literacy analyses (Smith, 1996), particular attention was given to modeling effects of age in preliminary analyses. Both age and age² (i.e., age-squared) were selected for use in regressions because the preliminary calculations indicated that the effects of age had a strong quadratic effect, often

corresponding to inverted-U-shaped effects of age on outcomes of interest. Educational attainment, measured on an interval scale, was represented by the variable YRSED, as defined in the table. The binary
variable LD is defined in terms of whether or not respondents indicated
they had a learning disability through self-report.[4]

The literacy variable was computed as the average of the prose, document, and quantitative scores. Because the prose, document, and
quantitative literacy proficiencies assessed with the NALS instruments
are very highly intercorrelated and effectively unidimensional for many
practical purposes, the three proficiency scores were averaged into a
composite literacy proficiency score (Reder, Chapter 4). To preserve
NALS' multiple imputation methodology, plausible values for these average proficiency scores were approximated by arithmetic averages of
the corresponding plausible values for each of the three scales. SEM
models were estimated separately for each plausible value of the combined literacy proficiency. Model parameters were then averaged across
the set of plausible, value-based estimates. Standard errors for these
model parameters included a component that averaged the standard errors associated with the separate plausible, value-based estimates as well
as a component derived from the variation among the plausible, values-
based standard error estimates.

To take the complex sampling design of NALS into account in computing standard errors of sample statistics for the SEMs, a design effect
correction was utilized. Preliminary analyses constructed bootstrap estimates of ordinary least squares regression coefficients. These boot-
strapped standard errors ranged between 1.2 and 1.4 times the
corresponding standard errors calculated when NALS data were assumed to be drawn from a simple random sample. A conservative design
effect of 2.0 was therefore adopted for use in subsequent analyses.[5]

STRUCTURAL EQUATION MODELS OF RECIPROCAL
EFFECTS OF LITERACY AND EDUCATION

Figure 10.5 displays a version of Model (C) from Figure 10.4, specifying the background variables of age, gender, minority status, learning
disabilities status, and parental education.[6] To explore usefulness of these
models for describing empirical relationships in the NALS data, the
structural equation model shown in Figure 10.5 was fitted to the data.
Overall, this reciprocal effects model fits the data extremely well. The
maximum likelihood fit of the expected (model-based) covariance matrix
to the observed covariance matrix is based on a design-weighted sample
size of 8,235.[7] A likelihood-ratio χ^2 test of the fit of this reciprocal effects
model compared to the perfect-fitting saturated model ($\chi^2 = 1.85$, df $=$
1, p $= 0.174$) indicates that we cannot reject the null hypothesis that the

Figure 10.5
Structural Equation Estimates for the Reciprocal Effects Model (Model C)

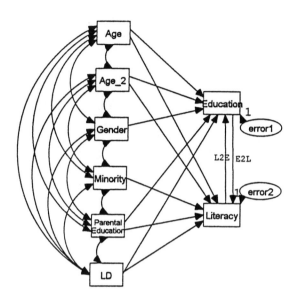

reciprocal effects model fits these data perfectly.[8] Similarly, a frequently used index of the goodness of fit for structural equation models, the root mean square error of approximation (RMSEA), has a value of 0.010, indicative of a very close fit (Browne & Cudeck, 1993).

Each arrow between a pair of variables in the figure represents a causal path leading from one variable to the other. Such paths are understood to be unidirectional. For example, the presence of the path leading from *education* to *literacy* in this model indicates that changes in years of educational attainment lead to changes in literacy proficiency. Conversely, the path leading from *literacy* to *education* represents the direct impact of literacy proficiency on years of educational attainment.

The coefficient associated with a given path indicates both the relative strength and sign of the corresponding influence. The absolute magnitude of the path weight is a measure of the strength of the relationship, whereas the sign of the coefficient indicates whether increases or decreases in one variable are associated with increases or decreases in the other variable. A design-weighted maximum likelihood method was used to estimate the standardized regression coefficients displayed in the figure. These standardized coefficients from the various paths are readily comparable in terms of the relative potency of their influence.

For example, the *education* → *literacy* path has a weight of 0.339, indicating that an increase of, say, one standard deviation in educational

Table 10.2
Structural Equation Analysis of the Reciprocal Effects Model (Model C)

Path	Standardized Coefficient	t
Literacy --> Education	.234	7.04
Education -> Literacy	.339	12.60
Parental Education --> Literacy	.186	12.98
Parental Education --> Education	.359	23.00
Age --> Literacy	.724	14.12
Age^2 --> Literacy	-.938	-18.37
Age --> Education	.861	13.97
Age^2 --> Education	-.804	-12.31
LD --> Literacy	-.149	-18.25
LD --> Education	-.075	-7.04
Minority --> Literacy	-.242	-30.87
Gender --> Education	.024	2.77

attainment is associated with an increase of about one-third of a standard deviation in literacy proficiency. The positive sign of this coefficient indicates that increases (decreases) in *education* are associated with increases (decreases) in *literacy*. The simultaneous *literacy → education* path has a coefficient of 0.234. Notice the standardized *literacy → education* coefficient is somewhat smaller than the *education → literacy* coefficient, indicating that education has a more potent effect on literacy proficiency than vice versa; the literacy development effects are stronger than the literacy selection effects.

Table 10.2 summarizes the model's path coefficients and associated tests of statistical significance. The path coefficients in the table are maximum likelihood estimates; the corresponding t-values indicate whether or not the path coefficients differ from zero in a statistically significant ($p < .05$) manner. In this table, *all* of the t-values are statistically significant. Notice that both the *education → literacy* and the *literacy → education* paths are statistically significant (i.e., have nonzero coefficients). If either of these critical paths were not significantly different from zero, the model would reduce to either a literacy development model (Model A) or a literacy selection model (Model B). Since each of these alternative models is a special case of the more general reciprocal effects model, the difference in overall fit of the models can be statistically tested as well. Neither the literacy development model ($\chi^2 = 40.09$, df = 1, p < .001) nor the literacy selection model ($\chi^2 = 117.43$, df = 1, p < .001) comes close to fitting the NALS data as well as the reciprocal effects model.

The multiple R^2 values for the *education* and *literacy* variables, corresponding to the proportion of its variance accounted for by the variables leading to it through one or more paths, are 0.396 and 0.539, respectively. This reciprocal effects model thus accounts for 40% of the variance in educational attainment and 54% of the variance in literacy proficiency. Overall, the model accounts for 52% of the variance in this set of variables.[9]

Notice in Table 10.2 that both the linear and quadratic terms were significant in modeling the effects of age on education and literacy. For each variable, curvilinear effects of age are indicated by the significant coefficients of the second-order term, *age²*. The regression coefficient for *age* was positive whereas the coefficient for the *age²* term was negative, indicating an inverted U-shaped relationship between age and each of these variables. This indicates that intermediate-aged adults tended to have the largest values of education and literacy, whereas the relatively young and relatively old have lower values when other background variables are held constant. Effects of age in cross-sectional surveys such as NALS are likely to be complex to interpret, because increasing age may reflect both *maturational effects* of growing older as well as *cohort effects* of different historical epochs (among which patterns of educational attainment and literacy differed). The youngest adults might not yet have completed their education and literacy development (even though our subsample was restricted to individuals not in school at the time of the survey), whereas the older adults tended to have been educated and acquired literacy skills in a much earlier historical era in which individuals typically completed less schooling and acquired less literacy proficiency. Age has similarly shaped profiles in both education and literacy, with direct effects of similar magnitude on both education and literacy.

Parental education had statistically significant, direct effects on both educational attainment and literacy proficiency. The direct effects were considerably stronger on educational attainment than on literacy proficiency. This finding may be theoretically and practically important, as it suggests that the ways in which parents influence their progeny's educational success and their literacy development may be distinct. Tentative as these interpretations are at this point, the findings do suggest that further research should try to differentiate the mechanisms involved and to identify more effective ways for parents to support their children's education and literacy development.

Minority status had a significant negative effect on literacy proficiency.

Since this variable is coded 1 for individuals who are members of racial or ethnic minorities and is coded 0 for non-Hispanic white adults, the large negative coefficient indicates that minority adults have substantially less literacy proficiency after the effects of other variables are taken into account. Evidently, minority and nonminority students leave school at the same levels of attainment with very different levels of literacy skill. Although equity-directed efforts at closing gaps in graduation rates have been relatively successful, the remaining literacy skill gaps between minority and nonminority students leaving school with comparable amounts of education are a major cause for concern (Reder, 1993).

Gender has a relatively weak, but statistically significant, effect on educational attainment, with men obtaining more education than women do when other variables are statistically controlled. There is no significant gender difference in overall literacy abilities in these data, either, though that path is not represented in the model for reasons noted earlier.

LD had significant direct effects on both education and literacy. The negative sign of these coefficients indicates that self-reported learning disabilities were associated with decreases in educational attainment and literacy proficiency. Judging from the magnitudes of the *LD* → *literacy* (−.149) and *LD* → *education* (−.075) coefficients, the direct effects of learning disabilities on literacy are somewhat stronger than on educational attainment. But the finding that LD impacts educational attainment even after the effects of LD on literacy are taken into account is noteworthy. It suggests that educational interventions for learning disabilities should target a broader set of factors than just literacy development. According to this model, the total effects (direct effects plus indirect effects) of learning disabilities on educational attainment correspond to nearly two years of schooling (−1.96 years), and the total effects of LD on literacy proficiency are −63.1 points on the proficiency scale. Thus, these effects not only are statistically significant, but may be extremely important from a practical perspective.[10]

RECIPROCAL EFFECTS OF EDUCATION AND LITERACY ON SOCIAL AND ECONOMIC OUTCOMES

The reciprocal effects model examined in the preceding section can be readily extended to examine the simultaneous effects of background variables, education, and literacy proficiency on various social and economic outcomes. The reciprocal effects model with outcome variables is displayed in Figure 10.6. The SEM diagrammed in the figure adds an endogenous outcome variable to the basic reciprocal effects model considered earlier. The model shown in Figure 10.6 assumes that the outcome variable is affected by both literacy and educational attainment

Figure 10.6
Structural Equation Model for Reciprocal Effects Analysis of Social and Economic Outcomes

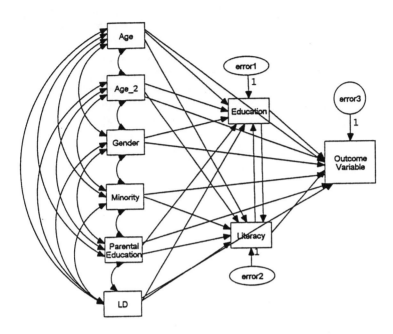

(as well as by the other background variables in the model) but that the outcome variable itself does *not* directly affect either literacy or educational attainment.

The analytical framework of this structural equation model enables us to examine the relative effects of educational attainment and literacy proficiency on important social and economic outcomes. Furthermore, by examining the effects of background variables on an outcome variable within the framework of this model, we can determine how such variables as parental education and minority status directly affect important social and economic outcomes beyond what can be expected from their indirect effects mediated through educational attainment and literacy proficiency. This model is being used to analyze the reciprocal effects of literacy and education on a range of outcome variables (Reder, in preparation). For present purposes, an illustrative example will be worked out for the outcome variable of annual earnings.

To predict annual *earnings*, the model was applied to the subpopulation of individuals who reported *some* employment and earnings for the year preceding the interview. The NALS subsample meeting these and the previously mentioned criteria had a size of 11,620.[11] The reciprocal effects model was fitted to predict log earnings. The maximum likelihood estimates fit the NALS data quite well, according to several goodness-of-fit indicators. A likelihood ratio chi-square test was conducted to compare the relative fit of the reciprocal effects model to the perfect-fitting saturated model: $\chi^2 = 0.52$, df $= 1$, p $= 0.469$. This result indicates that the reciprocal effects model fits the data as well as the saturated model. The adjusted goodness-of-fit index (AGFI) was 0.999, and the RMSEA was less than 0.001, indicative of a very well fitting model. The reciprocal effects model estimated R^2 values of 0.326, 0.477, and 0.262 for education, literacy, and log annual earnings, respectively. The total coefficient of determination for the structural equations was 0.523.

Table 10.3 displays maximum likelihood standardized regression co-efficients for the paths in the model and their associated t-values. All t-values listed were statistically significant at the .05 level, except for *minority → log earnings* and *gender → education*, which were not reliably different from zero. The structural equations for education and literacy were quite similar to their counterparts in the previous reciprocal effects model estimated earlier; coefficients of paths leading into *education* and into *literacy* exhibited the same general pattern as they did earlier. In addition, both literacy and education had strong positive effects on earnings, with literacy and educational attainment having approximately the same-size direct effect on earnings.

Parental education again exerted significant positive effects on both education and literacy, and again its effects were much stronger on educational attainment than on literacy. Parental education also exerted a statistically significant direct effect on earnings, but a much smaller one than on either education or literacy.

Age exhibited the same-shaped quadratic direct effect we saw before on both education and literacy and, now in this model, also on earnings. An inverted-U shape is generated in each equation by the positive co-efficient for *age* and negative coefficient for *age²*. The youngest and oldest individuals, with other variables equated, had less education, literacy proficiency, and earnings than their midaged counterparts.

LD, as in the previous analysis, had significant negative effects on both education and literacy, again with stronger effects on literacy than on educational attainment. Notice that LD had a significant direct negative effect on earnings even after its strong negative effects on education and literacy are taken into account.

An extremely important finding is that the *minority → earnings* path coefficient was *not* statistically significant. This indicates that with *both* educational attainment *and* literacy proficiency held constant, there was no significant difference in earnings between minority and nonminority individuals. Not shown here is the related finding that if only educa-

Table 10.3
Structural Equation Coefficients for (Log) Annual Earnings

Path	Standardized Coefficient	t
Literacy --> Education	.149	3.55
Education --> Literacy	.399	11.66
Literacy --> log Earnings	.143	9.09
Education --> log Earnings	.167	11.11
Parental Education --> Literacy	.179	10.14
Parental Education --> Education	.371	18.69
Parental Education--> log Earnings	.031	2.33
Age --> Literacy	.533	8.30
Age^2 --> Literacy	-.595	-9.68
Age --> Education	.958	13.09
Age^2 --> Education	-.816	-11.24
Age --> log Earnings	1.317	20.70
Age^2 --> log Earnings	-1.195	-18.84
LD --> Literacy	-.138	-13.53
LD --> Education	-.083	-6.27
LD --> log Earnings	-.025	-2.17
Minority --> Literacy	-.247	-25.29
Minority --> log Earnings	-.010	-0.80*
Gender --> Education	.006	0.57*
Gender --> log Earnings	.277	24.52

*not significant ($p > .05$).

tional attainment is held constant, there are significant gaps between minority and nonminority groups. These results should prompt us to refine our concept of educational equity, which for nearly half a century since *Brown v. Topeka Board of Education* has emphasized equalizing educational attainment between minority and nonminority groups. As important as that equity goal has been (and there has been remarkable progress made in equalizing educational attainment among groups), the present findings and other data indicate that equity of social and economic outcomes in our society will likely require educational equity not only in terms of degrees attained but in terms of literacy proficiency. (See Reder, 1993, in preparation, for a more detailed treatment of these issues.)

In sharp contrast is the strong direct effect of gender on earnings evident in Table 10.3. Even with education and literacy equated within the framework of the model, there is a large, significant effect of gender on earnings. At equal levels of educational attainment and literacy proficiency, women earn substantially less than men do. Race/ethnicity and gender inequities are thus patterned very differently. Members of minority groups tend to complete less education and to develop lower levels of literacy proficiency but have comparable earnings, given equal levels of both education and literacy. Women, on the other hand, tend to have equivalent levels of education and literacy but nevertheless earn less than men.

CONCLUSIONS

Evidence gathered by this study indicates that both literacy development and literacy selection processes must be represented in models of how education and literacy influence social and economic outcomes. The structural equation analyses indicate that the reciprocal effects model fit the NALS data very well, according to a number of goodness-of-fit indicators considered. Although this chapter examined only the outcome variable of annual earnings, other work in preparation with the same model finds substantially similar results with a wide variety of outcome variables (Reder, in preparation). Literacy development processes, in which increasing amounts of schooling directly cause increased literacy proficiency, are stronger than literacy selection effects, whereby varying amounts of literacy proficiency are reflected in how much schooling individuals complete.

Of course, despite the excellent fit of the reciprocal effects model to the NALS data, considerable caution is appropriate in interpreting these results. Both literacy development and literacy selection are dynamic processes that are assumed to have occurred earlier in the lives of the adult population NALS surveyed in a cross-sectional manner. All that can be said with a reasonably high degree of confidence at present is that the reciprocal effects model fits the cross-sectional NALS data very well; the snapshot taken of individual adult characteristics at a fixed point in time is very much as expected, given that the reciprocal effects operated as specified earlier in adults' lives. Clearly, longitudinal data sets—in which individuals' progress through school and their literacy proficiencies are measured repeatedly over time—will provide more powerful tests of the theory. Hopefully, future analyses of such longitudinal data will enable such refinements to take place.

With that caveat in place, there is nevertheless much of interest that has been learned from the present cross-sectional analysis. The reciprocal effects SEMs have enabled us to begin differentiating the effects of important background variables on literacy from their effects on educational attainment. Most important in the results examined in this chapter are those related to parental education, minority and gender status, and self-reported learning disabilities. In each case, after taking into account the reciprocal effects of literacy and schooling on each other, the relative potency of the variable's direct influence on education differs from its direct effect on literacy.

Consider first the findings for parental education. Although parental education significantly influenced both the educational attainment and literacy proficiency of their children (as adults), the direct effects on progeny's educational attainment were much stronger than the direct effects on literacy proficiency. Evidently, parental education influences children's eventual adult level of educational attainment—whether mediated through resources in the home, attitudes about education, assistance with schoolwork, or financial support—much more strongly than it influences the level of adult literacy reached. Although these results suggest that parental influences on education and on literacy are mediated through different processes, additional research is needed to clarify these findings and their implications for educational practice.

The model also indicates that self-reported learning disabilities had direct effects on both educational attainment and literacy proficiency. The finding that LD had strong effects on literacy comes as no surprise, of course, as learning disabilities are so often closely related to poor literacy skills. But the finding that LD had direct effects on educational attainment even after controlling for literacy proficiency may be worth further research, as it suggests that factors other than (NALS-measured) literacy are likely involved in the educational outcomes of individuals with learning disabilities (see Chapter 11, this volume, for further discussion of this point).

Perhaps the most striking findings of this inquiry have to do with the effects of minority status and gender on earnings. Results indicate that although minority and gender are each associated with profound inequities in the labor market, those inequities are differentially structured with respect to education and literacy. Gender inequities in earnings persist even when both educational attainment and literacy are equated between men and women. Minority-based inequities, on the other hand, disappear when and only when *both* educational attainment and literacy proficiency are equated between minority and nonminority groups. According to our findings, even when educational attainment is taken into account, there are major differences between minority and nonminority groups' literacy proficiency, and these residual literacy differences are directly associated with earnings gaps. It was suggested that educational equity must expand from a focus on just educational attainment to a focus on both educational attainment and literacy proficiency.

None of these topics, of course, are comprehensively addressed by the relatively simple reciprocal effects models considered in this chapter. Further research is needed to extend these findings and develop appropriate implications for policy and practice in adult education and literacy. Nevertheless, the reciprocal effects model seems to hold promise for advancing our understanding of the ways in which literacy and education support one another and jointly contribute to important social and economic outcomes.

NOTES

1. The literacy proficiency plotted is the average of the individual's prose, document, and quantitative scale scores. The graph has a highly similar shape if plotted for any one of the three scales separately.

2. NALS sample and weighting designs actually included corrections for estimated undercount in the 1990 census, which totaled approximately 3 million adults (U.S. Bureau of the Census, *Report of the Committee on Adjustment of Postcensal Estimates*, August 7, 1992).

3. Because cyclical paths of arbitrary length can be constructed between a background variable and either education or literacy (by going back and forth one or more times between literacy and education), the total effects of a background variable on education or literacy cannot always be identified or estimated; such *nonrecursive* models (in which such cycling can occur) in some cases may be *nonidentifiable* or may be *unstable* in some cases in which parameter estimates are identifiable (Goldberger, 1972).

4. See Vogel and Reder (Chapter 11) for further discussion of the relationship between self-report and other identification criteria for learning disabilities (e.g., school-identification).

5. For computing standard errors, this means that NALS data were assumed to come from simple random samples of half the corresponding size.

6. Notice that one path from an independent (exogenous) variable to each dependent (endogenous) variable is omitted from the model; this is necessary for parameters of the model's structural equations to be *identifiable* (Goldberger, 1972). The two omitted paths, *gender* → *literacy, and minority* → *education*, are very weak and have relatively little influence on estimation of the remaining model parameters.

7. The term *design-weighted* indicates that NALS sample weights are adjusted so they remain proportional and sum to a design-effect corrected sample size.

8. It is worth noting that the saturated model serving as a baseline of perfect fit (against which to compare the fit of the reciprocal effects model) includes a covariance to be estimated between the error variables associated with *education and literacy*. The reciprocal effects model, on the other hand, assumes these two errors or disturbances to be uncorrelated. The results of the chi-squared test indicate that we should accept the more parsimonious model in which the errors are assumed to be uncorrelated.

9. This corresponds to a total coefficient of determination for the structural equations of 0.519.

10. More detailed analyses and discussion of self-reported learning disabilities in the NALS data are available elsewhere (Reder & Vogel, 1997; Chapter 11, this volume).

11. The design-weighted size of this subsample is 5,810.

REFERENCES

Browne, M. W., & Cudeck, R. (1993). Alternative ways of assessing model fit. In K. A. Bollen & J. S. Long (Eds.), *Testing structural equation models* (pp. 136–162). Newbury Park, CA: Sage.

Collins, M. A., Brick, J. M., Kwang, K., & Stowe, P. (1997, May). *Measuring participation in adult education.* (Technical Report NCES 97–431). Washington, DC: U.S. Department of Education, National Center for Education Statistics.

Goldberger, A. S. (1972). Structural equation methods in the social sciences. *Econometrika, 40,* 979–1001.

Joreskog, K. G. (1973). A general method for estimating a linear structural equation system. In A. S. Goldberger & O. D. Duncan (Eds.), *Structural equation models in the social sciences* (pp. 85–112). New York: Seminar Press.

Kirsch, I. S., Jungeblut, A., Jenkins, L., & Kolstad, A. (1993). *Adult literacy in America: A first look at the results of the National Adult Literacy Survey.* Washington, DC: National Center for Education Statistics, U.S. Department of Education.

Miller, G. A. (1988). The challenge of universal literacy. *Science, 241,* 1293–1299.

Olson, D. R. (1977). From utterance to text: The bias of language in speech and writing. *Harvard Educational Review, 47,* 257–281.

Reder, S. (1993, September). "Literacy and equity." Paper presented at 23d annual Congressional Black Caucus Legislative Weekend, Washington, DC.

———. (in preparation). *Literacy, equity and societal outcomes.*

Reder, S., & Vogel, S. A. (1997). Lifespan employment and economic outcomes for adults with self-reported learning disabilities. In P. J. Gerber & D. S. Brown (Eds.), *Learning disabilities and employment* (pp. 371–394). Austin, TX: Pro-Ed.

Resnick, D. P., & Resnick, L. B. (1977). The nature of literacy: An historical exploration. *Harvard Educational Review, 47,* 370–385.

Scribner, S., & Cole, M. (1981). *The psychology of literacy.* Cambridge: Harvard University Press.

Smith, M C. (1996). Differences in adults' reading practices and literacy proficiencies. *Reading Research Quarterly, 31,* 196–219.

Stedman, L. C., & Kaestle, C. F. (1987). Literacy and reading performance in the United States from 1880 to the present. *Reading Research Quarterly, 22,* 8–46.

Young, M. B., Morgan, M., Fitzgerald, N., & Fleishman, H. (1994). *National evaluation of adult education programs. Executive Summary.* Washington, DC: U.S. Department of Education.

11

Literacy Proficiency among Adults with Self-Reported Learning Disabilities

Susan A. Vogel and Stephen Reder

A well-known reality among individuals with learning disabilities (LD) has been that learning disabilities are a lifelong condition. However, until most recently, studies that assessed reading and written language abilities of adults with LD focused on small samples of adults with LD who had been evaluated at university or hospital-affiliated clinics (Gottesman, 1994; Johnson, 1994; Johnson & Blalock, 1987; Silver & Hagin, 1964, 1985) or attended small private special education or preparatory schools, colleges, or universities with comprehensive support services (Adelman & Vogel, 1990; Bruck, 1992; Rawson, 1968; Rogan & Hartman, 1976, 1990; Spekman, Goldberg, & Herman, 1992). The most consistent finding from these studies is that adults with LD have continued difficulty in reading of single words and limited reading vocabulary and comprehension and that performance varies by cognitive abilities and educational attainment level (Adelman & Vogel, 1990; Rogan & Hartman, 1990).

This should not come as any surprise. It has been well established that 70–90% of individuals with learning disabilities have difficulties in the acquisition and use of their own native language, including oral and written language (Blalock, 1982; Gajar, 1989; Vogel, 1982, 1990; Vogel & Konrad, 1988; Vogel & Moran, 1982) and the underlying phonological, syntactic, morphological, and semantic aspects of language (Blalock, 1982; Gottesman, 1994; Johnson & Blalock, 1987; Liberman, 1983). However, the deficits vary and cover a broad range of skills. The range in literacy skills has been found to vary from 4th grade reading level (Frauenheim & Heckerl, 1983; Johnson, 1994; Gottesman, 1992, 1994) to high school level and beyond (Rawson, 1968; Adelman, O'Connell, Konrad, & Vogel, 1993; Adelman & Vogel, 1990). Grouping individuals by educational attainment allowed this difference to be readily apparent in the follow-up study conducted by Rogan and Hartman (1990). Those who had not graduated from high school scored between 4th and 6th grade level on reading and spelling, those who completed high school had reading and spelling skills between the 5th and 13th grade level, and those who had graduated from college scored between the 9th and 14th grade level.

The purpose of the present chapter is to report on literacy proficiency of adults with self-reported learning disabilities (SRLD) and explore variations within literacy proficiency by gender as well as the implications of these findings for adult educators, LD teachers, and literacy providers.

METHOD

Because the purpose and design of the (NALS) National Adult Literacy Survey have been covered thoroughly elsewhere in this volume, they will not be described here. It is important to note that the three literacy scales as measured by the NALS are so highly intercorrelated as to be effectively unidimensional (see Chapter 4). Therefore, the prose, document, and quantitative scores were averaged for each individual into a composite literacy score for the purposes of this chapter.

The Target Population

The target population for the analyses reported here is defined as a subpopulation of individuals living in the United States who met five conditions: (1) were born in the United States; (2) spoke English before entering school; (3) did not report having mental retardation; (4) were not students at the time of the survey; and (5) were age 25–64. The target population is restricted to native-born individuals who spoke English before entering school because of the concern that individuals who first attended foreign schools would not have spoken English at the time they started school in the United States, and their literacy proficiency might have been adversely affected. Finally, individuals who are currently students were excluded from the study because their educational attainment would have still been in a state of flux. Of the 24,944 individuals in the household sample (drawn from a population of 191 million adults in the nation age 16 and above), 14,519 satisfied the five selection criteria (referred to as the non-SRLD population) consisting of 8,232 females and 6,242 males. This target sample represents 100.6 million individuals meeting the five conditions for inclusion; there were 48.2 million males (48%) and 52.2 million females (52%).

The SRLD Population

Respondents answering yes to the question, "Do you currently have a learning disability?" were designated as the SRLD population in this study. Despite the frequent use of self-identification as an indicator of learning disabilities, the false-positive and false-negative rates of misclassification in the general adult population of this indicator with respect to other assessment techniques are unknown. In addition, neither the reliability nor the validity of the measure has been established. Within the target sample, 392 individuals (representing 2.8 million adults) indicated that they had a learning disability. Among those with SRLD, there were more men (56%) than women (44%).

Racial/Ethnic Background

The incidence of SRLD among the 25–64-year-old target population was 3.6% for African Americans and 2.7% for non-African Americans. Alternatively, the percentage of African Americans in the SRLD population was 11.5% versus 15.1% among the non-SRLD. The overall percentage of African Americans was 11.6%. A likelihood ratio chi-square test was conducted, and the data indicated that there was no significant interaction found (chi-square=2.26, df=1, p=0.13); that is, there was no significant difference in the incidence of SRLD between the African-American and non-African-American populations. Therefore, for the purposes of this chapter, no other disaggregation-by-race analyses were conducted.

Data Analysis Strategies

The basic data for this study are reported in terms of SRLD status (the non-SRLD population and the SRLD population) and by gender, that is, for males and females with and without SRLD. Descriptive statistics (e.g., SRLD prevalence rates, gender ratios, or averages of such variables as literacy proficiency by categories of another variable) are estimated for the subpopulations using NALS survey case weights. Several inferential statistics were utilized to carry out significance tests: likelihood-ratio t-tests were used to compare the means of a variable in two groups such as males and females; likelihood-ratio chi-square tests of independence were carried out to examine the possible interaction of SRLD and gender; and analyses of variance (ANOVAs) were conducted to compare the means of a variable and SRLD status on literacy proficiency. All such inferential tests were conducted using "design-weighted" data in which the NALS survey weights are rescaled to sum to one-half of the target sample or subsample size for a given analysis; this rescaling effectively compensates for the complex hierarchical sampling design of NALS, which is less efficient than simple random sampling (Reder, 1995).

Definition of Age and Literacy Variables

Although the total NALS sample age range was 16 and older, only individuals between the ages of 25 and 64 were included in this study. Age at the time of the interview was grouped into four age categories (25–34, 35–44, 45–54, and 55–64). Individuals' NALS scores were averaged across the three scales into composite literacy scores based on Reder's findings (Chapter 4).

RESULTS

For ease of exposition, the members of the target population with SRLD are designated the "SRLD population" whereas members of the target population without SRLD are designated the "non-SRLD population."

Prevalence and Gender Distribution

Of the target population meeting the five selection criteria, 2.9% self-reported having a learning disability. As can be seen in Figure 11.1, the gender distribution in the non-SRLD population was 48% male and 52% female, corresponding to a male:female ratio of .9:1.1. Given that in most genetic studies and samples of self-referred and research-identified individuals there is approximately a 1.3:1 male to female ratio, it was not surprising that the same pattern was seen among the adults with SRLD. As can be seen in Figure 11.1, there were slightly more males (56%) than females (44%) self-reporting a LD, representing a 1.3:1 male:female ratio.

Literacy Proficiency by SRLD Status and Gender

Table 11.1 displays the mean and standard deviation of literacy proficiency by SRLD status and gender. The mean composite literacy scores for adults in the non-SRLD and SRLD populations were 289 (SD=51) and 222 (SD=75), respectively. Although the main effect of SRLD status on literacy is significant (F=4089.06; df=1,7244; p < .001), the main effect of gender on literacy is not statistically significant (F=2.07; df=1,7244; p = .151). A two-way analysis of variance for literacy proficiency as a function of SRLD status and gender was carried out, and the analysis confirmed that there was a significant interaction for literacy proficiency as a function of SRLD status and gender (F=6.40; df=1,7244; p = .012). Therefore, the significant interaction for literacy proficiency as a function of SRLD status and gender can be attributed to only the significant main effect for literacy. As was anticipated, the adults in the non-SRLD population scored significantly higher than the adults with SRLD. Moreover,

Figure 11.1
Gender Distribution for NLD and SRLD*

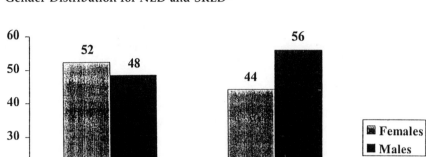

*Self-reported learning disabilities.

the difference between the two means (65 points) represents more than one standard deviation within the non-SRLD population. This difference is significant in both statistical and practical terms. While adults in the non-SRLD population performed, on average, at NALS Level 3, which has been identified by the National Education Goals Panel (1993) as meeting the national literacy goal, adults with SRLD performed on the average at Level 1 (225 is the cut score between Level 1 and Level 2). Lastly, the fact that there is not a significant main effect of gender indicates that men and women generally do not perform differently on the NALS literacy tasks, consistent with the overall results reported by Kirsch et al. (1993). Inspection of Table 11.1 indicated the nature of this interaction; although males perform only slightly better than females in the non-SRLD population (291 versus 287), in the SRLD population the females performed significantly better than the males (221 versus 206).

An alternative method to assist in understanding the impact of SRLD on literacy proficiency is provided in Figure 11.2, which shows the percent of each group scoring at the five NALS-defined proficiency levels using the composite literacy score. As can be seen, five times the percentage of adults with SRLD as without SRLD scored within Level 1 (57% as compared to 11%), while the reverse is the case for Level 4; that is five times as many adults without SRLD as with SRLD scored within Level 4.

One surprising finding confirming other studies and clinical observa-

Table 11.1
Literacy Proficiency for Each Group by Gender

Group	Mean	SD
General Population	288.73	51.16
Males	290.85	53.42
Females	286.79	48.93
SRLD Group	212.76	74.89
Males	206.28	76.65
Females	221.04	72.16

tion is that learning disabilities exist on a continuum from mild to severe. We can only speculate that the nature of their LD did not affect written language, or alternatively, they had already overcome their learning disability. However, because the numbers are fairly small at Level 5, this finding will have to be interpreted cautiously until replication studies are conducted. (See Figure 11.2.)

Literacy Proficiency in Males and Females

As noted in Table 11.2 and revealed in Figures 11.2 and 11.3, the mean literacy score for females in the non-SRLD population was almost identical to that of the males, that is, four points lower. Figures 11.2 and 11.3 provide visual confirmation of the striking similarity between males' and females' performance on the NALS within the non-SRLD population. In contrast to the non-SRLD population, there is a slightly larger discrepancy between the males and females in the SRLD population and in the reverse direction: the mean literacy score for the females with SRLD was 15 points higher than for the males. This finding contradicts previous studies of school-age individuals in which females with LD had significantly more severe reading disabilities, that is, poorer academic achievement skills, than their male peers. We interpret these contradictory findings as related to bias of ascertainment in school-identified populations. There is a growing body of evidence (Vogel, 1990) that documents that hyperactive boys are more likely to be referred for assessment for a suspected learning disability than girls with the same degree of reading difficulty (Shaywitz, Shaywitz, Fletcher, & Escobar, 1990). When girls are referred for assessment and identified in the public schools as having a learning disability, they are usually lower in intelligence, are more se-

Figure 11.2
Literacy Level for Total NLD and SRLD* Groups

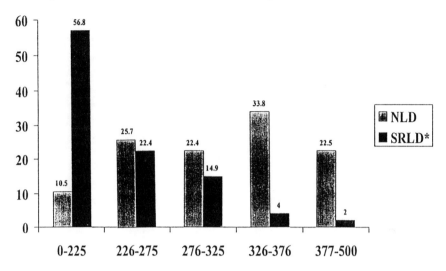

*Self-reported learning disabilities.

verely impaired readers, and are older than their male counterparts (Payette & Clarizio, 1994; Vogel, 1990).

Prevalence and Gender Distribution by Literacy Proficiency

It should not be at all surprising that the prevalence of SRLD is dramatically higher among those performing at Level 1 as compared to the
higher literacy levels. Table 11.3 reveals that 13% of all individuals scoring at Level 1 (the lowest literacy proficiency level) had SRLD. The prevalence rate declines abruptly at Level 2 to 2.4% and to approximately 1
% or less at Levels 3 and 4. Interestingly, 2.2% of all individuals at the
highest literacy level had SRLD, thus confirming earlier research findings
regarding the occurrence of LD at all levels of severity. It is interesting,
however, that individuals still considered themselves as having a learning disability, even though they had acquired a high level of literacy
proficiency.

When the prevalence rate for males and females at each level was
examined, an interesting pattern emerged. Fifteen percent of all males
scoring at Level 1 had SRLD, as compared to only 11% of the females
with SRLD, indicating a 36% higher incidence of males with SRLD as
compared to females among those at the lowest literacy proficiency level.
In contrast, the prevalence rate of males and females with SRLD is almost
identical for those scoring at Levels 2, 3, or 4.

Table 11.2
Prevalence of SRLD by Literacy Level and Gender

Group	Level 1	Level 2	Level 3	Level 4	Level 5
Total	13.0%	2.4%	1.0%	< 1.0%	2.2%
Males	15.3%	2.9%	< 1.0%	< 1.0%	2.7%
Females	10.7%	2.0%	< 1.0%	< 1.0%	1.4%

DISCUSSION

It was not surprising that adults with SRLD did significantly more poorly than the adults in the non-SRLD population on the NALS. What was unexpected, however, was that so many would score so poorly among those with SRLD; more than half performed at Level 1. The frequency and severity of the literacy deficiencies among adults with SRLD attest to the stubborn persistence of literacy problems throughout adult life.

Since 2% of the adults with SRLD scored at Level 5, it would appear that either they had overcome their SRLD or perhaps had a math disability rather than a language-based LD. If the former were the case, it appears that they had substantially overcome their reading disability. Yet, they still perceived themselves as having a learning disability. Apparently, SRLD is not just a reading problem, not just a "school" problem, but a cluster of symptoms that are pervasive and resistant to change (Bruck, 1992; Johnson, 1994; Vogel, 1985).

Unlike the usual research studies in which significant findings make "headlines," it is precisely the lack of significant differences in literacy proficiency among males and females with SRLD that is the most important finding in regard to gender and literacy proficiency. Formerly, researchers reported that girls with school-identified LD had significantly more severe reading disabilities than boys (Vogel, 1990). However, it has now become evident that literacy proficiency differences in prior studies more often reflected what, how, and when children were referred for special services rather than the severity of their reading disability per se (Vogel, 1990). In addition, utilizing district or regional samples of school-identified LD individuals resulted in findings that could not be generalized to the population as a whole.

As compared to the non-SRLD population, there is a minimal, nonsignificant difference in the gender distribution of the SRLD population (1.3: 1) as compared to the non-SRLD population (.9:1 male: female ratio), with slightly more males than females in the SRLD population and

Figure 11.3
Literacy Level for Females and Males with SRLD*

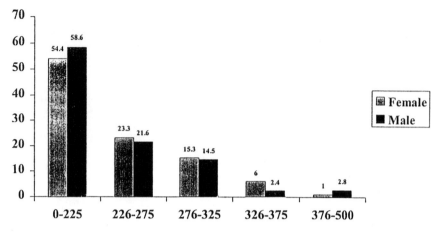

*Self-reported learning disabilities.

slightly more females than males in the non-SRLD population. However, as compared to findings from clinic-identified and school-identified samples, this difference is minimal. For example, the gender distribution of those with LD in the National Longitudinal Transition Survey (NLTS) sample was 3.5:1, typical of the LD school-identified population (U.S. Department of Education, 1995; Wagner, 1991).

Self-report has been used in several other national surveys. For example, one national database in particular that has relied exclusively on self-reported disabilities in adults began in 1985 asking respondents if they had learning disabilities. Moreover, this database is the most frequently cited source for determining the number of students with disabilities enrolled in U.S. colleges and universities (Henderson, 1995). These data are collected by the Cooperative Institutional Research Program (CIRP), which is based at the University of California–Los Angeles and is supported by the American Council on Education (ACE), and the findings are published by the federally funded clearinghouse known as HEATH (Higher Education and Adults with Handicaps). Since these data were first collected in 1978, the CIRP has consistently relied on self-reported (SR) disabilities and has provided the most comprehensive national, regularly updated statistics to date regarding the prevalence of full-time, first-time college and university freshmen with self-reported disabilities, including those with self-reported LD (Henderson, 1995). Nonetheless, self-reported LD raises many questions regarding self-perceptions and alternative definitions of LD used by these adults. What we do know, however, is that there is good precedence for the use of

Table 11.3
Prevalence of SRLD by Educational Attainments

Group	0-8	9-12	HS Diploma/ GED	Some College	College Degree
Total	15.1%	5.6%	2.1%	1.5%	1.0%
Males	18.0%	7.7%	2.4%	1.6%	.6%
Females	11.7%	4.0%	1.9%	1.4%	1.2%

self-report to determine the prevalence of disabilities in the nation as a whole.

To summarize, adults with SRLD had significantly lower NALS literacy proficiency than those without SRLD. More than half of the adults with SRLD (57%) scored at Level 1 as compared to only 11% in the non-SRLD group. However, 21% scored at Level 3 or above, and 2% had even performed at the highest level. This study confirmed that learning disabilities occur across the continuum of literacy proficiency. Moreover, the one-fifth who had achieved at a level commensurate with the non-SRLD population (Level 3 or above) still recognized the persistence of their learning disabilities. These results confirm that learning disabilities are a lifelong condition and have a significant impact on the acquisition of literacy skills. Moreover, the lower the literacy proficiency, the higher the prevalence rate of SRLD. Thirteen percent of the adults who scored at Level 1 had SRLD as compared to the overall prevalence rate of 2.9%. In contrast, there was no contribution of gender to literacy acquisition. Gender ratios of those who scored within Levels 2, 3, and 4 were approximately 1:1.1, with slightly more females than males at each level other than at the lowest one, where there were about 50% more males than females (1.5:1). This finding was thought to relate to the finding that males more often than females experience more severe LD.

IMPLICATIONS

The finding that severe literacy problems persist into adulthood in slightly more than half of the adults with SRLD has important implications for LD teachers, literacy providers, adult basic educators, workplace literacy instructors, and those responsible for professional preparation and staff development in the fields of literacy, learning disabilities, and adult education. All of these individuals will benefit from learning about the National Institute for Child Health and Human Development Learning Disability Research Programs (NICHD) (Lyon,

1995). The five LD research centers and the five multidisciplinary research programs funded by NICHD have already made many major contributions to our understanding of the neurobiological correlates, causes, identification, and treatment of the most common type of learning disability, namely, a language-based learning disability sometimes referred to as dyslexia. Findings indicate that the most effective method to teach individuals with severe reading disabilities is to use a direct, systematic, and explicit instructional program to teach phonemic awareness, sound-symbol relationships, and reading comprehension strategies in an integrated fashion. The challenge now is to implement these techniques in adult education and confirm their effectiveness with adults as well.

NOTE

This research was supported, in part, by a grant from the ACLD Foundation and contract R117Q0003 to the National Center on Adult Literacy from the U.S. Department of Education, Office of Educational Research and Improvement. The findings and opinions expressed here are those of the authors and do not necessarily reflect the views of the foundation or any institution or agency.

REFERENCES

Adelman, P. B., O'Connell, J., Konrad, D., & Vogel, S. A. (1993). The integration of remediation and subject-matter tutoring: Support at the college level. In S. A. Vogel & P. B. Adelman (Eds.), *Success for college students with learning disabilities* (pp. 206–239). New York: Springer-Verlag.

Adelman, P. B., & Vogel, S. A. (1990). College graduates with learning disabilities—Employment attainments and career patterns. *Learning Disability Quarterly, 13*(3), 154–166.

Blalock, J. (1982). Persistent auditory language deficits in adults with learning disabilities. *Journal of Learning Disabilities, 15,* 604–609.

Bruck, M. (1992). Persistence of dyslexics' phonological awareness deficits. *Developmental Psychology, 28,* 874–886.

Frauenheim, J., & Heckerl, J. (1983). A longitudinal study of psychological and achievement test performance in severe dyslexic adults. *Journal of Learning Disabilities, 16,* 339–347.

Gajar, A. H. (1989). A computer analysis of written language variables and a comparison of compositions written by students with and without learning disabilities. *Journal of Learning Disabilities, 22*(2), 125–130.

Gottesman, R. L. (1992). Literacy and adults with severe learning difficulties. *Journal of the National Association for Adults with Special Learning Needs, 2*(1), 48–53.

———. (1994). The adults with learning disabilities: An overview. *Learning Disabilities: A Multidisciplinary Journal, 5*(1), 1–14.

Henderson, K. (1995). *College freshmen with disabilities—A triennial statistical profile.*

Washington, DC: American Council on Education, HEATH Resource Center.

Johnson, D. (1994). Clinical study of adults with severe learning disabilities. *Learning Disabilities: A Multidisciplinary Journal, 5*(1), 43–50.

Johnson, D., & Blalock, J. (Eds.). (1987). *Young adults with learning disabilities.* Orlando: Grune & Stratton.

Kirsch, I. S., Jungeblut, A., Jenkins, L., & Kolstad, A. (1993). *Adult literacy in America: A first look at the results of the National Adult Literacy Survey.* Washington, DC: National Center for Education Statistics, U.S. Department of Education.

Liberman, I. Y. (1983). A language-oriented view of reading and its disabilities. In H. Myklebust (Ed.), *Progress in Learning Disabilities.* Vol. 5. New York: Grune & Stratton.

Lyon, G. R. (1995). Research initiatives in learning disabilities: Contributions from scientists supported by the National Institute of Child Health and Human Development. *Journal of Child Neurology, 10* (supplement No. 1), 120–126.

National Educational Goals Panel (1993). *The 1993 national educational goals panel report.* Washington, DC: U.S. Government Printing Office.

Payette, K., & Clarizio, H. (1994). Discrepant team decisions: The effects of race, gender, achievement, and IQ on LD eligibility. *Psychology in the Schools, 31,* 40–48.

Rawson, M. (1968). *Developmental language disability: Adult accomplishments of dyslexic boys.* Baltimore: Johns Hopkins University Press.

Reder, S. (1995). *Literacy, education, and learning disabilities.* Portland, OR: Northwest Regional Educational Laboratory.

Rogan, L. L., & Hartman, L. D. (1976). *A follow-up study of learning disabled children as adults. Final report.* Evanston, IL: Cove School. ERIC Document Reproduction Service No. ED 163–728.

———. (1990). Adult outcome of learning disabled students 10 years after initial follow-up. *Learning Disabilities Focus, 5*(2), 91–102.

Shaywitz, S., Shaywitz, B., Fletcher, J., & Escobar, M. (1990). Prevalence of reading disabilities in boys and girls: Results of the Connecticut Longitudinal Study. *Journal of the American Medical Association, 264,* 998–1002.

Silver, A. A., & Hagin, R. A. (1964). Specific reading disability: Follow-up studies. *American Journal of Orthopsychiatry, 34,* 95–102.

———. (1985). Outcomes of learning disabilities in adolescence. *Annals of the American Society for Adolescent Psychiatry, 12*(14), 197–213.

Spekman, N. J., Goldberg, R. J., & Herman, K. L. (1992). Learning disabled children grow up: A search for factors related to success in the young adult years. *Learning Disabilities Research and Practice, 7*(3), 161–170.

U.S. Department of Education. (1995). *Seventeenth annual report to Congress on the implementation of IDEA.* Washington, DC: U.S. Government Printing Office. ERIC Document Reproduction Service No. ED 386 018.

Vogel, S. A. (1982). On developing LD college programs. *Journal of Learning Disabilities, 15,* 518–528.

———. (1985). Learning disabled college students: Identification, assessment, and outcomes. In D. Duane & C. K. Leong (Eds.), *Understanding learning dis-*

abilities—International and multidisciplinary views (pp. 179–203). New York: Plenum Press.

———. (1990). Gender differences in intelligence, language, visual-motor abilities, and academic achievement in students with learning disabilities: A review of literature. *Journal of Learning Disabilities, 23*(1), 44–52.

Vogel, S. A., & Konrad, D. (1988). Characteristic written expressive language deficits of the learning disabled: Some general and specific intervention strategies. *Journal of Reading, Writing, and Learning Disabilities International, 4,* 88–99.

Vogel, S. A., & Moran, M. (1982). Written language disorders in learning disabled college students: A preliminary report. In W. Cruickshank & J. Lerner (Eds.), *Coming of age: The best of ACLD* (Vol. 3, pp. 211–225). Syracuse: Syracuse University Press.

Wagner, M. (1991). *Youth with disabilities: How are they doing? The national longitudinal transition study of special education students.* Menlo Park, CA: SRI International.

PART III

Broader
Perspectives in
Adult Literacy

12

Family Literacy and Adult Education: Project FLAME

Flora V. Rodríguez-Brown and
Maureen A. Meehan

Parent involvement is often viewed as the missing link to school success for all children. It is believed that if parents were more involved, they would provide schools with support toward higher achievement levels for their children. Up to now, parent involvement has often been seen as the provision of opportunities for parents to participate in school activities, such as Parent–Teacher Organization (PTO) meetings, parent–teacher conferences, assemblies, and the like. Most recently and in response to the heterogeneity of our school population, the parent involvement paradigm has been shifting toward not only a participatory but a parental support perspective. From this perspective, schools not only expect parents' participation in school activities but also are providing parents with opportunities to learn how to help their children in their schooling. Through this approach, it is expected that the discontinuities between home and school will be attenuated, and children will come to school better prepared to learn and succeed. Currently, family literacy programs have been developed as a way to gear parent involvement toward activities that enhance both parents' and children's literacy skills while also improving home–school relations. This chapter deals directly with issues of parent involvement and literacy in the Hispanic community by describing a program that has proven to be successful with this population.

FAMILY LITERACY AS A COMPONENT OF
PARENT INVOLVEMENT

In a heterogeneous and multicultural society, it is not enough to simply provide parents with ideas to help their children. A parental support component also needs to deal with enhancing the parents' literacy skills and help them become aware of their own knowledge and capabilities for helping their children. Nuckolls (1991) believes that the education of children is enhanced when the parents or caregivers are also involved in advancing their own literacy. In fact, according to Nickse, Speicher, and Buchek (1988) and Van Fossen and Sticht (1991), parents who see themselves as active and effective learners will more consciously engage in their children's literacy development. Studies of parents' views and understanding of literacy suggest that their views about literacy strongly influence their interactions with their children and the schools (Eldridge-Hunter, 1992; Goldenberg, Reese, & Gallimore, 1992).

According to Goodman (1986) an important parental role is to model problem solving and to establish literacy practices that are critical in people's lives. From this perspective, family literacy programs should promote literacy as social practice and also focus on oral language interactions. The adult-directed activities can be carried out through adult education classes (English as a Second Language [ESL], General Educational Development [GED], basic skills) that emphasize the development of parents' self-images as readers and writers. Programs can convey the functional as well as enjoyment values of reading and writing. If parents develop a positive attitude toward these activities, they will be more likely to buy books and model reading and writing at home, thus creating home environments where literacy is highly regarded. Family literacy programs can also address common challenges of implementing a successful adult education program. Research indicates these programs tend to be low in intensity and have high dropout rates (Moore & Stavrianos, 1994). Also it appears many do not sufficiently improve literacy skills or enhance job opportunities (Duffy, 1992). However, recent research suggests successful programs share several features. Young, Morgan, Fitzgerald, and Fleishman (1994) explain how individualized curricula are more effective with adults. Also, programs with curriculum content related to students' needs and interests motivate adult learning. Programs that provide support services such as transportation, child care, and appropriate scheduling for participants are more successful in terms of attendance and long-term participation (Young et al., 1994). These are all components that can and should be included in effective family literacy programs. Within such a framework, family literacy programs have increased parents' literacy skills, enhanced parental participation in their children's education, and developed parents as school resources in an era of economic cutbacks and shrinkage of instructional resources.

Although family literacy programs may follow a variety of approaches to promote literacy-enhancing practices for both children and parents (Auerbach, 1989; Edwards, 1988; Kerka, 1991; Nickse, 1989, 1990, 1991; Ryan, 1991; Shanahan, Mulhern, & Rodríguez-Brown, 1995), most provide parents with

1. Support for their own literacy skills development, which will, in turn, support the literacy development of their children;
2. Survival literacy development skills that enable them to better meet social, economic, and educational demands for themselves and their children;
3. Explicit or implicit support to be able to support their children's literacy development and school success;
4. Support in understanding parenting issues;
5. Planned opportunities for parent–child interactions that emphasize modeling and transfer of skills and support among both children and adults;
6. Opportunities to enhance collaboration and networking as they work toward contributing to the school's success.

THEORETICAL PERSPECTIVES FOR PROGRAM PLANNING

By definition, family literacy programs should recognize the relevance of the family in children's learning. The programs should be an extension of the family rather than an extension of the school environment, and the family should be recognized as a learning unit (Nickse & Englander, 1985). By placing learning within the family context, program activities become more relevant and meaningful to participants. This position is supported by Freire (1970), Heath (1983), and Street (1984). However, not all programs are developed from a critical perspective. Some programs are planned according to a functional approach (Rodríguez-Brown & Mulhern, 1993). That is, programs are planned according to what outsiders or schools think are the needs of the parents and their children. Within this perspective, parents are seen as teaching "structured academic activities that reinforce schoolwork" (Simich-Dudgeon, 1987, p. 3).

By contrast, a critical perspective recognizes that families need to identify with the program content and be collaborators in learning rather than just recipients of information (Rodríguez-Brown & Mulhern, 1993). According to Gadsden, "[P]ractitioners and family literacy learners are constructors of the context of teaching, learning and knowledge generation" (1983, p. 36). This type of program is broader in perspective and better situated within the daily lives of the families, which, in turn, provides the social context for richer resources to family living and learning. These programs are planned in coordination and consultation with the participating families, and the most successful ones encourage extensive parent input into program planning (Auerbach, 1989; Rodríguez-Brown & Mulhern, 1993). Within this framework, the acquisition of literacy skills is seen in relation to the context and use of language (Heath, 1983; Moll, 1992), and literacy becomes more meaningful to the students as it relates more directly to their lives (Freire, 1970; Freire & Macedo, 1987). Within the critical literacy perspective, it is believed that the success of a program is more lasting if the program is allowed to evolve from a functional to a more critical perspective as the program is implemented (Rodríguez-Brown & Mulhern, 1993). These programs become more relevant to the needs of the population and are more readily incorporated into the community.

Critical family literacy programs recognize that families differ not only in their socioeconomic and sociocultural backgrounds but in their racial, ethnic, cultural and religious affiliations. Program planners need to consider the strengths and challenges these families and communities bring and listen to their needs and concerns in order to design appropriate family literacy programs (Ferdman, 1990). This critical approach, in turn, motivates participants to change their relationship with the school and the community on a long-term basis (Gadsden, 1995). According to Auerbach (1989), the incorporation of these cultural and social issues and concerns into the program enhances participation.

Functional and critical literacy has been presented as theoretical perspectives in the development of family literacy programs. While the functional perspective is based on what program planners believe are the literacy needs of families participating in a program, the critical perspective takes into account what the families bring to the program and builds a program that is directly relevant to their strengths and needs. It is believed that a program based on participants' strengths and needs is especially relevant for culturally and linguistically-diverse populations as, in this case, Hispanics.

FAMILIES AS RESOURCES IN CRITICAL LITERACY PROGRAMS

Successful family literacy programs recognize families are a source of information and a resource to be used in developing programs that deal with both adults' and children's literacy. Families know what they need and what works for them. They can help design appropriate literacy activities and identify literacy knowledge and information needed by parents to be able to make educated decisions about their lives and those of their children.

A critical perspective in family literacy program planning requires that programs make use of, or build upon, the knowledge that families already possess. These programs incorporate cultural and social issues into the program in order to enhance participation. By connecting already existing knowledge to new knowledge, families recognize, use, and value their new learning. The approach also facilitates the integration of new learning with already existing structures or traditions. This enhances literacy learning for both adults and children and contributes to improved home–school relations. This interactive process allows for the sharing of knowledge between program planners and the population they serve, thus establishing program relevance and lasting effects for the community. Literacy programs that allow for this interaction and exchange of knowledge adopt a critical perspective in which they build upon what families already possess rather than impose ideas and/or activities upon communities.

LITERACY AND THE HISPANIC COMMUNITY

Hispanics are the most undereducated major segment of the U.S. population, a particular concern since census data show that 1 of every 12 Americans is of Hispanic origin. Forty-three percent of the 19-year-old and older Hispanic population are not in school and do not have a high school diploma (National Council of La Raza, 1990). Combined, Hispanic adults have the fewest years of schooling (10.2 years), compared to 12.8 years for whites and 11.6 for blacks (National Adult Literacy Survey). While in school, Hispanics at all grade levels lag far behind their Anglo peers in reading and writing achievement (Applebee, Langer, & Mullis, 1987). As adults, they also displayed lower literacy proficiency as measured by the NALS (Kirsch, Jungeblut, Jenkins, & Kolstad, 1993). Hispanic performance, which ranged from 206 to 218 on the prose scale, did not vary greatly among subpopulations (Mexican, Cuban, Puerto Rican, Central/South American). However, this was 68–80 points less than for whites (mean prose score of 286) and 29 to 31 points less than for blacks (mean prose of 237). Even after controlling for levels of educational attainment, there is cause for concern. On average, whites outscored Hispanics by 71 points on prose. After controlling for education, there was still an average 40-point difference. Controlling for education did mediate the differences between blacks and Hispanics at a high school level and above.

Age is also an apparent factor. In comparing whites and Hispanics in the 16–18-and 19–24-year-old age brackets, there is a little more than a year difference in educational attainment (1.1 and 1.4, years respectively) but a 47-to 57-point difference in prose literacy. For the 25–39-year age cohort, there is nearly a three-year difference in education and an 88-

point difference in prose literacy. Clearly, younger parents (16–24) in family literacy programs may seem to have similar educational experiences, yet the Hispanic parents may very well have lower literacy proficiencies. Among 25–39-year-old parents, the Hispanic parents may have a somewhat larger discrepancy in years of school, accompanied by a substantial difference in proficiency.

Finally, the NALS data confirm that nativity is significant to English literacy. Not surprisingly, persons born in the United States tend to be more proficient in English than those born outside the country, who are more likely to have learned English as a second language. This also holds true for Hispanics. Those born in the United States, many of whom may be bilingual, outperform those born outside this country.

Solutions to low achievement require broad-based solutions; neither the school nor the home will fulfill the literacy needs of populations at risk—regardless of racial origin or cultural and linguistic differences. In school settings, research indicates that interactive, meaning-based instruction that draws on children's social, cultural, and linguistic strengths is successful with Hispanic students (Serna & Hudelson, 1993; Moll & Greenberg, 1991). Unfortunately, the instruction of low-income, minority students tends to emphasize decontextualized skills and rote learning (Delgado-Gaitan, 1991; Delgado-Gaitan & Trueba, 1991). Research on Latino families shows that parents are highly concerned with the success of their children, but they are uncertain about the American educational system (Delgado-Gaitan, 1992; Goldenberg & Gallimore, 1991).

PARENT INVOLVEMENT IN HISPANIC COMMUNITIES: VALUING LITERACY

Because literacy is social and cultural in nature, it tends to develop best within the context of the family and in the daily lives of families. Recently, demographic changes have altered the configuration of the "family." Increasing numbers of mothers are working outside the home, and single-parent families and language minority children have increased in the United States. These changes affect parents' participation in their children's education for several reasons (e.g., lack of time, financial constraints, poor English proficiency, or low educational levels). Within this social context, research shows that Latino parents view teachers as experts and so are unlikely to interfere with what they see as the teacher's role (Flores, Taft, & Diaz, 1991). Lack of fluency in English and limited years of schooling result in Hispanic parents' feelings of inadequacy for helping their children with homework or communicating with the school. In turn, this lack of involvement may be interpreted by the teacher as lack of interest in the children's education. Yet the notion that poor linguistic minority or immigrant families do not value or support literacy development has been refuted widely (Delgado-Gaitan, 1987; Diaz, Moll, & Mehan, 1986; Goldenberg, 1987a; Taylor & Dorsey-Gaines, 1988). Parents in these groups may not directly work on literacy skills development or home activities, a fact that is incongruent with what supports school success in the United States. Yet these families are interested in their children's education and willing to help in their school success (Delgado-Gaitan, 1990; Epstein, 1990; Goldenberg & Gallimore, 1991).

Heath (1983), Moll (1992), and others have studied how the daily cultural activities of ethnic and cultural minorities in the United States affect language practices and socialization. Also, Goldenberg, Reese, and Gallimore (1992) suggest that there are significant differences in literacy behaviors of parents who value education. For example, middle-class parents tend to use stories for entertainment, while low-income parents may emphasize explicit instruction (Baker, Sonnerschein, Serpell, Fernandez-Fein, & Scheer, 1994). This work suggests that learning languages cannot be separated from learning how to be competent in participating in activities where different languages are used. So in helping linguistic minorities learn a new language, we also are concerned with their learning how the new culture, language, and society are interrelated. Therefore, family literacy is an appropriate approach to address the academic needs of the Latino community in order to enhance Latinos' success and achievement (Ada, 1988; Quintero & Huerta-Macias, 1990). Research demonstrates the centrality of the concept of "familia" in the cultural descriptions of Latino people (Abi-Nader, 1990), and meeting the needs of the family is one of the greatest motivations for success in the Latino culture. Since literacy learning is a culturally bound activity, by increasing the opportunities for families to learn and use literacy at home, it is possible to smooth discontinuities between home and school and facilitate literacy learning.

A FAMILY LITERACY MODEL: PROJECT FLAME-FAMILY LITERACY: APRENDIENDO, MEJORANDO, EDUCANDO

In response to the need to smooth discontinuities between home and school and from the perspective that Hispanic parents are genuinely interested in the education of their children, Project FLAME-Family Literacy: Aprendiendo, Mejorando, Educando was created with the belief that Hispanic parents need support in understanding ways to help their children (Shanahan, Mulhern, & Rodríguez-Brown, 1995). The program is an intervention designed with community and parent input in order to address parents' and children's literacy needs. Through the program, school success is placed in the context of "familia" in order to increase parental efficacy in providing and improving their childrens' literacy learning.

Project FLAME was developed as a community project based in schools or community agencies and run by the university. The project as designed is directed to parents of children who are three to nine years old. It was originally designed to provide literacy training and support to Latino parents who want to learn English as a second language, improve their basic skills, or take the GED, which, in turn, will enhance their chances to better influence their children's literacy and achievement. Although the program serves the Hispanic community, we believe that the program can be replicated in other communities and with different racial and ethnic populations.

Project FLAME was implemented in September 1989. The program was funded through grants from the U.S. Department of Education for six years and currently is funded through private donations. We served about 60 families per year in three schools during the first three years. Currently, we serve about 200 families whose children attend eight different schools in Chicago. In return for our services, the families agree to participate in interviews and testing and give the codirectors authorization to receive the testing scores from their children currently attending Chicago public schools.

Program Design

Project FLAME is based on four assumptions. First, we believe that a supportive home environment is essential to literacy development. Second, we believe that parents can have a positive effect on their children's learning. Third, we believe that parents who are confident and successful learners will be the most effective teachers of their children. Fourth, we believe that literacy is the school subject most likely to be influenced by the social and cultural contexts of the family.

Underlining these assumptions is a set of objectives: (1) to increase the ability of LEP (limited English proficiency) parents to provide literacy opportunities for their children; (2) to increase LEP parents' ability to act as positive literacy models; (3) to improve the skills of LEP parents so that they can more effectively initiate, encourage, support, and extend their children's literacy learning; and (4) to increase and improve relationships between LEP families and schools. In relation to these objectives and throughout this chapter the term "limited English proficiency" is defined as an inability to fully understand and/or operate within an all-English-speaking environment. Generally, a limited English proficient individual will have trouble understanding abstract, noncontextualized language.

All of these objectives are supported by research that shows the impact of each of these areas in relation to children's learning and achievement (Edwards, 1988; Feitelson & Goldstein, 1986; Gallimore & Goldenberg, 1989; Goldenberg, 1987a; Heath, 1986; Janiuk & Shanahan, 1988; Mulhern, 1991; Nickse, Speicher, & Bucheck, 1988; Silvern, 1988; Teale, 1984). In order to fulfill these objectives, Project FLAME addresses literacy within four areas that support the relevance of parents' impact in their children's education. These areas are literacy opportunity, literacy models, literacy interactions, and school–home relationships.

Literacy Opportunity

A supportive home environment provides children with the opportunity to use literacy. To do well with school literacy learning, children need to be familiar with a culture of literacy, a culture that is rich in literacy materials including books, magazines, and writing implements. The availability of materials provides children with the opportunity to see literacy in action and to experiment with literacy. Children with such opportunities do best in school, and the provision of such opportunities alone has been found to be a powerful stimulus to literacy learning of young children (Wheeler, 1971).

Often Hispanic families do not have reading or writing materials in the home because the parents themselves have limited reading abilities. Even when literacy materials are available, often parents do not share them with their children in fear that the books will be damaged or misused (Mulhern, 1991).

Through visits to public libraries and learning to analyze the characteristics of books relevant for their children's ages, Project FLAME teaches parents to locate and select appropriate books, magazines, and other literacy materials for their children; how to increase the amount of library use by the families; and how to increase the availability of literacy materials in the home for the children, including appropriate reading and writing materials. After each project session, parents are given ideas for activities to follow up at home with their children.

Literacy Models

A literacy model is defined as a significant person in the child's environment who uses literacy in an open and obvious manner. Children who see their mothers and fathers reading and writing do best in school reading achievement (MetriTech, 1987). Children who have appropriate models attempt to imitate literacy behaviors of their parents and older siblings. Efforts to improve a mother's strategies for reading to her children have been successful in improving children's literacy learning with Hispanic children (Gallimore & Goldenberg, 1989) and other low Socio-economic Status (SES) children (Edwards, 1988).

Hispanic parents often do not share their literacy with their children (Gallimore & Goldenberg, 1989). Sometimes this is because the parents have very limited literacy skills or at least limited literacy skills in English. Even when literacy is available, they do not necessarily make a point of sharing it with their children because they do not recognize the power and value of the activity.

Sometimes parents, in their zeal to provide English to their children, do not provide a rich, active language environment (Heath, 1986). Studies show that parents are more likely to serve as effective literacy models and participate in their children's literacy learning when they see themselves as effective learners (National Center for Family Literacy, 1991; Nickse, Speicher, & Buchek, 1988; Van Fossen & Sticht, 1991). Project FLAME's program is designed to encourage parents to increase their own English literacy and language use and to draw their children's attention to this behavior. Specifically, Project FLAME encourages parents to use reading and writing in the company of their children, to draw their children's attention to their more subtle uses of reading and writing, and to improve their own English proficiency and literacy skills.

Literacy Interaction

Literacy interaction refers to any direct exchange between parents and their children that is intended to enhance children's literacy knowledge. This includes formal direct instruction, but it also includes less formal activities such as reading to children or encouraging them to pretend to read or write. Such interactions have a positive influence on children's learning (Tobin, 1981), yet LEP parents are less likely to know the most productive and powerful ways to help their children to become literate.

Children who are read to often are more successful in school than are those who do not receive such experiences (Feitelson & Goldstein, 1986). It is believed that such reading acquaints children with story structures and literacy conventions (Teale, 1984). However, it has been found that parents are not equally effective in how they read to their children (Shanahan & Hogan, 1982). Parents in this program are shown how to read to their children more effectively and how to talk with their children about books. They are also taught how to use language experience activities to broaden their children's awareness and understanding of literacy (Janiuk & Shanahan, 1988).

Parents are instructed about how to use songs, games, and other language activities that can increase children's phonemic awareness and other skills (Tobin, 1981). Parents are shown how to encourage children's invented writing (Henderson & Beers, 1981). FLAME teaches specific techniques that have been found to mediate such influences. Specifically, LEP parents learn that they can share books with their children more and in ways that will enhance children's literacy learning (regardless of their own literacy level); how to create simple language-experience activities; how to play simple language games with their children that enhance literacy learning; and to be more aware of the literacy resources available in their community. In this way parents become aware of their power in influencing the learning of their children.

Home–School Relationships

Home–school relationships involve all interactions between parents and the school. Parents need to understand what their children's teachers are trying to accomplish, and teachers need to know of the parents' concerns and aspirations. Research shows that Hispanic children's literacy knowledge is highest in situations in which teachers and parents maintain frequent contact with each other (Goldenberg, 1987b). It has also been shown that cultural and social discontinuity between school and home can interfere with literacy learning and that such discontinuities are more likely for the LEP child (Silvern, 1988). This program is designed to act as an early outreach between school and parents, attempting to smooth some of the potential discontinuity.

Specifically, Project FLAME attempts to increase contact between families and neighborhood schools, particularly with regard to improving early communication about literacy learning and home–school cooperation; improve relations and increase mutual respect between LEP parents and school personnel; and increase LEP parents' self-confidence in their ability to communicate with the teachers and administrators in their children's schools. To achieve these goals, Project FLAME shares information with parents about the teacher's role in the classroom and organizes parents' visits to classrooms in order to observe teachers. Also, parent–teacher sessions are scheduled where the parents and teachers exchange ideas about their specific expectations for the children and their schooling.

PROGRAM STRUCTURE

Project FLAME is described in terms of four dimensions or areas of literacy learning, and these dimensions are linked to one another. The program activities are designed with the idea that each will contribute to more than a single goal simultaneously, although each activity is likely to contribute a greater effect to one or another of the goals. A productive home literacy culture is necessarily complex, and program activities recognize and reflect this subtle intricacy.

The instructional design of the program includes two integrated components, "Parents as Learners" and "Parents as Teachers." The "Parents as Learners" sessions include instruction in either basic skills, English as a second language, or GED training, depending on the needs of project participants. The bimonthly "Parents as Teachers" sessions are in Spanish, the language the parents know best, and they focus on the four areas of home literacy influence: literacy opportunity (increasing the range of literacy materials available in the home); literacy modeling (encouraging parents to model literacy uses to children); literacy interactions (demonstrating ways to engage in literacy activities with children); and home–school relationships (providing opportunities for teacher–parent discussions and classroom observation). The topics that are presented include the following:

Creating Home Literacy Center—Creating a literacy activity center in a box, including pencils, crayons, paper, scissors, paste, magazines, pictures, and so on. How to make one, how to use it.

Book Sharing—The most effective ways to share books with children. How to talk about books and share books when your own literacy is limited.

Book Selection—Quality criteria for selecting books appropriate for children's needs and interests.

Library Visit—Public library tour, complete with applications for library cards.

Book Fairs—Parents buy (with coupons) English- or Spanish-language books for their children.

Teaching the ABCs—Simple ways to teach letters and sounds. Emphasis on language games, songs, and language experience activities.

Children's Writing—How young children write and ways to encourage home writing.

Community Literacy—How parents can share their own literacy uses with their children during marketing and other daily activities.

Classroom Observations—Classroom visitations to gain sense of how their children are taught in the schools.

Parent–Teacher Get-Together—Guided discussions about children's education with teachers and principals.

Math for Your Child—Games and activities for helping children to understand numbers and arithmetic.

How Parents Can Help with Homework—Ways parents can monitor and help with children's homework even when they can't do the homework themselves. Some of the sessions require that parents work together with their children, while others allow parents to interact with the program leaders and each other without their children present. When parents are in meetings without their children, baby-sitting services are provided. These services are also available as appropriate when parents are receiving ESL or adult literacy instruction.

The twice-weekly "Parents as Learners" sessions (ESL, basic skills, or GED classes) focus on specific educational needs of the parents and are connected to the "Parents as Teachers" sessions. The adult education component is used as a vehicle to help parents to become models of literacy use for their children. Although these sessions are designed to enhance parents' literacy skills, they also are tied into the "Parents as Teachers" component of FLAME. For instance, parents may develop books for their children during the ESL sessions, an activity that clearly increases "literacy opportunity"; or an ESL class may focus on how to share particular books in English with their children ("literacy interaction").

In addition to the specific activities described here, there are a number of less structured meetings or get-togethers such as a Summer Leadership Institute in which parents are encouraged to share with each other their progress and their concerns (not limited to literacy) and also hear speakers addressing community issues and educational themes. These meetings are a source of information for shaping content and procedures of project activities.

Originally, we had graduate and undergraduate students teaching ESL, GED, and/or basic skills and sharing knowledge in both the "Parents as Teachers" and "Parents as Learners" sessions, but the program was later expanded by adding a "Training of Trainers" component. In this component we have trained about 30 parents per year to plan and deliver the "Parents as Teachers" sessions provided through Project FLAME. Using parents as trainers has added more relevance to the literacy topics, since the presenters are parents who have previously participated in FLAME and live in the community where the program is delivered. Also, this model develops capacity for the community to keep the program in existence when the university is no longer able to offer the program.

EFFECTIVENESS OF PROJECT FLAME

Every year, each participating family is interviewed to check their qualifications for the program, which includes having a child between three and nine years old. Besides demographic data, the interview includes a section on literacy activities and materials at home. Another section requests that parents rate the objectives of the project using a Lickert-type scale. The purpose of the ratings is to learn about the parents' interest on the different components of the project and to determine any change in their interests over the time they participate in the program.

It is beyond the purpose of this chapter to present all the data supporting the effectiveness of the program, but data collected between 1992 and 1995 and described elsewhere (Mulhern, 1991; Rodríguez-Brown & Mulhern, 1993) have provided information about FLAME participants and their attitudes and literacy behaviors, both before and after their participation in Project FLAME. Analyses of parents' pre–post uses of, and attitudes toward, literacy at home show significant changes in the areas of literacy opportunity and literacy interactions.

These changes appear to impact children's school performance. Each year the children of FLAME participants who are three to six years old are pre-and post-tested in order to determine if our work with the parents has an effect on the children's learning and their preparedness for school. For this purpose, children are given a letter recognition test, a test of print awareness, and the Boehm Test of Basic Concepts. The tests are administered in either Spanish or English, depending on the children's proficiency in those languages. Statistical analyses (e.g., t-tests) show significant gains ($<.001$) from pre-to post-test in all areas tested. FLAME researchers also conducted a comparative study. During the third year of the project, one of the FLAME schools agreed to allow us to test a class of preschoolers (three-to five-year-olds). The purpose was to compare their performance to a group of three-to five-year olds whose parents participated in Project FLAME. Because there were pretest differences among the groups (i.e., the FLAME group scored significantly lower on the test of print awareness [$p<.02$] and lowercase letters [$p<.0001$]), ANCOVA was used to control for pretest differences. The results indicate that no significant differences existed among the two groups by the end of the school year. These results show that although Project FLAME children lagged behind the comparison children in several areas related to literacy at pretest, they generally caught up during the months their families participated in the program. The children managed to do this despite the fact that a larger proportion of comparison children were in preschool or kindergarten.

The test scores of the children whose mothers were involved in the project provided some information that allows us to evaluate the effectiveness of the project on the children's literacy skills. Clearly, the children acquired additional skills when their families were involved with the project. This occurred even though the children experienced no direct intervention. The intervention was aimed at the parents, individuals who typically have very limited literacy skills themselves, limited experience with school, and limited English proficiency.

CONCLUSION

Because parent involvement is seen as a necessary and valued tool for students' school success, family literacy programs can provide a support system for family participation in literacy events that enhance both schooling and learning opportunities for everyone. Family literacy programs, such as Project FLAME, can be successful with families who have limited proficiency in English and whose children are often at risk for academic failure.

Family literacy programs offer learning and opportunity for everyone. When programs are developed within the context of the family, they can validate parents' knowledge and enhance the image of parents as models in learning. Also, with linguistic minority parents such as Hispanic immigrants, family literacy programs entice parents to share literacy with their children in the language they know best (Cummins, 1986; Shanahan, Mulhern, & Rodríguez-Brown, 1995), thereby validating the home language as a learning tool while both the parents and children learn English. Family literacy programs also provide a structure that allows the development of networks among families in the community. Because of these benefits, family literacy programs should be seen as a feasible way to enhance adult education and parent involvement. If we are to achieve the literacy goals outlined in Goals 2000, family literacy programs such as Project FLAME have a critical role to play in developing the literacy skills of parents and children in language minority families.

REFERENCES

Abi-Nader, J. (1990). A house for my mother: Motivating Hispanic high school students. *Anthropology and Education Quarterly, 21,* 41–58.

Ada, A. F. (1988). The Pajaro Valley Experience: Working with Spanish-speaking parents to develop children's reading and writing skills in the home through the use of children's literature. In T. Skutnabb-Kangas & J. Cummins (Eds.), *Minority education: From shame to struggle* (pp. 223–238). Clevedon, England: Multilingual Matters.

Applebee, A. N., Langer, J. A., & Mullis, I. (1987). *Learning to be literate in America.* Princeton, NJ: Educational Testing Service.

Auerbach, E. R. (1989). Toward a socio-contextual approach to family literacy. *Harvard Educational Review, 59,* 165–187.

Baker, Z., Sonnerschein, S., Serpell, R., Fernandez-Fein, S., & Scheer, D. (1994). *Contexts of emergent literacy: Everyday home experiences of urban prekindergarten children.* Athens, GA: National Reading Research Center, University of Georgia and University of Maryland.

Cummins, J. (1986). Empowering minority students: A framework for intervention. *Harvard Educational Review, 56,* 18–36.

———. (1988). *Empowering minority students*. Sacramento: California Association for Bilingual Education.

Delgado-Gaitan, C. (1987). Mexican adult literacy: New directions for immigrants. In S. R. Goldman & H. Trueba (Eds.), *Becoming literate in English as a second language* (pp. 9–32). Norwood, NJ: Ablex.

———. (1990). *Literacy for empowerment: The role of parents in children's education*. London: Farmer Press.

———. (1991). Involving parents in schools: A process of empowerment. *American Journal of Education, 100*, 20–41.

———. (1992). School matters in the Mexican American home: Socializing children to education. *American Educational Research Journal, 29*, 495–513.

Delgado-Gaitan, C., & Trueba, H. (1991). *Crossing borders: Education for immigrant families in America*. New York: Farmer Press.

Diaz, S., Moll, L., & Mehan, H. (1986). Socio-cultural resources in instruction: A context specific approach. In California State Department of Education (Ed.), *Beyond language: social and cultural factors in schooling of language minority children* (pp. 187–229). Los Angeles: California State University.

Duffy, T. M. (1992). What makes a difference in instruction? In T. G. Sticht, M. J. Bieler, & B. A. McDonald (Eds.), *The intergenerational transfer of cognitive skills: Vol. 1: Programs, policy and research issues*. Norwood, NJ: Ablex.

Edwards, P. A. (1988, December). "Lower SES mothers' learning of book reading strategies." Paper presented at the annual meeting of the National Reading Conference, Tucson, AZ.

Eldridge-Hunter, D. (1992). Intergenerational literacy: Impact on the development of the story-book reading behaviors of Hispanic mothers. In C. K. Kinzer & D. J. Leu (Eds.), *Literacy research, theory and practice: Views from many perspectives*. Forty-first yearbook of the National Reading Conference (pp. 101–110). Chicago: National Reading Conference.

Epstein, J. (1990). School and family connections: Theory, research and implications for integrating sociologies of education and family. In D. Unger & M. Sussman (Eds.), *Families in community settings: Interdisciplinary perspectives* (pp. 96–126). New York: Haworth Press.

Feitelson, D., & Goldstein, Z. (1986). Patterns of book ownership and reading to young children in Israeli school-oriented and non-school-oriented families. *Reading Teacher, 39*, 924–930.

Ferdman, B. (1990). Literacy and cultural identity. *Harvard Educational Review, 60*, 181–204.

Flores, B., Taft, R., & Diaz, C. (1991). Transforming deficit myths about learning, language and culture. *Language Arts, 68*, 369–379.

Freire, P. (1970). *Pedagogy of the oppressed*. New York: Seabury Press.

Freire, P., & Macedo, D. (1987). *Literacy: Reading the word and the world*. South Hadley, MA: Bergin and Garvey.

Gadsden, V. (1995). Representations of literacy: Parents' images in two cultural communities. In L. Morrow (Ed.), *Family Literacy: Connections in schools and communities* (pp. 167–183). Newark, DE: International Reading Association.

Gallimore, R., & Goldenberg, C. (1989, March). "School effects on emergent literacy experiences in families of Spanish speaking children." Paper presented at the annual meeting of the American Educational Research Association, San Francisco.

Goldenberg, C. (1987a). Low-income Hispanic parents' contributions to their first grade children's word recognition skills. *Anthropology and Education Quarterly, 18,* 149–179.

———. (1987b). Roads to reading: Studies of Hispanic first graders at risk of reading failure. *National Association for Bilingual Education Journal, 11,* 235–250.

Goldenberg, C., & Gallimore, R. (1991). Local knowledge, research knowledge and educational change: A case study of early Spanish reading improvement. *Educational Researcher, 20,* 2–14.

Goldenberg, C., Reese, L., & Gallimore, R. (1992). Effects of literacy materials from school on Latino children's home experience and early reading achievement. *American Journal of Education, 100,* 497–536.

Goodman, Y. (1986). Children coming to know literacy. In W. Teale & E. Sulzby (Eds.), *Emergent literacy: Writing and reading* (pp. 1–40). Norwood, NJ: Ablex.

Heath, S. B. (1983). *Ways with words.* Cambridge, U.K.: Cambridge University Press.

———. (1986). Socio-cultural context of language development. In State of California, Department of Education (Eds.), *Beyond language; Social and cultural factors in the schooling of language minority students* (pp. 143–186). Los Angeles: California State University.

Henderson, E. & Beers, J. (Eds.). (1981). *Developmental and cognitive aspects of learning to spell.* Newark, DE: International Reading Association.

Janiuk, M. T., & Shanahan, T. (1988). Applying adult literacy practices in primary grade instruction. *Reading Teacher, 41,* 880–887.

Kerka, S. (1991). *Family and intergenerational literacy.* (ERIC Digest # No.111). Columbus, OH: ERIC Clearinghouse on Adult Career and Vocational Education. (ERIC DRS Number 334–467).

Kirsch, I. S., Jungeblut, A., Jenkins, L., & Kolstad, A. (1993). *Adult literacy in America.* Washington, DC: National Center for Education Statistics.

MetriTech (1987). *The Illinois reading assessment project: Literacy survey.* Champaign, IL: Author.

Moll, L. (1992). Bilingual classroom studies and community analysis: Some recent trends. *Educational Researcher, 21,* 2, 20–24.

Moll, L., & Greenberg, J. B. (1991). Creating zones of possibilities: Combining social contexts for instruction. In L. C. Moll (Ed.), *Vygotsky and education.* New York: Cambridge University Press.

Moore, M. & Stavrianos, M. (1994). *Adult education reauthorization: Background.* Washington, DC: CSR.

Mulhern, M. (1991, February). "The impact of a family literacy project on three Mexican-immigrant families." Paper presented at the UIC Literacy Colloquium, Chicago, University of Illinois at Chicago.

National Center for Family Literacy (1991). *The effects of participation in family literacy programs.* Louisville, KY: National Center for Family Literacy.

National Council of La Raza (1990). *Hispanic education: A statistical portrait—1990.* Washington, DC: NCLR.

Nickse, R. S. (1989). *The voices of literacy: An overview of intergenerational and family literacy programs*. Washington, DC: U.S. Department of Education.

————. (1990). *Family literacy in action: A survey of successful programs*. Syracuse, NY: New Reader Press.

————. (1991). "A typology of family and intergenerational literacy programs: Implications for evaluation." Paper presented at the annual meeting of the American Educational Research Association, Chicago.

Nickse, R. S., & Englander, N. (1985). *Collaborations for literacy and intergenerational reading project*. Boston: Trustees of Boston University.

Nickse, R. S., Speicher, A. M., & Buchek, P. C. (1988). An intergenerational adult literacy project: A family intervention/presentation model. *Journal of Reading, 31*, 634–642.

Nuckolls, M. (1991). Expanding students' potential through family literacy. *Educational Leadership, 41* (1), 45–46.

Quintero, F., & Huerta-Macias, A. (1990). Learning together: Issues for language minority parents and their children. *Journal of Educational Issues of Language, Minority Students, 10*, 41–56.

Rodríguez-Brown, F. V., & Mulhern, M. (1993). Fostering critical literacy through family literacy: A study of families in a Mexican-immigrant community. *Bilingual Research Journal, 17* (3 & 4), 1–16.

Ryan, K. (1991). *An evaluation framework for family literacy programs*. ERIC Document Reproduction Service No. 331–029.

Serna, I., & Hudelson, S. (1993). Becoming a writer of Spanish and English. *Quarterly of the National Writing Project and the Center for the Study of Writing and Literacy, 15* (1), 1–5.

Shanahan, T., & Hogan, V. (1982). Parent reading style and children's print awareness. In J. A. Niles & L. A. Harris (Eds.), *Searches for meaning in reading/language processing and instruction*. Thirty-Second Yearbook of the National Reading Conference. Chicago: National Reading Conference.

Shanahan, T., Mulhern, M., & Rodríguez-Brown, F. V. (1995). Project FLAME: Lessons learned from a family literacy program for linguistic minority families. *The Reading Teacher, 48*, 586–593.

Shanahan, T., & Rodríguez-Brown, F. V. (1993, April). "Project FLAME: The theory and structure of a family literacy program for the Latino community." Paper presented at the annual meeting of the American Educational Research Association, Atlanta, GA.

Silvern, S. (1988). Continuity/discontinuity between home and early childhood education environments. *Elementary School Journal, 89*, 147–160.

Simich-Dudgeon, C. (1987, March). Involving limited English proficient parents as tutors in their children's education. *ERI/CLL News Bulletin, 10* (2).

Street, B. M. (1984). *Literacy in theory and practice*. Cambridge, U.K.: Cambridge University Press.

Taylor, D., & Dorsey-Gaines, C. (1988). *Growing up literate*. Portsmouth, NH: Heinemann.

Teale, W. (1984). Reading to young children: Its significance for literacy development. In H. Gollman, A. Oberg, & F. Smith (Eds.), *Awakening to literacy* (pp. 110–121). Portsmouth, NH: Heinemann.

Tobin, A. W. (1981). "A multiple discriminate cross validation of the factors associated with the development of precocious reading achievement." Dissertation, University of Delaware.

Van Fossen, S., & Sticht, T. G. (1991). *Teach the mother and reach the child: Results of the intergenerational literacy action research project.* Washington, DC: Wider Opportunities for Women.

Wheeler, M. E. (1971). "Untutored acquisition of writing skill." Dissertation, Cornell University.

Young, M., Morgan, M., Fitzgerald, N., & Fleishman, H. (1994). *National evaluation of adult education programs: Final report.* Arlington, VA: Development Associates.

13

Adult Literacy and Health Care

Joanne R. Nurss

INTRODUCTION

> I had some papers, but didn't know they were prescriptions, and I walked around for a week without my medication. I was ashamed to go back to the doctor, but a woman saw the papers I had and told me they were prescriptions. It's bad to not know how to read.

> I've had a lot of illnesses, but I preferred to stay home until I get better by taking anything I can. Because being asked to fill this out, to fill that out, I be embarrassed to ask for help, to ask for them to fill them out for me. They might get upset so I stay home.

These comments all too clearly summarize the predicament of people with low functional health literacy trying to care for themselves without adequate understanding of their written health care instructions. Is this unusual? Unfortunately, it is not. Forty-two percent of indigent patients at urban hospitals could not comprehend directions for taking medication on an empty stomach; 26% could not read and understand the slip telling when their next appointment was scheduled; 60% could not understand a standard hospital informed consent form (Williams, Parker, Baker, Parikh, Pitkin, Coates, & Nurss, 1995). The problem is especially acute in elderly patients, over 80% of whom have low functional health literacy. According to Doak, Doak, and Root (1985), about 23 million American adults may not be able to understand the health care information given to them. The National Adult Literacy Survey (Kirsch, Jungeblat, Jenkins, & Kolstad, 1993) suggests that one in five adults have difficulty with "everyday" literacy tasks of modest difficulty and complexity, such as completing a deposit slip or locating the time or place of a meeting (p. xiv). Very likely these adults would also have difficulty reading common medical information such as prescription labels or appointment slips.

FUNCTIONAL HEALTH LITERACY

Current usage of the term "adult literacy" encompasses the adult's level of proficiency in reading, writing, numeracy, oral communication, and problem solving. Frequently, this proficiency is reported in academic terms, using designations such as grade level scores. These assessments may be meaningful for adults seeking to obtain a GED (General Equivalency Diploma) or to engage in postsecondary education. For most adults, however, grade level designations are meaningless. More useful is information about the adequacy of their literacy for daily activities— at home, on the job, in the community, in other words, about how functional their literacy skills are for everyday life. This latter definition is explored in the research reported in this chapter. Functional health literacy refers to the adequacy of the adult's literacy to read and comprehend materials encountered in typical health care settings and necessary to positive health outcomes. Of particular concern is skill in reading and comprehending both written text and numerical information (numeracy).

Assessment of Functional Health Literacy

Assessment of adult literacy is frequently done by using standardized measures such as the Test of Adult Basic Education (TABE), Adult Basic Literacy Examination (ABLE), Wide Range Achievement Test-Revised (WRAT-R), or Test of English as a Foreign Language (TOEFL). These measures may be appropriate for assessment of literacy in preparation for academic instruction. They do not, however, provide adequate information about functional literacy. In order to assess functional literacy, the measure must use actual text or materials used in a real-life setting, for example, the adult's skills in reading and comprehending a bus schedule, a checkbook, consumer warning labels, or directions for assembling a toy. The National Adult Literacy Survey (NALS) assessed functional literacy of prose, document, and quantitative texts. There are two measures of functional health literacy reported in the literature. The Rapid Estimate of Adult Literacy in Medicine (REALM) assesses the patient's skill in reading a list of 66 health-related words (Murphy, Davis, Long, Jackson, & Decker, 1993). Scores are interpreted as "estimates of literacy," not as grade equivalents. The REALM is easy to give, taking only about two to three minutes to administer and score. It can be done by personnel in any medical clinic or hospital. The authors report good reliability (test-retest, $r = .98$) and criterion validity with correlation coefficients ranging from .88 to .97 with the SORT-R, PIAT-R, and WRAT-R (Murphy et al., 1993). However, the REALM does not assess comprehension or understanding of the words read, only their pronunciation. Attempts to translate REALM into Spanish were unsuccessful due to the nature of the Spanish language (Nurss, Baker, Davis, Parker, & Williams, 1995). The REALM does not completely meet the need for a test of functional health literacy that assesses adults' skills in reading and understanding health-related materials in English and Spanish.

The Test of Functional Health Literacy in Adults

The Test of Functional Health Literacy in Adults (TOFHLA) was developed to meet this need (Parker, Baker, Williams, & Nurss, 1995). TOFHLA assesses adults' skills in reading and comprehending both text and numerical statements encountered in a typical health care setting. The Numeracy section is a 17-item test using actual prescription vial labels and hospital forms. It assesses the patient's skill in understanding written directions for taking medicines, monitoring blood glucose, keeping clinic appointments, and obtaining financial assistance. Items are presented on cue cards that patients read before responding to oral questions. The overall difficulty of the Numeracy items on the Gunning Fog index is grade 9.4. The score on the 17-item test is multiplied by a constant to yield a score of 0 to 50. The Reading Comprehension section of TOFHLA is a 50-item modified Cloze test over three passages of varying difficulty. Every 5th to 7th word is omitted in each passage. The adult reads the passage and selects which of four words best fits in each blank, for example:

Your doctor has sent you to have a———X-ray.
    a. stomach, b. diabetes, c. stitches, d. germs.

The passages were selected from instructions for preparation for an upper gastrointestinal series, the patient rights and responsibilities section of a Medicaid application form, and a standard hospital informed consent form. The readability levels of the passages on the Gunning Fog index are grades 4.3, 10.4, and 19.5, respectively.

TOFHLA was developed and field-tested on 256 patients in the medical walk-in and emergency care clinics at a large urban hospital in Atlanta serving primarily indigent African-American patients. Patients' visual acuity was tested using the Rosenbaum handheld vision chart. Using a criterion of 20/50, 11% were excluded from the pilot sample.

Table 13.1
Reliability of the Test of Functional Health Literacy in Adults (TOFHLA) and Validity of the TOFHLA when Compared with the Rapid Estimate of Adult Literacy in Medicine (REALM) and the Wide Range Achievement Test-Revised (WRAT-R)

	English (n =200)	Spanish (n = 203)
Reliability		
Spearman-Brown	0.92	0.84
Cronbach's alpha	0.98	0.98
Validity (r)[1]		
REALM	0.84*	—
WRAT-R	0.74*	—

[1]The REALM is not valid in Spanish, and the WRAT-R is not available in Spanish.
*$p < 0.001$ by Spearman's rank correlation.

Subsequently, a large-print (14-point font) version was developed for patients with visual acuity 20/70 to 20/100. Pilot testing was also done at an urban hospital in Los Angeles using a Spanish version of TOFHLA for Spanish-speaking patients. To create the Spanish TOFHLA, all passages were translated into Spanish, and a bilingual literacy expert checked the translation and developed the Cloze deletions and options, creating as equivalent a test as possible. Table 13.1 gives the reliability and validity correlations for the English and Spanish versions of TOFHLA. TOFHLA is an individually administered test, taking about 20 minutes to administer and score. A short form of the TOFHLA is currently being piloted.

Both the REALM and the TOFHLA provide an assessment of adults' functional health literacy. The TOFHLA, while requiring more time to administer, is a more comprehensive measure including the adult's understanding of text and numeracy passages.

PREVALENCE OF LOW FUNCTIONAL HEALTH LITERACY IN ADULTS

TOFHLA was used to measure patients' functional health literacy in two urban, public hospitals in Atlanta and Los Angeles (Williams, Parker, Baker, Parikh, Pitkin, Coates, & Nurss, 1995). A total of 2,659 predominantly indigent and minority patients were assessed: 1,892 English-speaking and 767 Spanish-speaking. Patients were approached in the acute care clinics of the two hospitals by trained research assistants. After obtaining informed consent, they were given a demographic questionnaire, the Rosenbaum handheld vision chart, and the TOFHLA. Patients with visual acuity from 20/70 to 20/100 were given a large-print (14-point font) version of the TOFHLA, those with visual acuity 20/50 or better were given the regular version, and those with 20/100 or worse were excluded. Other exclusionary criteria were under 18 years of age, too ill to participate, native language other than English (except Spanish speakers in Los Angeles, who were given the Spanish TOFHLA), unintelligible speech, and uncooperative behavior. In Atlanta, 7% of those approached were excluded; in Los Angeles, 5%.

Scores on the TOFHLA group adults into three levels of functional health literacy—adequate (75–100), marginal (60–74), and inadequate (0–59). A total of 47.4% of patients in Atlanta and 61.7% Spanish-speaking patients and 22.0% English-speaking patients in Los Angeles had low (inadequate or marginal) functional health literacy. That is, they were unable to read and understand directions for taking the correct dosage of a prescribed medication, clinic appointment slips, or instructions for preparation for an upper gastrointestinal tract radiographic procedure. They also were unable to read and understand the Medicaid Rights and Responsibilities passage and directions for taking medications on an empty stomach or taking all of a prescribed medication. Age was highly correlated with TOFHLA scores, but number of years of schooling did not reliably identify functional health literacy.

Inadequate functional health literacy may be a barrier to patients' understanding of diagnoses and receiving high-quality medical care. For example, patients who cannot read and understand the Medicaid Rights and Responsibilities do not understand what care to expect or what is required of them as patients. Patients who do not understand how to take prescribed medications are likely to become sicker and to need emergency care. Unless the health care environment is modified, it can be assumed that at least half of the patients in urban hospitals are unable to read and understand the materials presented to them. The problem is even more acute for some groups of patients.

Special Populations

Diabetic

Diabetes is a chronic disease for which patients need to be able to manage their own medical care. It is essential for patients to be able to read and understand their prescribed diet, directions for monitoring their blood glucose or administering insulin, and suggested modifications in medication when they are ill. There have been numerous studies to develop educational materials for diabetic patients. However, very few have considered the reading difficulty of the materials or the literacy level of the patients. Designing diabetes education materials on a lower literacy level significantly improves patients' understanding of the materials (Kicklighter & Stein, 1993), but what literacy level is most appropriate has not been studied. If diabetes patients cannot read and understand the instructions provided to them, they will be unable to comply with medical directions and are likely to become ill more frequently.

A study (Nurss, El-Kebbi, Gallina, Ziemer, Musey, Lewis, Liao, & Phillips, 1996) was undertaken using the TOFHLA to assess the functional health literacy of patients with diabetes in order to provide diabetes education materials and procedures they can understand. Data were collected from four sites at an urban public hospital: the Diabetes and Medical Clinics at the main hospital and two satellite clinics. An additional sample was collected from follow-up patients at the Diabetes Clinic. Of the total sample of 131 patients, 86% were African American and 14% Caucasian. Procedures and exclusion criteria, including visual screening, were essentially the same as in the study of the prevalence of low literacy previously described (Williams et al., 1995).

The incidence of low literacy (inadequate or marginal functional health literacy) was significantly higher in the population of patients with diabetes than in the general hospital population ($p = .000$). Nearly three-fourths of the established patients with diabetes and more than half of the new patients had low functional health literacy. These increased numbers are, most likely, due to the fact that the sample of patients with diabetes was significantly older than the general hospital population (mean age 57 versus 40 years), and older patients have been shown to have lower literacy (Kirsch et al., 1993; Williams et al., 1995).

The mean functional health literacy level (inadequate = 1, marginal = 2, adequate = 3) for all patients in the diabetes study was 1.8, with the new patients at the Diabetes Clinic having a significantly ($p = .0097$) higher level of functional health literacy (2.2) than those at the other sites (satellite clinics = 1.8 and 1.9; Medical Clinic = 1.6; follow-up patients at the Diabetes Clinic = 1.3). According to these scores, these patients have marginal functional health literacy at best, with the majority of patients having inadequate functional health literacy. This older population with poorer vision is likely to have difficulty reading and understanding written medical instructions and to need diabetes education geared to their functional health literacy level. They are likely to be sicker and to have more medical problems and, therefore, more need for education and printed materials to instruct them in diet, glucose monitoring, and sick day management. They are less likely to be able to accurately measure and adjust their insulin dosage. Low functional health literacy is an even greater problem for them than for the general population.

Elderly

The elderly have more chronic health problems than younger patients requiring them to follow a medical regime (medications, daily monitoring, tests, etc.). Unfortunately, they are also most likely to have low functional health literacy. In the study of the prevalence of low functional health literacy in hospital patients (Williams et al., 1995), older patients had the lowest literacy scores. The majority of patients 60 years or older had inadequate functional health literacy (81% in Atlanta, 71% of Spanish-speaking patients and 48% of English-speaking patients in Los Angeles). In the study of patients with diabetes (Nurss et al., 1996), there was a clear link among age, vision, and literacy. Older patients had both poorer vision and lower functional health literacy. In all of these studies, patients were screened for visual acuity and provided a large-print version of TOFHLA, if needed. Further, the NALS survey also reported that persons 54 years of age and older were likely to be in the lowest categories of literacy (Kirsch et al., 1993). Similarly, Weiss, Reed, & Kligman, 1995) studied persons 60 years and older and found that 32.2% had reading skills below the fourth grade level. They reported that these persons obtain much of their health information from television, a satisfactory solution for general information but not for specific directions for their own health care. Elderly persons with chronic medical problems are most in need of health care services and, with low literacy, most at risk for taking medications incorrectly and suffering adverse medical consequences.

Other Special Populations

Other research is currently considering the prevalence of low literacy among other special populations, including chronic diseases such as asthma, hypertension, and arthritis. It is hypothesized that functional health literacy influences contraceptive knowledge, attitudes, and behaviors as well (Parker, Williams, Baker, & Nurss, 1996). Davis, Arnold, Jackson, Glass, and Sentell (1996) report that lower reading levels on the REALM correlated significantly with less knowledge about mammography and with more negative attitudes about screening mammograms. It has been proposed that illiteracy (or low functional literacy) is a contributing factor in poisonings (Mrvos, Dean, & Krenzelok, 1993). More study is needed to ascertain the effect of low functional health literacy on the health status of persons with specific chronic diseases and to determine the role of low functional health literacy in prevention and wellness.

LITERACY AND SHAME

Particularly disturbing in many of these studies is the finding that patients do not readily report to health care personnel that they have difficulty reading and comprehending medical forms, perhaps due to shame. In a study to address this issue (Parikh, Parker, Nurss, Baker, & Williams, 1996), English-speaking patients were assessed with the TOFHLA. Of the 202 patients tested, 43% were found to have inadequate or marginal functional health literacy. When asked if they had any difficulty reading or understanding written materials given to them at the hospital, only two-thirds of those with low functional health literacy admitted to having difficulty. These patients were then asked if they feel ashamed or embarrassed about their difficulty reading. Only 40% of those with low functional health literacy admitted feeling shame. The stigma placed on being illiterate in our society is so great that 67% of the low literate sample had never told their spouse they could not read; 53% had not told their children; and 19% had told no one.

Similarly, in the study of diabetes patients' functional health literacy (Nurss et al., 1996), despite the low levels of academic attainment within the sample, only 13.6% reported that reading medical forms is either very hard or impossible. Moreover, only 26% report asking someone to help them read the forms and information that they receive from the hospital. Of those who do ask for help, family members are the most commonly asked helper (64.3%), with neighbors asked second most often (21.4%). Patients are least likely to ask their doctor or nurse for help (3.6%).

Low literacy carries a stigma in our society. Persons who do not have adequate literacy skills have been shown to have feelings of inadequacy, fear, and low self-esteem (Beder, 1991; Clabby & Belz, 1985). Although they know they cannot read, they are unable or unwilling to admit this problem, even when their health is at risk. It is very difficult to assist these low literate persons when they are too embarrassed to ask for help. Clearly, health care providers must alter the environment so that everyone has equal access to health care. Staff training is needed to provide a shame-free environment in which patients feel comfortable requesting help without being stigmatized. Staff members must be aware of the types of help patients may need and be ready to offer it without asking.

LITERACY AND HEALTH OUTCOMES

In the low literacy prevalence study, patients were also questioned about their overall health and use of health care services during the three months prior to their assessment (Baker, Parker, Williams, Clark, & Nurss, in press). Patients with inadequate functional health literacy were more likely to describe their health as poor than patients with adequate literacy. In Atlanta, patients with inadequate functional health literacy were more likely than those with adequate literacy to have been hospitalized during the last year, even after adjusting for health status, age, and economic level. Thus, it appears that low literacy is strongly associated with self-reported poor health, and patients with inadequate functional health literacy may be more likely to be hospitalized.

Needed Research

What these studies have clearly shown is the prevalence of low literacy among urban hospital patients. A very large majority of these patients are unable to read and understand their health care documents, including medication instructions. What does that mean in practical terms?For the patients, it certainly means shame, confusion, and, very likely, poor health outcomes. We are currently studying the effects of low functional health literacy on compliance with medical instructions. It seems logical to assume that these patients do not follow all their medical directions and are very likely to end up back at the clinic or the emergency room with severe medical problems. If this is the case, not only are the patients failing to receive high-quality medical care, but they are incurring unnecessary costs to themselves and/or the health care system. Longitudinal studies are needed to verify these connections.

PROPOSED MODIFICATIONS TO SERVE PATIENTS WITH LOW FUNCTIONAL HEALTH LITERACY

Low functional health literacy is a pervasive problem in the United States. No doubt it affects the quality of patients' health care and may well increase health care costs. Certainly, it makes patients feel ashamed. One solution to the problem is to provide written materials on an easier readability level, using a more reader-friendly format, simple graphics or illustrations, and culturally sensitive examples. These materials can be used for all patients with positive results as verified by a study of a short, simply written polio vaccine information pamphlet with instructional graphics (Davis, Bocchini, Fredrickson, Arnold, Mayeaux, Murphy, Jackson, Hanna, & Paterson, 1996). Both high- and low-income-level parents, regardless of reading level, preferred the easier-to-understand pamphlet.

Another suggestion is staff training to help hospital staff be more aware of, and sensitive to, low literate patients. Patients frequently report that hospital staff stigmatize them if they realize that they cannot read forms. Staff members need to realize that statements such as, "I forgot my glasses" or "I broke my glasses" are frequently codes for, "I need help reading and filling out these forms." Once it is determined that a patient needs assistance with written material, the staff might suggest that the patient bring someone to help him or her read, a friend or family member who can serve as a surrogate reader at the hospital and at home.

The use of audio- or videotapes to explain directions, such as the preparation for an upper gastrointestinal series, would be easy for the patient to check out and take home. They can be used with family members or friends and can be played as many times as needed for complete understanding. Videotapes are expensive to produce but should be effective. Even the low-income patients in the Williams et al. (1995) study were more likely to have access to a videocassette recorder (VCR) than to a telephone!

Not only do materials need to be simply written and prepared in an easy-to-understand format, but they also need to be culturally sensitive and culturally relevant. Illustrations and vocabulary should be familiar to the target group and should take into consideration the life circumstances of the patients. For example, if a special diet is prescribed, the materials could present recipes modifying foods commonly eaten in that culture for a low-fat or low-sugar diet. Consideration could also be given to the ease of obtaining ingredients with food stamps when shopping at markets on public transportation. Diabetes occurs commonly among African-American women over the age of 50 years. They often are the cook for an extended family and must prepare foods that are appropriate to their diet but that will also be eaten by other family members. Other issues to consider include the culture's view of health and diet. In some cultures, being overweight is desirable; in others, being underweight is desired.

Finally, new models of health care education and training need to be considered. Instead of onetime lecture classes at the hospital or clinic, community-based education using trained peer educators is being studied. Initial studies in both the African-American and Hispanic communities using trained peers to teach patients with diabetes about their diet and care have been very successful (Auslander, Haire-Joshu, Houston, & Fisher, 1992; LaGreca, Auslander, Greco, Spetter, Fisher, & Santiago, 1995). Further research needs to be done to determine how such a program could be generalized and whether it would be just as successful with volunteers or the patient's own community network as with paid peer educators.

The link between literacy and health care is just beginning to be explored. As health care providers become more aware of their patients' literacy needs, health care will improve, and patient outcomes will be more positive. Persons with low functional health literacy are unable to do everyday literacy tasks such as reading prescription labels. It is incumbent on the health care community to provide an atmosphere in which the person feels comfortable asking for help and to provide the support needed. It is also important for literacy providers to work with health care personnel to make modifications in materials and procedures as suggested earlier. These changes should create an environment in which the patient who just stays home is comfortable coming to the hospital for treatment. It is heartening to see the growing awareness and interest of health care providers in the issue of patient literacy (Forster, 1996; Miles & Davis, 1995). Patients will be the beneficiaries of this heightened concern.

NOTE

The work presented in this chapter is based on research supported, in part, by the Robert Wood Johnson Foundation and completed by Ruth M. Parker, M.D., Mark V. Williams, M.D., David W. Baker, M.D., Emory University School of Medicine, and Joanne R. Nurss, Ph.D., Georgia State University. Appreciation is also expressed to project staff members Ron Hall and Nina Parikh.

REFERENCES

Auslander, W. F., Haire-Joshu, D., Houston, C. A., & Fisher, E. B. (1992). Community organization to reduce the risk of non-insulin-dependent diabetes among low-income African-American women. *Ethnicity and Disease, 2,* 176–184.

Baker, D. W., Parker, R. M., Williams, M. V., Clark, W. S., & Nurss, J. R. (in press). The relationship of patient reading ability to self-reported health and use of health services. *American Journal of Public Health.*

Beder, H. (1991). The stigma of illiteracy. *Adult Basic Education, 1,* 67–78.

Clabby, J. F., & Belz, E. J. (1985). Psychological barriers to learning: An approach using group treatment. *Small Group Behavior, 16,* 525–533.

Davis, T. C., Arnold, C., Jackson, R. H., Glass, J., & Sentell, T. (1996). Relationship of knowledge and attitudes about screening mammography to literacy level in low income women. Abstract. *Journal of General Internal Medicine, 11* (supplement 1), 122.

Davis, T. C., Bocchini, J. A., Fredrickson, D., Arnold, C., Mayeaux, E. J., Murphy, P. W., Jackson, R. H., Hanna, N., & Paterson, M. (1996). Parent comprehension of polio vaccine information pamphlets. *Pediatrics, 97* (6), 804–810.

Doak, C. C., Doak, L. G., & Root, J. H. (1985). *Teaching patients with low literacy skills*. Philadelphia: J. B. Lippincott.

Forster, J. (1996). Health literacy: How poor literacy leads to poor health care. *Patient Care: The Practical Journal for Primary Care Physicians. 30* (16), 94–127.

Kicklighter, J. R., & Stein, M. A. (1993). Factors influencing diabetic clients' ability to read and comprehend printed diabetic diet material.*The Diabetes Educator, 4* (6), 627–630.

Kirsch, I. S., Jungeblat, A., Jenkins, L., & Kolstad, A. (1993). *Adult literacy in America: A first look at the results of the National Adult Literacy Survey*. Washington, DC: National Center for Educational Statistics, U.S. Department of Education.

LaGreca, A. M., Auslander, W. F., Greco, P., Spetter, D., Fisher, E. B., & Santiago, J. V. (1995). I get by with a little help from my family and friends: Adolescents' support for diabetes care. *Journal of Pediatric Psychology, 20* (4), 449–476.

Miles, S., & Davis, T. (1995). Patients who can't read: Implications for the health care system. Editorial. *Journal of the American Medical Association, 274* (21), 1719–1720.

Mrvos, R., Dean, B. S., & Krenzelok, E. P. (1993). Illiteracy: A contributing factor to poisoning. *Veterinarian and Human Toxicology, 35* (5), 466–468.

Murphy, P. W., Davis, T. C., Long, S. W., Jackson, R. H., & Decker, B. C. (1993). Rapid Estimate of Adult Literacy in Medicine (REALM): A quick reading test for patients. *Journal of Reading, 37*, 124–130.

Nurss, J. R., Baker, D. W., Davis, T. C., Parker, R. M., & Williams, M. V. (1995). Difficulties in functional health literacy screening in Spanish-speaking adults. *Journal of Reading, 38*, 632–637.

Nurss, J. R., El-Kebbi, I., Gallina, D. L., Ziemer, D. C., Musey, V. C., Lewis, S., Liao, Q., & Phillips, L. S. (1996). *Diabetes in African-Americans: VIII. Functional health literacy of low-income patients with diabetes*. Manuscript submitted for review.

Parikh, N. S., Parker, R. M., Nurss, J. R., Baker, D. W., & Williams, M. V. (1996). Shame and health literacy: The unspoken connection. *Patient Education and Counseling, 27*, 33–39.

Parker, R. M., Baker, D. M., Williams, M. V., & Nurss, J. R. (1995). The Test of Functional Health Literacy in Adults (TOFHLA): A new instrument for measuring patients' literacy skills. *Journal of General Internal Medicine, 10*, 537–541.

Parker, R. M., Williams, M. V., Baker, D. W., & Nurss, J. R. (1996). Literacy and contraception: Exploring the link. *Obstetrics and Gynecology, 88*, 72S–77S.

Weiss, B. D., Reed, R. L., & Kligman, E. W. (1995). Literacy skills and communication methods of low-income older persons. *Patient Education and Counseling, 25*, 109–119.

Williams, M. V., Parker, R. M., Baker, D. W., Parikh, N. S., Pitkin, K., Coates, W. C., & Nurss, J. R. (1995). Inadequate functional health literacy among patients at two public hospitals. *Journal of the American Medical Association, 274* (21), 1677–1682.

Index

Contributors

ERNEST DAVENPORT is Associate Professor of Educational Psychology at the University of Minnesota-Twin Cities.

JEREMY D. FINN is Professor of Education at SUNY-Buffalo.

LYNN FRIEDMAN is Assistant Professor of Education at St. Mary's University, Winona, MN.

SUSAN B. GERBER is a graduate student at SUNY-Buffalo.

ANDREW HARTMAN is Director of the National Institute for Literacy in Washington, D.C.

JOSEPH HOWARD is Professor at the Community College of Philadelphia.

ALICE JOHNSON is a Program Staff member at the National Institute for Literacy in Washington, D.C.

DAVID KAPLAN is Associate Professor of Educational Studies at the University of Delaware, Newark, DE.

IRWIN S. KIRSCH is Executive Director of the Literacy Learning and Assessment Group at the Educational Testing Service in Princeton, NJ.

MAUREEN A. MEEHAN is Assistant Director at the Center for Literacy, the University of Illinois–Chicago.

JOANNE R. NURSS is Professor of Educational Psychology and Director of the Center for the Study of Adult Literacy at Georgia State University in Atlanta.

WAYNE S. OBETZ is Research Associate, Office of Instructional Research, at the Community College of Philadelphia.

STEPHEN REDER is Associate Professor of Psychology, at Portland State University, Portland, OR.

FLORA V. RODRÍGUEZ-BROWN is Professor of Curriculum and Instruction at the University of Illinois–Chicago.

JANET K. SHEEHAN is Assistant Professor of Educational Psychology at Northern Illinois University in DeKalb.

PAUL SIMON (U.S. Senator, Retired) is Director of the Public Policy Institute at Southern Illinois University at Carbondale.

M CECIL SMITH is Associate Professor of Educational Psychology at Northern Illinois University in DeKalb.

RICHARD L. VENEZKY is Unidel Professor of Educational Studies and Professor of Computer and Information Sciences at the University of Delaware, Newark, DE.

SUSAN A. VOGEL is Professor of Special Education at Northern Illinois University in DeKalb.

ISBN 0-275-95786-1

90000>

EAN

9 780275 957865

HARDCOVER BAR CODE